CHANGE AND CONTINUITY IN THE MIDDLE EAST

Also by M. E. Ahrari

ETHNIC GROUPS AND U.S. FOREIGN POLICY

OPEC – THE FAILING GIANT

THE DYNAMICS OF OIL DIPLOMACY: Conflict and Consensus

THE GULF AND INTERNATIONAL SECURITY: 1980s and Beyond

THE MIDDLE EAST IN TRANSITION

THE PERSIAN GULF AFTER THE COLD WAR

Change and Continuity in the Middle East

Conflict Resolution and Prospects for Peace

M. E. Ahrari
Professor of National Security and Strategy
Armed Forces Staff College
Norfolk, Virginia

First published in Great Britain 1996 by
MACMILLAN PRESS LTD
Houndmills, Basingstoke, Hampshire RG21 6XS
and London
Companies and representatives
throughout the world

A catalogue record for this book is available
from the British Library.

ISBN 0–333–63314–8

First published in the United States of America 1996 by
ST. MARTIN'S PRESS, INC.,
Scholarly and Reference Division,
175 Fifth Avenue,
New York, N.Y. 10010

ISBN 0–312–12866–5

Library of Congress Cataloging-in-Publication Data
Change and continuity in the Middle East : conflict resolution and prospects for peace / [edited by] M. E. Ahrari.
p. cm.
Includes bibliographical references and index.
ISBN 0–312–12866–5 (cloth)
1. Middle East—Politics and government—1979– I. Ahrari, Mohammed E.
DS63.1.C514 1996
956.05—dc20 95–30548
CIP

10 9 8 7 6 5 4 3 2 1
05 04 03 02 01 00 99 98 97 96

Printed in Great Britain by
Ispwich Book Co Ltd
Ipswich, Suffolk

For my sister Khadija and my niece Nasreen, the two most loving ladies of my life;

and

for all those who are struggling to bring about peaceful change in the Middle East, while maintaining the best traditions from the past.

Contents

List of Maps, Figures and Table

Acknowledgements

The original seed for this study was sown when I co-directed a conference, with Professor James Daddysman of Alderson-Broaddus College, on Contending Issues of the Middle East during the Summer of 1993. When I originally wrote the conference proposal, the world around the Middle East was undergoing a number of changes. So, I decided on the present theme of change and continuity.

As can be imagined, the issue of change and continuity is almost too slippery to handle. At the same time it is too intriguing to avoid. The Cold War is history, and so is the Soviet Union. The most significant recent event for the Middle East, however, was the Gulf War of 1991. Since it was brought about as a result of an invasion of one Arab state by another, it gave the Arab world a very serious jolt, causing serious disarray among the Arab leadership.

The American handling of the Gulf War became a source of comfort for the Israelis. They could see that they could depend on American military power. The war was also convincing proof for a number of Gulf states that they could also count on Washington for their security. These contradictory emotions – disarray mixed with confidence – became the stuff from which emerged the peace negotiations concerning Arab–Israeli conflict as a whole. One can only point to a major change related to these negotiations – the PLO–Israeli peace process – that resulted in the establishment of limited self-rule for the Palestinians. Even though no one can yet say with any amount of certainty that this process will be successful, its very materialization has changed the overall shape of strategic affairs.

As one ponders the nuances of this development, one also wonders whether Syria and Israel will come to some sort of a *rapprochement* at any time in the near future. At the same time, the fate of the PLO–Israeli peace process remains very fragile and equally tenuous. Jordan and Israel, on the other hand, appear to be well on the road to a 'warm' peace. Yet there is a notion of continuity with the past in the Middle East in the shape of the unremitting arms race, manifestations of religious extremism, authoritarian rule, Saudi-Iranian rivalry, Iran's 'Janus-faced' foreign policy which causes such consternation and confusion among its Gulf neighbours, and a continuing American resolve to exclude Iran from the future security arrangements in the Persian Gulf. Anyone performing a systematic analysis of the strategic affairs of the Middle East will be hard-pressed to find a bottom-line type of statement as to which element – change or continuity – dominates the 1990s, and the situation is likely to remain the same in the next decade. Perhaps that is one of the reasons why the Middle East is so intriguing. It has ceaselessly baffled even those who have spent their lives living and operating within the region. In any case, from the perspective of the United States, this region deserves a careful and continuous watch. I hope this study makes some contribution in that direction.

Views expressed by all the contributors in this volume are their own. I want to express my utmost gratitude to a number of individuals who have been an important part of my professional life at the Armed Forces Staff College. The two individuals who deserve a special mention are Brigadier General Marvin Esmond, Commandant of the Armed Forces Staff College, and Colonel Leonard ('Jack') Walls, Chief-of-Staff to the Commandant. Both went out of their way to accommodate my research-related requirements. Colonel Thomas Wilson, Dean of the Joint and Combined Warfighting School, also encouraged me to concentrate on my writing by working around a very demanding teaching schedule.

No reader can really understand the significance of a good editor. Only a writer can. I have been very fortunate in having the services of a qualified professional in Dr William K. Riley, who is our official editor at the Staff College. I cannot count the number of occasions when I wanted him to edit my writing 'asap'. The best thing about Bill is that he is not only a fine editor, but he is so cheerfully accommodating in this regard. I cannot thank him enough for his professional services.

The other members of the Editorial department, Cheryl Edwards, Katherine ('Kat') Smith (especially Kat), and Brenda Griffith have been very helpful in providing their services.

Thanks are due to Dr Armin Ludwig of the US Air War College for drawing the maps.

The library staff at the Armed Forces Staff College has done its utmost to assist me with getting inter-library loans, chasing footnotes, etc. I especially wish to mention Mary Louise O'Brien and Marie Harrison. Credit is also due to Ms Gayle Nicula, Director of the AFSC Library, for maintaining such an efficient staff.

Last but not least, the constant cheer and support of my family and friends has done the most to fuel my productivity. The four individuals who should be mentioned are my father, my sister, my brother and my niece, Nasreen. I also want to make a special mention of Judy Robbins, a dear friend, who will never know how helpful her cheerful notes and her love have been to me during moments of fatigue and frustration.

Notes on the Contributors

THE EDITOR

M. E. Ahrari is a Professor of National Security and Strategy and Associate Dean of the Joint and Combined Warfare School at the United States Armed Forces Staff College. Between 1990 and 1994, he served as a Professor of Middle East and West Asian Affairs at the United States Air War College. He is a specialist in American policy process – with special reference to foreign and defence policies, major-power relations in the Middle East, and the political economy of oil. He has written or edited five books, and co-authored one monograph. His latest books are *The Persian Gulf after the Cold War* (1993) and the co-authored monograph, *The Middle East in Transition* (1994). He has also published extensively in professional journals in the United States, the UK, and Asia.

OTHER CONTRIBUTORS

Nader Entessar is Professor of Political Science and International Studies and Chairman of the Division of Social Sciences at Spring Hill College in Mobile, Alabama. He has written or edited six books and numerous articles in scholarly journals on the Middle East, Europe, and North America. His most recent publications are *Kurdish Ethno-nationalism* (1992) and *Iran and the Arab World* (1993).

Aaron Karp is Research Coordinator and Adjunct Professor of International Studies at Old Dominion University in Norfolk, Virginia. Previously he was an analyst with the Stiftung Wissenschaft und Politik, Ebenhausen, Germany, and Arms Trade Project Leader at the Stockholm International Peace Research Institute. His publications include the *Report of the UN Secretary-General on South Africa's Nuclear and Missile Capability* (1991) and *Ballistic Missile Proliferation: the Politics and Technics* (1995).

James H. Noyes has been a Research Fellow at the Hoover Institution since 1985. He also served as Deputy Assistant Secretary of Defense for Near Eastern, African, and South Asian Affairs in the Nixon and Ford

Administrations. His publications include *The Clouded Lens: Persian Gulf Security and U.S. Policy* (1979, revised 1981). He also co-edited with M. E. Ahrari *The Persian Gulf after the Cold War.*

Raymond Picquet is a Senior Analyst at the EAI Corporation in Fairfax, Virginia. He has over 13 years of experience in the defence industry, ten of which have been dedicated primarily to chemical weapons (CWs) or were CW-related research.

Brigid Starkey is associate Director of Project ICONS, which is an international negotiations simulation project used in educational institutions and applied settings for negotiation training. Her publications include 'The OIC and International Islamic Cooperation' (1994) and 'Foreign Policy in the Muslim World: A Dialogue Between State and Society' (1992).

List of Abbreviations

AMAL	Afwaj al-Muqawwama al-Lubnanyyia
ASEAN	Association of South East Asian Nations
CENTO	Central Treaty Organization
DOP	Declaration of Principles
ECO	Economic Cooperation Organization
FIS	Islamic Salvation Front
GCC	Gulf Cooperation Council
GOIC	Gulf Organization for Industrial Consulting
HAMAS	Harakat al-Muqawwama al-Islamiyya
ICO	Islamic Conference Organization
KDP	Kurdish Democratic Party
KDPI	Kurdish Democratic Party of Iran
NIF	National Islamic Front
OPEC	Organization of Petroleum Exporting Countries
PFLP	Popular Front for the Liberation of Palestine
PKK	Kurdish Workers Party
PLO	Palestine Liberation Organization
PUK	Patriotic Union of Kurdistan
RCD	Regional Cooperation for Development
SLA	South Lebanese Army
UN	United Nations
UNHCR	United Nations High Commisioner for Refugees
USCENTCOM	United States Central Command
WMD	Weapons of Mass Destruction

Introduction

M. E. Ahrari

One of the truisms of the Middle East is that its environment is the most fertile for enduring conflicts. In general, and without necessarily being all-inclusive, three broad categories of major conflicts emerge in this area. The first category contains issues that appear to linger on and defy attempts to find solutions, or those which may not be resolved because political realism becomes one of the chief obstacles to finding solutions for them. The second category includes those conflicts with deeper roots, and there may not now (or even ever) be a clear-cut solution for them. The third category contains conflicts that have arisen within a decade or so, and have threatened the political stability of one or more countries of that area. In this study, selected issues in these categories will be analyzed.

The Arab–Israeli conflict certainly belongs to the first category. It is an issue that still appears intractable. Such an observation should not be taken to imply that this issue has not undergone many changes since the creation of the State of Israel in 1948. Indeed, it underwent numerous phases strictly in terms of the attitudes of Arab states and Israel towards each other, and towards the ways in which this conflict could be resolved. For instance, despite a series of clashes between 1948 and 1956, and despite conquering a substantial part of Egyptian territory as a result of the Suez Crisis, Israel could not translate its military victories into a lasting political settlement and was forced to withdraw. Similarly, by formally announcing the creation of the Palestine Liberation Organization (PLO) in 1964, and by calling for the 'liberation of Palestine', members of the Arab League implied, for the first time, their resolve to settle this conflict through military force.[1] This Arab action also enabled the emergence of a powerful Palestinian identity. One only has to look back at the significance of the role of Palestinian nationalism since then to see the way it has affected the intractability of the conflict.

From the Israeli side, this conflict became quite complicated after the 1967 War, which gained parts of Egyptian, Syrian, and Jordanian territories for the Jewish state, and, most notably, Jerusalem. For the first time since its creation, Israel was also able to turn these territories into long-term (if not permanent) political realities. The territories also became the most powerful bargaining chips in the hands of Israeli leaders for extracting diplomatic recognition from Arabs. The Camp David Agreement of

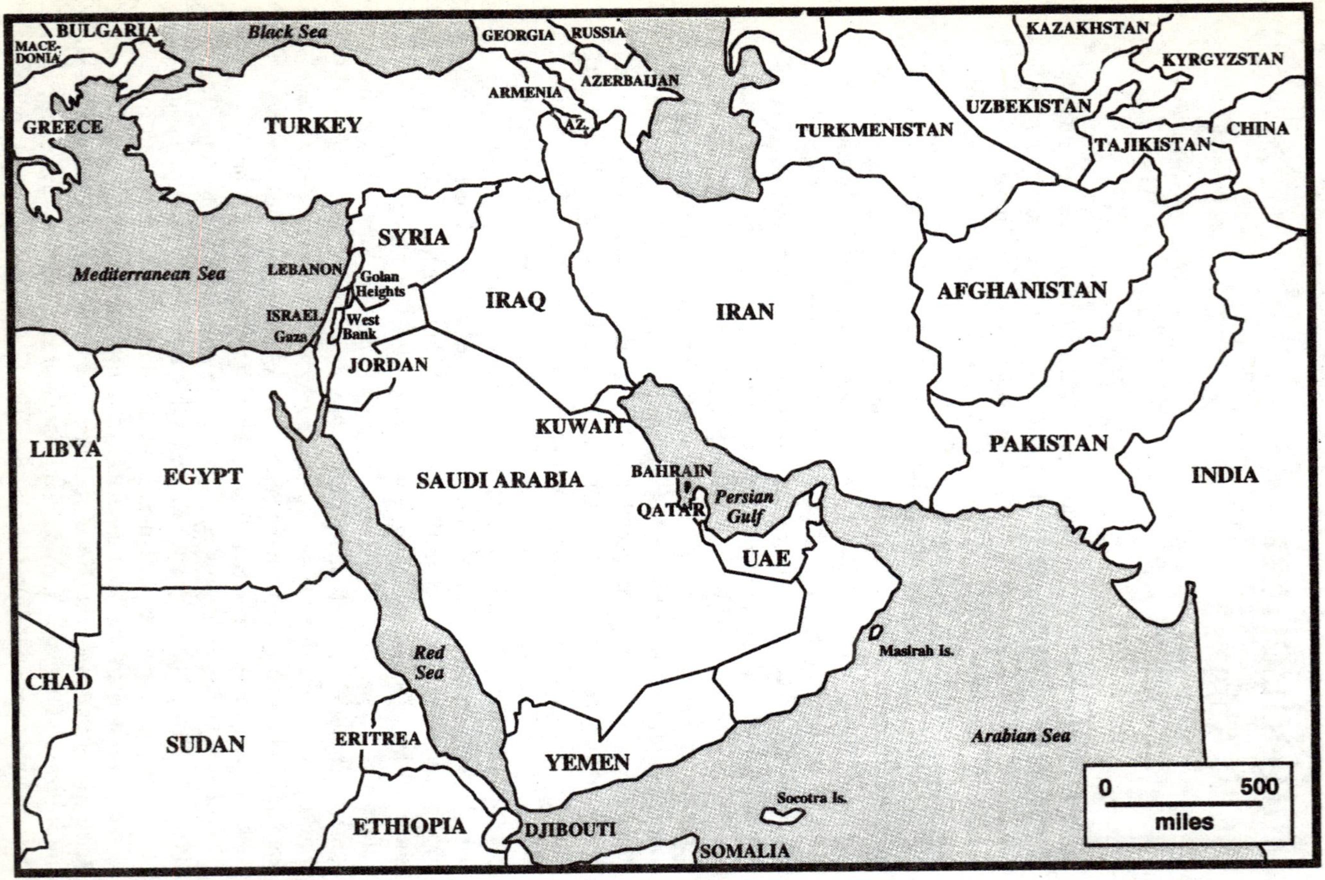
BULGARIA
MACE-DONIA
GREECE
Black Sea
TURKEY
GEORGIA
RUSSIA
ARMENIA
AZERBAIJAN
AZ.
KAZAKHSTAN
KYRGYZSTAN
UZBEKISTAN
TURKMENISTAN
TAJIKISTAN
CHINA
SYRIA
Mediterranean Sea
LEBANON
Golan Heights
ISRAEL
Gaza
West Bank
JORDAN
IRAQ
IRAN
AFGHANISTAN
PAKISTAN
INDIA
KUWAIT
BAHRAIN
QATAR
Persian Gulf
UAE
SAUDI ARABIA
LIBYA
EGYPT
CHAD
SUDAN
Red Sea
ERITREA
ETHIOPIA
DJIBOUTI
SOMALIA
YEMEN
Socotra Is.
Masirah Is.
Arabian Sea
0
500
miles

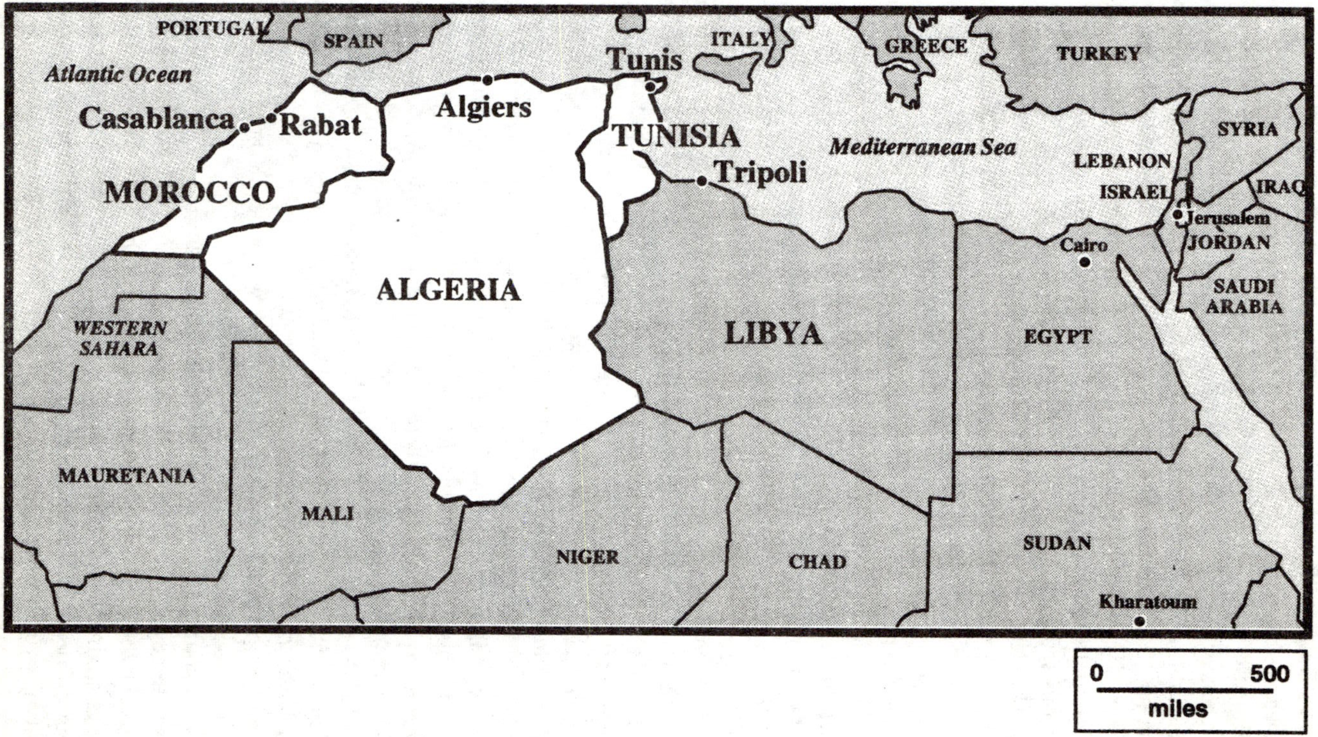

Map 2 The Maghreb and its neighbours

1978–79 epitomizes the success of this Israeli objective. This agreement also became the basis in the 1990s of territorial exchanges with Syria and Jordan. After a prolonged refusal to trade territory for peace, Israel made a major concession by granting self-rule to the Palestinians in the Gaza and Jericho areas. This agreement was signed as the climax of an international drama on 13 September 1993, and the whole world witnessed the happy occasion. Since then, not to the surprise of the observers of the Middle Eastern political scene, the PLO–Israeli peace process has suffered numerous setbacks.

In 'The Peace Process and its Critics', Ahrari examines the intricacies of the peace negotiations between Israel and its Arab counterparts. A substantial portion of this chapter deals with the PLO–Israeli aspect of the Arab–Israel conflict. In the next section, Ahrari discusses the roles of what he calls the new 'rejectionist' front. The post-Cold War rejectionists of peace include Iran, the Hizbollah (Party of God) of Lebanon, and the Hamas (or Islamic Resistance Party) of the occupied territories. While acknowledging the important influence of Iran on the political thinking and activities of the Hizbollah, he dismisses any suggestion that Hamas is significantly influenced by Iran. Hamas' attitude towards the peace process, according to him, is largely determined by its own calculations regarding the political realities of the occupied territories. One of the results of the Iranian revolution is the presence of Iran in Lebanon through the so-called 'Party of God' (Hizbollah). Iran has been able to develop this organization as a source of terror and instability through the use of its own 'Revolutionary Guards'. The alliance between Syria and Iran has been crucial for this purpose. In fact, the Syrian–Iranian role regarding the use of Hizbollah emerges as a perfect example of Machiavellian politics. Iran used this alliance to obtain a powerful politico-military presence in Lebanon. Syria, especially in the aftermath of the dismantling of the Soviet Union and the end of the Cold War, could (and did) rely on Hizbollah to put pressure on Israel. This was done by allowing that organization to launch intermittent rocket attacks on northern Israel. These events also served Iran's purpose in the sense that they had the potential to undermine the peace process, since peace was a development that was unacceptable to Iran.

Even though Syria was an important participant in the peace negotiations with Israel, it could play the 'Hizbollah card' in order to put pressure on Israel to be more forthcoming on the issue of the Golan Heights. Given a longstanding Israeli refusal to buckle under such tactics, one wonders whether President Hafez Assad of Syria has 'indeed' learned anything about the overall Israeli negotiating posture. The Iranian role on this issue might be more in response to its own domestic radical groups. It is possible that by giving the green light to (if not actually instigating) these intermittent attacks, Rafsanjani might be placating the radical groups, as both pragmatists and hardliners continue to jockey for position in the domestic politics of Iran. Ahrari is of the view that of the four dimensions of the peace process covered in his chapter (viz., the PLO–Israel, Syria–Israel, Jordan–Israel, and Lebanon–Israel) the one involving the Palestinians is the most significant. 'Even though the PLO is the weakest entity, since it is not negotiating as the representative of an existing nation state,' he writes, 'any derailment of the peace process between the PLO and Israel is destined to cause considerable turbulence in and around Israel.'

The Kurdish question also belongs to the first category of conflicts. The Kurds have pursued their dream of nationhood with little success. Since they are scattered throughout a number of countries (Iran, Iraq, Turkey, Syria, Azerbaijan and Armenia) their own aspiration to statehood clashes with the sovereignty of all those countries. They have been exploited on numerous occasions by all their neighbours, and even by countries outside the area such as the United States and Israel. Mullah Mustafa Barzani, who is regarded as father of the Kurdish nation, correctly – albeit sadly – labelled his people as 'the orphans of the universe'. This issue recently captured world attention in the aftermath of the Gulf War of 1991. The Kurdish uprising following that war and Saddam's brutal suppression of it became reasons for the United States, Britain, and France to establish a no-fly zone in northern Iraq. The Kurds have had some form of self-rule since 1992, but it may not last if Saddam finds an opportunity to unleash his fury on them.

Nader Entessar's chapter, 'Kurdish Conflict in a Regional Perspective', is an interesting study of its various dimensions. Perhaps the most recent aspect of this ancient conflict is the resolve shown by the aforementioned Western nations to protect the Kurds. The author emphasizes the fact that Iran, Turkey and Iraq continued their policies of using the Kurds for their respective strategic advantages whenever possible. Consequently, the Kurdish Question will continue to affect relationships between these three neighbours. A good example of this reality is discussed by Entessar. The *de facto* establishment of a Kurdish state in 1992 resulted in a quasi-formal arrangement between Iran and Turkey to deal with the Kurds. Even though neither of these countries wants to see the emergence of an independent Kurdistan, Iran and Turkey, according to Entessar, appear to be pursuing different policies. Turkey is inclined toward co-operating and forging closer links with major Iraqi–Turkish parties. Iran, on the contrary, 'has remained suspicious of both the ultimate goals of the Kurdish government and Turkish motives in the region'. Iran suspects that through its conciliatory policies towards the Kurds, Ankara really has the geopolitical objective of 'directly or indirectly', 'altering the balance of power in the region'.

Another old aspect of this conflict that remains highly relevant in the post-Cold War years is the fact that neither Iran, Turkey nor Iraq is likely to change its staunch opposition to the creation of an independent Kurdish state. In fact, any autonomy the Kurds acquire at one time, such as that which they have gained since the Gulf War of 1991, is likely to be only temporary. Iran, Iraq and Turkey continue to view such a development with the utmost suspicion, as a precursor to the creation of an independent Kurdistan and thus a development that should be crushed before it reaches full bloom.

The second category of conflicts contains such issues as the role of Iran in the Persian Gulf and other regions of the Middle East, the role of Islam in the post-Cold War environment, and democracy versus Islam as a means of government and an agent of stability. Two developments related to the Iranian revolution of 1978–79 made it a source of concern for the states of the Arabian peninsula. Firstly, there was the fact that this was an uprising against a monarchical regime, making it a nightmarish reality for the sheikhs of the neighbouring states. Second, by intermittently threatening to export this revolution to the Arabian peninsula, Iran convinced those countries that they had better strengthen their own collective security. The Iran–Iraq war of 1980–88 added a further sense of urgency to their need to respond to the Iranian manoeuvres. The Arabian states responded by creating the Gulf Cooperation Council (GCC). The United States viewed the Islamic revolution in Iran and the Soviet invasion of Afghanistan that occurred in December of 1979 as ominous developments for its own strategic interests. The eventual response from Washington emerged in the form of the creation in January 1983 of the Central Command (USCENTCOM), a military organization aimed at stabilizing the Persian Gulf, western Asia and contiguous areas.

The Arab perception of Iran has gone through some noteworthy changes since the end of the Iran–Iraq War in 1988. Of course, a major reason for this change was related to two regional developments. The first was the death of Khomeini in June 1989. The second development was Saddam Hussein's decision to invade Kuwait in August 1990. Even though the Gulf War of 1991 (Operation Desert Storm) brought about the dismantling of Iraqi military might for the foreseeable future, Saddam still remains at the helm. In the 1990s, Iran appears to be sending mixed signals regarding its intentions towards its neighbouring states. Iran's neighbours remain wary and continue to view Iran as a potential threat. In the 1990s, Iranian foreign policy activism is being blamed for political turbulence in North Africa.

It is a reality of the 1990s that the legitimacy of the Revolution in Iranian domestic politics has become more important than any living person, inside or outside the government. While Khomeini was alive, he epitomized the Revolution. In that sense, he could do no wrong; or alternatively, he could make a mistake as major as waging an eight-year-long war with Iraq, and then end it by merely issuing a statement. No person of that stature is living in Iran today. So, the Revolution itself – a phenomenon as opposed to a person – has taken the place of Khomeini. Everyone else – including President Ali Hashemi Rafsanjani or even Khomeini's successor, Ali Khameini – has to prove their political worth by living up to that phenomenon.

This reality is making the domestic politics of Iran not only highly contentious, but equally difficult as an atmosphere in which a politician can survive. The domestic litmus test for the survival of an Iranian politician is to constantly prove his loyalty to the Revolution by adopting policies that appear to be in harmony with it. However, the West is increasingly putting pressure on Iran to bring it back into the fold of nation-states by trying to force it to adopt conventional policies. Even if such policies are not aimed at an explicit abandonment of the Revolution itself, their vigorous pursuit by any Iranian politician is likely to trigger charges of treason from a number of radical groups which remain quite active in their pursuit of power, thereby keeping the pragmatic forces from getting too strong.

President Rafsanjani is definitely qualified for the difficult role of balancing these contradictory domestic and international pressures. If he were to survive for another five years, the prospects for the emergence of Iran as more of a conventional nation-state (as opposed to an agent of revolution) would improve tremendously. In the final analysis, the long-term survival of a regime depends largely on the ability of its leaders to create economic development. When the Revolution has run its course, the people want to enjoy a decent standard of living and a peaceful life. Even the 'perpetual' aspect of the cultural revolution of the People's Republic of China in the 1970s turned out to be a farce. Once this reality has penetrated the psyche of the Iranian masses – probably in the 1990s – the facade of the perpetuality of this Revolution is also likely to become history.

The essay by Ahrari, Starkey, and Entessar, 'Iran, The Persian Gulf, and the Post-Cold War Order', is an examination of the complex role of Iran. They start their chapter with the following important questions: Is the Islamic Republic poised to fully re-enter the prevailing international system? Or is it a dangerous renegade state which threatens the core principles of that system? They say that 'there is no definitive answer as yet'. Elaborating further on this point, they write, '...Iran continues to stand at a crossroads. It faces some nations which continue to try to actively engage it in constructive international business and diplomacy. It faces others which feel it is reprehensible to do business openly with a regime whose internal and external policies have often been deemed to be unethical and even criminal. Ultimately, the future course taken by Teheran may well be determined by which side proves the stronger and by the internal dynamics of a struggle for dominance that is still being played out.'

In the 1990s, according to these authors, Iran's neighbours remain highly perplexed and indecisive as to whether they ought to engage Iran in the economic and security-related issues faced by them or to isolate Iran as a response to its 'sinister' motives. These authors remain similarly perplexed about the 'conflictual'and the 'dangerously Janus-faced' foreign policy of the Islamic Republic of Iran. Despite this confusion, they observe that Iran is 'too strategically significant to be excluded from any lasting security arrangements in the region'. They further add that, 'logic compels one to conclude that only by including Iran in future regional security arrangements would the United States and other great powers be able to stabilize the Persian Gulf'.

Islamic resurgence is an issue that has become quite relevant for the politics of the Middle East, especially since the advent of European colonialism. The decline and downfall of the Ottoman empire lent this movement an almost permanent stature. Various movements in different Muslim countries (Arab as well as non-Arab) have surfaced and resurfaced from time to time, questioning the legitimacy of existing regimes, and even causing their instability. But no permanent solution related to Islamic resurgence can be found, because the movement seeks to establish Islamic government in the various countries, a concept which defies all attempts at precise definition. Various groups of Muslim scholars find themselves strongly disagreeing with each other's descriptions of what an Islamic government ought to look like. There might be agreement over such matters as having *Sharia* (Islamic law) as the basis of governance, but then strongly divergent views emerge on such issues as how strictly a government should adhere to the *Sharia*. What should be the basis for selecting (or electing) the top decision-makers? What qualifications should they have for holding office? Should opposition parties be allowed or not? What should be the role of opposition parties? What basis should the opposition be allowed to use for evaluating the performance of the government? These questions barely scratch the surface of the controversy over the concept of Islamic government. It is an idea which was put into practice in a different age. Whether this concept can be applied in its purest form in a highly differentiated world that is fast reaching the twenty-first century is a question that defies a definite answer. Since there is no agreement over the precise form of Islamic government, any version of it is likely to raise a storm of controversy from those who strongly favour a different version. Since Islam as the last monotheistic religion is applicable to the *Umma* (i.e., the Muslim community) until the end of this world, the controversy related to Islamic government is not likely to fade away in the coming years or even decades.

Ahrari's chapter, 'Islam as a Source of Continuity and Change in the Middle East', is an examination of the role of Islam in historical and contemporary political settings. One aspect of Islam that is usually missed by most students of the Middle East was captured by Albert Hourani when he wrote,

> With the full articulation of the message of Muhammad in a universal community obedient to divine command, what was significant in history came to an end. History could have no more lessons to teach, if there was change it could only be for the worse, and the worse could only be cured, not by creating something new but by renewing what had once existed.[2]

This issue has been one of the major sources of cataclysmic change in the Middle East. Only since the Islamic revolution in Iran has its relevance to the contemporary Muslim world been resuscitated.

Another source of contention between the West and the Muslim world is secularism. Expanding on this issue, Ahrari writes, '... the chasm between Islam and secularism appears not only to be a permanent one, but even seems to be widening'. In the post-World War II era, a number of the newly independent states of the Middle East adopted secularism in order to acquire the credentials of modernity and its attendant promise. By doing so, they unwittingly (or even perhaps wittingly) attempted to create a distance between themselves and Islam, thereby accepting the European argument that only by giving up the 'archaic'world view and lifestyle of Islam could they enjoy the technological and cultural advances of the twentieth century. However, given the miserable record in terms of economic performance of a number of these secular governments, they are coming under growing pressure from Islamicist groups whose slogan is 'Islam is the solution'. 'This slogan', concludes Ahrari, 'may or may not be transformed in the near future into concrete solutions to the socio-economic problems faced by a great many of them. However, many of these governments will continue to face increasing challenges from within to abandon secularism.'

A related controversy in the Middle East is the issue of Islam versus democracy. Even though no clear-cut argument can be made that Islam and democracy are mutually exclusive, more often than not they are pursued along lines of mutual exclusivity. There are elements of both compatibility and incompatibility between Islam and democracy. Both underscore individual participation. During the rule of the four caliphs – the enlightened ones or the *Khulafa-e-Rashidun* – who followed Prophet Mohammed, even an ordinary citizen could publicly question their actions. However, with the advent of later dynasties, this tradition was replaced by the notion of absolute rule by the caliphs, who claimed both political and religious authority. This makes it difficult to determine whether their absolute political rule justified their unquestioned role in religious affairs, or whether they simply claimed this unquestioned authority by virtue of their religious title as 'defenders of Islam'.

Both democracy and Islam emphasize majority rule, but in different senses. In a democracy, this majoritarian bias is reflected in sheer numbers. Islam, on the contrary, rejects the majoritarian principle based on numbers alone. Islam's position is that no man-made laws can be passed which contradict the laws of God (i.e., those of Islam) merely because a numerical majority wishes to do so. But in a country in which Muslims are in the majority, Islamic laws must be promulgated. Islam's rejection of majority rule based on numbers alone is one of the least understood phenomena in the West.

Islam also emphasizes majority rule through the doctrine of *Ijma* (consensus) on issues of public concern. Even here, the consensus must not violate any Islamic precept. Both democracy and Islam emphasize the rights of minorities. Even in an Islamic state, minorities are both protected and allowed to practise (though not propagate) their faith.

Islam and democracy emphasize constraints on authority. Democracy guarantees these constraints on the authority of rulers through a number of constitutional and legal provisions. Islam, by the same token, emphasizes that a ruler must be accountable to the ruled, and will be questioned and even replaced if he violates the laws of God. However, the entire history of the Middle East is cluttered with examples of absolute rule in the name of Islam.

If the notion of compatibility between Islam and democracy is perceived to be on shaky ground, that of incompatibility may appear to be a bit more clear-cut. Democracy is aimed at promoting individualism. This notion involves self-gratification and the promotion of private goals, and it is the duty of a government to furnish a proper environment for the promotion of these variables. Islam, on the contrary, is about submitting oneself to the will of God. On this issue, there is a direct contradiction, indeed a clash, between Islam and democracy.

Self-gratification and the promotion of private goals in a number of democratic states allow for countless activities which, as long as they are not illegal, may even be anti-religious. Submitting oneself to the will of God, on the other hand, forces an individual to discipline him- or herself. It is possible, on an individual level, to find a happy medium between individualism and submission to the will of God. For instance, one may look for self-gratification in activities which remain within the acceptable bounds of Islam or select private goals which are not anti-Islamic. However, I am not sure whether such a happy medium can be found by everyone in a society at large. More importantly, who will ensure that the society at large is abiding by this happy medium? Such a watchdog activity, by definition, is anti-democratic. Thus, it becomes clear that this aspect at least of the conflict between Islam and the Western notion of democracy is unresolvable. Muslim countries have to evolve their own version of democracy, which is likely to be very different from liberal democracy as practised in the West.

In his essay, 'Assessing Prospects for Democracy in the Middle East', James Noyes deals with a controversial subject. The adoption of democracy as a system of government, he writes, has remained an idea with limited popularity. The secularists of the area have remained receptive to it by and large. However, even they have thought along the line of 'a single unopposed progressive party', which is not exactly what pluralistic democracy is all about. Noyes laments that 'Unfortunately, rather than the West's liberal democratic tradition it was its authoritarian, military and fascist strain which was influential [in the Middle East] after World War II.' In order to find 'a few elements' common to the absence of democracy, he focuses on a few Middle Eastern states. In the case of Iraq and Syria, the emphasis has been on militarism, one-party rule, and pan-Arabism. But for these countries, 'and elsewhere in much of the Middle East, it was not the absence of democracy's rudimentary forms during the Mandate period that inhibited democratic development, but rather, their misuse'. He labels Lebanon as a 'false' and only 'superficially a functioning democracy', where ancient clans are 'unable to define a common interest', where 'religion and clan leaders are focused exclusively on maintaining their power bases', and where foreign powers have been involved in 'constant intrigues' as Lebanon 'became a centre of espionage and propaganda warfare with newspapers and politicians alike often available to the highest bidder'. Egypt, according to Noyes, is an example of 'the strongest continuity of democratic potential', and a state that 'maintains a tantalizing flirtation with pluralistic forms'. However, in the 1990s, the worsening of economic conditions, increasing political violence by the Islamicists and repressive measures by the government do not bode well for the future of democracy in that country. In Egypt, as elsewhere in the Middle East, obstacles to democracy, notes the author, come from 'economic failures and statism,' and 'the enormous and largely dead-handed bureaucracies'. 'Thus, democracy's impeders include secular forces and are not confined to the catch-all "Islamicist" groups.' Noyes, like most Western observers of the Middle East, views the liberal potential in Islam as a positive step towards democratic pluralism.

The third category of issues in this study includes the future dynamics of security in the Persian Gulf, the arms race and its implications for regional stability in the Middle East. The Persian Gulf has been endowed with the largest oil reserves in the world. At the same time, this region has also been cursed by endemic political instability and intermittent turbulence. In less than twenty years, the area has been rocked by the Soviet invasion of Afghanistan, the Iranian revolution, the Iran–Iraq War, the Gulf War or 1991, and the Yemeni civil war of 1994. Mention of these major upheavals makes it easy to gloss over the attendant and even longer-lasting tensions between and among other states of the region. These tensions fuel the arms race that has remained so typical of the area. At the same time, as soon as one crisis ends, it seems that the Persian Gulf is only waiting for the next one to begin.

The security-related problem of the Persian Gulf appeared almost impervious to the competition between the superpowers during the Cold War years. The United States had maintained an overarching strategic dominance in the area until the Iranian Revolution, but could not stabilize the region. After the Iranian Revolution, the Gulf states were faced with one more major source of instability, namely the potential exportability of the Iranian revolution. When the long and bloody Iran–Iraq War ended in Iraq's favour, the oil sheikhdoms hoped that they could breathe a collective sigh of relief due to the fact that their sister Arab state, Iraq, had emerged as the victor. But before they could settle down in their seats, they were stunned to see Iraq – whose military might was substantially built up by money from the oil sheikhdoms – take over the tiny, oil-rich, Emirate of Kuwait. When the Gulf War of 1991 resulted in a sound beating for the Iraqi forces, the major issue for the Persian Gulf was the way in which collective security should be handled. But instead of being able to come up with a consensual security arrangement, they opted for the so-called 'Damascus Declaration'. The contentious aspects of this arrangement were only too obvious from the fact that it excluded Iran. The Damascus Declaration was designed to enable Egypt and Syria to station forces in the Arabian Peninsula in order to protect Saudi Arabia and Kuwait from future invasions (presumably from Iraq and Iran).

If the exclusion of Iran from this arrangement did not bring about its demise (I, for one, believe that the existence of Iran was a major obstacle to its implementation), then provision for the presence of Egyptian and Syrian forces on the Arabian Peninsula indeed turned out to be a non-starter. One is well-advised to recall the environment in which this arrangement was concluded. The Arab world was reeling from the shock of the invasion of one Arab state by another. How could the oil sheikhdoms have trusted two other Arab states who had had a long and powerful tradition of Arab nationalism, *à la* Iraq, to protect them?

In her essay, 'Post-Cold War Security in the GCC Region: Continuity and Change in the 1990s', Brigid Starkey identifies a number of new and old challenges faced by the Gulf Cooperation Council (GCC). One such challenge, according to the author, is that this entity 'must overcome the internal and external structural factors which have inhibited it from growing and strengthening as a regional security regime'. Secondly, the member states must place a high priority on the search for multilateral security solutions. Expanding further on this point, the author expresses a clear preference for a 'coherent and unified security strategy', rather than a 'patchwork approach which combines Saudi-style financial diplomacy with a newly-guaranteed American security umbrella, a stalled GCC+2 (Syria and Egypt) concept [i.e., the Damascus Declaration mentioned above], and a lone Omani voice calling for a re-emphasis on Gulf state self-reliance and a dialogue with the Islamic Republic of Iran'.

In addition, continues Starkey, the member-states 'must resolve competitive and contradictory goals in the area of security, as well as their many unsolved territorial disputes'. She concludes by noting that 'up to this point, [the GCC] has not been allowed to live up to its potential as an instrumental channel'. A substantial reason, according to her, is the 'imbalanced nature' of this organization, 'with Saudi Arabia largely outweighing its junior partners along every dimension of power'. If the GCC 'is to provide a true security regime for its members, it will have to expand to encompass all the nations of the broader Gulf region'.

The arms race in the Middle East remains the chief source of concern. There was some hope that the United States would play a leading role in decelerating it after the Gulf War of 1991. However, the overall drastic reduction in military expenditure that the major arms suppliers were forced to make as a result of the end of the Cold War required them to look for arms sales as a source of revenue to finance continuing military research and development. The Middle East has been regarded by all of them as a crucial source of such funds. Besides, in the absence of an arms control agreement among the major arms suppliers, no one supplier is willing to introduce unilateral reductions in its arms sales for fear of losing lucrative markets to its competitors. In the fertile crescent, Syria and Israel are continuing to arm themselves, their eyes fixed on each other's military preparedness. The Clinton Administration's decision to sell Israel F-15s and F-15Es is just another wrinkle that promises to further accelerate the arms race. In the Persian Gulf region, as previously noted, Iran and Saudi Arabia are spending enormous sums of money in arms purchases. Kuwait, since the restoration of its government, and the UAE are also listed as big spenders on arms.

Given the seriousness of the issue, two chapters are devoted to it. In 'Change and Continuity in the Middle East Arms Race', Aaron Karp claims that the race for military superiority 'has come to an end'. While one may be struck by the hyperbolic nature of this observation, the author does make a point regarding the stabilization of the conventional arms race in the Middle East. He sees this deceleration as 'a gentle process, almost invisible behind the rhetoric of political polarization and confrontation'. However, in Karp's view, the acquisition of the weapons of mass destruction might be emerging as an issue that warrants more urgent consideration in the Middle East than in South-east Asia or the Korean peninsula. Weapons of mass destruction also appear to be posing the 'greatest risk' of destabilization in the Gulf region. The spread of nuclear weapons is not imminent. But chemical and biological weapons 'have become weapons of choice' for a number of governments in the Middle East, notes Karp, and they are 'cultivated mainly to exert pressure on Israel's nuclear programme'. Ballistic missiles are quite widespread, with the total inventories of all Arab states at possibly over two thousand. This inventory does not include Iraq which, according to the author, is known to have received over 900 SCUD missiles. Karp expresses his grave concern over the potential acquisition of weapons of mass destruction by religious extremist groups in the Middle East for the purpose of perpetrating acts of political terrorism. He labels this as the chief source of destabilization.

Ray Picquet's chapter, 'Weapons Acquisitions and the Arms Race in the Middle East', deals with the high level of interest of Egypt, Israel, Iraq, Iran, Syria, Algeria and Libya in acquiring weapons of mass destruction (WMD). He refers to them as 'proliferation states'. The author observes that WMD proliferation in the Middle East is characterized by 'extraordinary efforts and ongoing competition'. Picquet goes on to add, 'Indeed, it is the presence of both [these] characteristics which makes the regional phenomenon so costly and so potentially dangerous.' He also looks at the arms race from the decision-making aspect in the aforementioned countries. From this perspective, he contends, 'armament decisions are typically multi-dimensional. They tend to involve more than strategic issues in order to include a range of political interests. They transcend domestic, foreign and defence policy both as a function of the complexity of political issues and objectives and of cost considerations.'

Acute economic asymmetries are likely to cause a considerable amount of turbulence in the Middle East in coming years. Since no separate chapter is devoted to the subject in this volume, I will briefly discuss some aspects of this issue here. A number of Middle Eastern countries are suffering from such problems as high fertility rates, high levels of unemployment, urban decay, infrastructure-related problems, slow rates of economic growth, statist policies, etc.

Several of the larger countries of the Middle East and North Africa show signs of the following four troublesome patterns of unemployment. Firstly, employment in urban areas is higher than it is in rural areas. Secondly, there is considerably more unemployment among younger than among older workers. Thirdly, the measured unemployment rates for women exceed those of men. Finally, educated workers are more likely to be unemployed than unskilled ones.[3] Of the above patterns, the age-related pattern is the most explosive politically, and may lead to cataclysmic changes in some of these countries. Table 1 shows the unemployment figures for selected Middle Eastern countries.

Table 1 Unemployment in selected Middle Eastern countries

Country	*Year*	*Age group*	*Unemployment rate*[4] %
Algeria	1990	15–19	64
	1990	20–24	45
	1990	25–29	17
Jordan	1991	15+	23.4
Egypt	1988	6–65	7.1
Morocco	1991	24–34	18

Statist development strategies in most Middle Eastern countries also contribute to unemployment. The proportion of the labour force employed by the government remains much less flexible than that in the private sector. 'Since labour market flexibility is positively associated with unemployment, large public sectors contribute to high rates of unemployment.'[5]

Another serious economic problem in the Middle East is related to capital shortage. One study labels it as a 'fundamentally institutional' problem. The statist policies of governments are contributing more than their fair share to depressing the efficiency of investment. Indigenous savers and investors are fearful of potential government decisions – either through nationalization or by issuing state decrees – to expropriate their savings. Consequently, they hold their savings in highly liquid assets or in overseas accounts.[6] Another study provides further insight into this problem by indicating that Arab overseas investments are in the order of $650 billion. When one compares the investment figures of Arab investors in the overseas markets with their investments in their own economies, this ratio emerges as 56:1.[7]

Even though the economies of the countries of the Persian Gulf region are doing much better than the economies of non-oil states in the Middle East, the former remain too vulnerable to price swings – especially since downward trends in prices have become the *sine qua non* of the oil markets of the 1980s and 1990s. Even attempts on the part of some of these oil states to diversify their economies have not significantly reduced their vulnerability to price volatility. It is interesting to note that, of all the Persian Gulf oil states, the Iraqi economy is most dependent on oil revenues, oil constituting 99 per cent of its total exports. However, because of the continuing UN-sponsored embargo of Iraqi oil, this figure does not reflect how much oil was exported from Iraq in the first quarter of 1995. For Qatar and Kuwait, the figure is 95 per cent. For Iran and Saudi Arabia, oil remains at 92 and 90 per cent of their total exports, respectively. Only the UAE emerges as an impressive example of economic diversification, with oil constituting only 71 per cent of its total exports.[8]

The real economic problem is that no dramatic endeavours are being made in the region to eradicate poverty and its related economic and social miseries. The most visible manifestation of misplaced priorities of all the states in this vast region – especially those of the oil-rich states of the Persian Gulf – is manifested in an almost never-ending quest for arms purchases on the part of a number of regimes. In the meantime, economic time-bombs continue to tick away in a number of Middle Eastern states with large populations.

In the concluding chapter, I return to the major theme of this book, that of change and continuity.

NOTES

1. 'Arab–Israeli Conflict', *The Middle East* (Seventh Edition), (Washington, DC: Congressional Quarterly Press, 1990), pp. 7–38.
2. As cited by M. E. Ahrari in his 'Islam as a Source of Continuity and Change', in this volume.
3. Allan Richards, 'Economic Roots of Instability in the Middle East', *Forces for Change in Southwest Asia* (Proceedings of a CENTCOM Conference, Tampa, Florida, 1993), pp. 245–64.
4. Ibid., p. 257.
5. Ibid., pp. 249–50.
6. Ibid., p. 254
7. Donald Hepburn, 'Observations from an Oil Vantagepoint: Focus – The Persian Gulf', *Forces for Change in Southwest Asia*, op. cit., pp. 279–302.
8. Ibid.

Part I Contemporary Dynamics of 'Old' Conflicts in the Middle East

1 The Peace Process and Its Critics: Post-Cold War Perspectives

M. E. Ahrari

BACKGROUND

The peace process in the Middle East should be examined for the treatment it has received from its critics, the New Rejectionist Front. The term 'rejectionist front' was used during the Cold War years to describe the activities of a number of Middle Eastern countries – Syria, Iraq and Libya – which rejected the notion of a political solution to the Arab–Israeli conflict. Since these countries were also allied with the former Soviet Union, the role of that superpower was depicted in the West as that of a 'spoiler'.

Even though Moscow played an important role in bringing about a negotiated withdrawal of the Arab and Israeli forces following the 1973 War, it found itself afterwards on the fringes of any scenario leading to a political solution of the overall Arab–Israeli conflict. It therefore suited Moscow for the rejectionist Arab states to maintain their hardline stance regarding a negotiated solution of the Arab–Israeli conflict, from which Moscow was almost certain to be excluded, throughout the 1970s and up until 1989. The Arab hardliners' rejection of a political solution gave them the power of veto over the peace process. As long as Moscow was willing and able to back their position, they could (and did) stall the peace process. In this sense, the relationship between the USSR and these hardline states was a symbiotic one.

The dismantling of the Soviet Union and the end of the Cold War also brought about an end to the power of veto of the rejectionist states in the Middle East. In the last two to three years of its existence, the USSR had abandoned its position of serving as a 'spoiler'. It also unequivocally advised President Hafez Assad of Syria and Chairman Yasser Arafat of the Palestine Liberation Organization (PLO) to initiate negotiations with Israel. No evidence of the Soviet resolve to abandon its erstwhile position

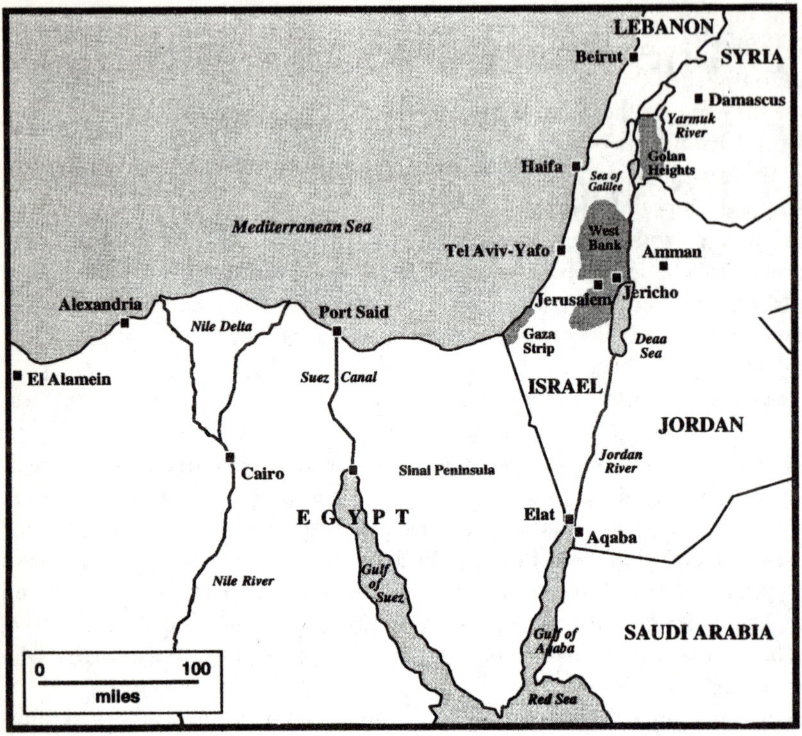

Map 1.1 Israel and its Arab neighbours

was more conclusive than its abandonment of its ally Iraq when the latter invaded Kuwait in 1990. The Desert Storm coalition could not have accomplished the sound defeat of the Iraqi forces if Moscow had not been on the side of the international coalition, insisting on Iraqi withdrawal from Kuwait.

In the last two to three years of its existence, the Soviet Union also stopped supplying arms to Syria in the latter's pursuit of achieving 'strategic parity' with Israel. Moscow's refusal to serve as a major source of arms was a serious jolt to both Syria and Libya. The latter Arab state never played a particularly crucial role as a rejectionist state because of its distance from the heart of the Arab–Israeli conflict – i.e., the territory occupied by Israel, especially after the 1967 War.

The Bush Administration's decision to initiate multi-track peace negotiations involving Israel, the PLO and a number of other Arab states was a major post-Cold War development in the Middle East. Two major taboos – the refusal of Israel and the PLO to recognize each other and negotiate on the modalities of the peace process, and the refusal of Syria to talk to Israel – were shattered, causing the old Rejectionist Front to be destroyed by the end of the 1980s.

The post-Cold War years witnessed the emergence of a new Rejectionist Front in the Middle East. This includes Iran, the Hizbollah ('the Party of God') of Lebanon and Hamas (Islamic Rejectionist Front) in Israel and the Territories. The decision to exclude Syria from this Rejectionist Front is a difficult one. Even though Syria has maintained an on-again-off-again posture of negotiating peace with Israel, its very decision to initiate a dialogue removes it from the ranks of those who condemn a negotiated resolution *per se* of the Arab–Israeli conflict. The phrase 'Arab-Israeli conflict' is used in a broad sense here. It includes not only the Israeli–Palestinian issue, but issues involving Israel, Syria and Jordan.

The 'peace process' is defined as the ongoing negotiations between the PLO and Israel which are aimed at expanding the scope of Palestinian self-rule in the Occupied Territory. Three additional dimensions of this phenomenon that will also be of concern in this chapter are the off-again-on-again negotiations between Syria and Israel, the peace treaty signed between Jordan and Israel in October 1994, and the stalled negotiations between Israel and Lebanon. A major thesis of this chapter is that, of the four dimensions of the peace process described above, the Palestinian one is the most significant. Even though the PLO is the weakest entity, since it cannot negotiate as a representative of an existing nation-state, any derailment of the peace process between the PLO and Israel is destined to cause considerable turbulence in and around Israel.

DIMENSIONS OF THE PEACE PROCESS: CONTINUITY AND MEGA-CHANGE

The signing of the Declaration of Principles (DOP) between the PLO and Israel brought about a mega-change in the conventional patterns of politics in the Middle East. Given the complexity and longevity of this conflict, a brief overview emphasizing the notions of continuity and change is in order.

From its very inception, this conflict was marred by a long-standing refusal of the Arabs to negotiate with Israel. The Arab states also adopted a powerful rhetoric calling for the destruction of the Jewish State. For its part, Israel also took a number of actions that demonstrated its own resolve not only to persist, but to persuade its Arab neighbours that it could be just as firm in its dealings with them as they were with it. For instance, Israel remained steadfast in refusing to allow even a partial resettlement of the Palestinian refugees within its borders. From its creation until its formal admission to the United Nations (UN) in 1949, Israel also refused to offer territorial concessions to the Arabs in return for resolving the conflict. The Israeli refusal on this issue became even more categorical after its entry into the UN.

Another aspect of Israeli security policy that had a long-term impact on the Arab–Israeli conflict was the adoption of a reprisal policy in 1952 by the Jewish State. Under this policy, Israel held the Arab governments responsible from whose territory terrorist attacks were launched. There was to be no doubt whether Israel would retaliate; the only question was the extent of the retaliation. This policy was especially important because it resulted in Jordan's decision in 1970 to expel the Palestinians, who were launching attacks on Israel from Jordanian territory. The Palestinians thus expelled went to Lebanon and continued their activities in that country.

The 1967 Arab–Israeli war was the decisive moment for the Jewish State. Israel captured the entire West Bank including Jerusalem, the Gaza Strip and the Golan Heights belonging to Jordan, Egypt, and Syria, respectively. For the Arabs, this war was a humiliating defeat. A number of other important developments in the Arab–Israeli conflict occurred as a result of this war. Firstly, the issue of land for peace became a viable political option, though its modalities remained an extremely contentious issue, especially as the Arab states showed no sign of political give and take. Secondly, the PLO emerged as a powerful force, using terrorism as a political weapon. Third, the issue of Eretz-Israel (or Greater Israel) became a bargaining chip for the Jewish hardliners and religious fundamentalists.

The humiliations suffered by the Arabs on the battlefield in 1967 sowed the seeds for the 1973 war. Lost honour had to be restored; Arab pride had to be reclaimed on the battlefield, where it had been lost only a few years previously. Thus, the 'October surprise' of 1973, which briefly went in favour of the Egyptian armed forces, was enough for Anwar Sadat to assume the mantle of a peacemaker. Only a few years after the 1973 War, Sadat went to Jerusalem as an Arab messenger of peace.

The phased Israeli withdrawal from the Sinai was carried out under the government of Menachem Begin, a terrorist during the British Mandate of Palestine turned peacemaker, who eventually won a Nobel peace prize, along with Sadat, for radically and permanently altering relations between the respective countries from belligerents to friendly neighbours. The Camp David Accords resulted in an Israeli withdrawal from Sinai, and the establishment of diplomatic ties between Egypt and Israel. Even though the peace between these two states was a 'cold' one (i.e., it did not result in the expansion of trade and cultural exchanges, etc.), it established a powerful precedent. The Israeli withdrawal was especially significant in that the rest of the Arab countries saw the real outcome of peace with Israel. Hafez Assad of Syria and Yasser Arafat of the PLO were watching, and were perhaps taking notes.

However, the possibility of an Israeli withdrawal from the West Bank was to become the most obdurate aspect of the Arab–Israeli conflict. In 1974, Gush Emunim appeared on the Israeli political scene. This group started the practice of creating illegal Jewish settlements near the Arab population centres. Before the emergence of this group, the 'land-for-peace' issue was already becoming a source of heated debate in Israel, Begin's Herut party being opposed to returning any of 'the land of historical Israel' to the Arabs. Even an Israeli war hero, former Defence Minister Moshe Dayan, a member of the previous Labour administration, was in favour of creating Jewish settlements in the territories occupied since the 1967 War, to use as bargaining chips. But the Gush Emunim position made the future settlement of the Arab–Israeli conflict even more difficult, for these settlements not only mushroomed between 1974 and 1994, but any attempt to stop or disband them created yet another taboo which promised to create enormous acrimony and divisiveness in the domestic politics of Israel.

The PLO, which was formally established at a summit conference of Arab leaders in 1964, was recognized by the Arab states as the sole representative of the Palestinians at another summit meeting in 1974. This increased status of the PLO, which Israel perceived as its chief nemesis, was a major source of concern for the leadership of the Jewish state, fearing that the growing political clout of the Arab oil states – especially since they had imposed a selective oil embargo on the United States and the Netherlands in 1973 – might be used again in the future to impel America to apply pressure on Israel to pull back from the Occupied Territories. The Jewish State extracted a promise from Washington that it would neither recognize nor establish a dialogue with the PLO until the latter recognized Israel's right to exist and accepted UN Resolutions 242 and 338.

While Israel was hardening its position by seeking political guarantees from Washington, complicating the internal realities by establishing Jewish settlements in the Occupied Territories and remaining strong militarily, the PLO was continuing its attacks on the Jewish State. When King Hussein of Jordan expelled the PLO from his kingdom in 1970, fearing Israeli reprisals in response to the Palestinian attacks from Jordan, the PLO found a new refuge in Lebanon. From that country, it continued its attacks on Israel.

There was much more to the Palestinian presence in Lebanon. The political balance between the Christians, Muslims and Druzes was also seriously disturbed. The growing power of the Palestinians was clearly perceived by the Maronite Christian elite as a threat to its dominance.[1]

The Lebanese Christians now had the option of playing the Israeli and Syrian cards to safeguard their political status. However, it was unfortunate for the Maronites that the Syrians and the Israelis had their own strategic agendas, whose pursuit was bound to prove deleterious to the political interests of the Maronites. When the domestic violence between various political factions escalated into a civil war in 1975, the Christian government of President Suleiman Franjieh requested Syria to intervene. President Assad, concerned about a potential Israeli intervention and its implications for Syrian interests, sent his troops into Lebanon. The Syrian entry into Lebanon only postponed Israeli intervention in that country by six years. It is interesting to note that this Syrian entry amounted to a *de facto* incorporation of Lebanon into a Greater Syria. Even the end of the Cold War did not result in the withdrawal of the Syrian forces.

The Israeli invasion of Lebanon in 1982 triggered a series of developments that continues to cast its ominous shadows in the 1990s over the future of peace negotiations between Syria, Israel and Lebanon itself. One of the noteworthy aspects of these developments was the US entry into Lebanon as a peacemaker in 1982, and its withdrawal after a series of violent operations by the Lebanese Islamicist groups, resulting in the death of 241 American military personnel. The retelling of those events is beyond the scope of this chapter. Suffice it to say that the entire Lebanese debacle, starting with the civil war and continuing into the 1990s, has altered the structure of Lebanese politics, possibly forever.

Writing in the mid-1990s, there is some hope that Lebanon might reacquire the vibrant economic status it had in the pre-civil war years. However, the Syrians are still in that troubled land, and the Hizbollah remains quite strong in southern Lebanon, intermittently clashing with Israel. Consequently, the future of peace between Lebanon and Israel remains uncertain. One major change that emerged from the Israeli invasion of Lebanon in 1982 was the expulsion of the PLO from Lebanon. Even though the PLO resettled in Tunisia, the significance of the Palestinian Question was never really diminished for those who continued to experience the humiliation resulting from the continued Israeli occupation.

In Iran, there was a major revolution in 1978–79 that established an Islamic Republic. The new government of Iran was attacked by Iraq in 1980, thus triggering a war that lasted almost throughout the entire decade. At one time, in 1987, when the tide of this war was going against Iraq, the Gulf Arab states became so preoccupied with the implications for their security of a potential Iranian victory that they did not attach ample significance to the resolution of the Palestinian issue as part of their strategic agenda.

In the meantime, King Hussein of Jordan and PLO Chairman Yasser Arafat continued their own search for a negotiating package that might become a basis for starting negotiations with Israel. The Arab states had already made public their willingness to negotiate with Israel in the 'Fez Summit peace proposal' in 1982. Using this proposal as a point of departure, Hussein and Arafat endeavoured to come up with some sort of agreement for an international peace conference that was acceptable to the National Unity (Coalition) Government of Israel, which was in power at that time. As might have been expected the socialist wing of the coalition, the Labour Party (Ma'arakh), was willing to negotiate within this framework; however the Likud (right-wing) faction remained fervently opposed to any negotiation in an international forum. The Arab and Israeli inability (or unwillingness) to make progress on a variety of conflicting proposals was leading implacably towards another period of *impasse* when an unprecedented development occurred in the Occupied Territories.

This was the *Intifada* (Uprising). This movement was totally indigenous to the Occupied Territories, and was a clear signal that their inhabitants were in no mood to leave their fate in the inept hands of the 'official' Arab leadership. It was the momentum created by this movement and the concomitant Israeli inability to deal with it that sowed the seeds for the secret Oslo Rounds of negotiations between the PLO and Israel a few years later. The PLO benefited from the *Intifada* in the sense that the movement continued to identify the PLO as its legitimate representative. In this respect, as in the decision to start the *Intifada*, the Palestinians of the Israeli Occupied Territories were definitely ahead of the entire 'official' Arab leadership. This was also a very bitter pill for the Israeli government to swallow, for it continued to identify the PLO as a 'terrorist' organization. However, the PLO had to fulfill the Israeli pre-condition of renunciation of violence and recognition of the rights of Israel to exist as a state before any direct dialogue could be established.

The decisive victory over the Iraqi forces by the international coalition in 1991 raised US prestige in the Middle East to a new height. The Bush Administration calculated that about the only way to safeguard the long-term interests of the US in that region was to create a radical momentum towards a peaceful resolution of the Arab–Israeli conflict. It should be borne in mind that a cardinal principle underlying US diplomacy in the Middle East has always been, first and foremost, the legitimization of the existence of Israel. Every related issue, including the Palestinian Question, has only been secondary to the survival and legitimacy of Israel. The post-Gulf War and post-Cold War environment was virtually tailor-made for pursuing a multilateral negotiating process that would lead to the general Arab recognition of Israel. Since the Jewish State felt it could rely on American defence, as provided during Desert Storm, it could also be expected to show ample confidence in a multilateral negotiating process.

The Arab leaders, on the other hand, were in a state of disarray in the aftermath of the Gulf War, especially since they had just experienced the shame of the aggression of one Arab state (Iraq) against another (Kuwait). To add insult to injury, they had to rely on the leadership of a coalition of three Western states – the United States, the UK and France – to play a leading role in this war. Inter-Arab unity, spasmodic though it had been from the 1960s to the 1980s, was at one of its lowest points. Inter-Arab confidence was equally shaky. A significant example of this phenomenon was the treatment accorded by Saudi Arabia and Kuwait to the 'Damascus Declaration', under which Egypt and Syria were to station troops in Kuwait to ensure the security of those two Arabian states. The two sheikhdoms did not want Egyptian and Syrian troops on their soil, obviously fearing possible intervention in their internal affairs. The Gulf sheikhdoms, through their behaviour, thus sent an unambiguous signal that they preferred to entrust their security to the three major Western powers – United States, UK, and France – before they trusted any of their sister

Arab states. The United States could not have had a more opportune moment in which to create a forum for a multilateral approach to the resolution of the Arab–Israeli conflict.

The first round of negotiations began in October 1991, in Madrid. By July 1993, the Israeli, Palestinian, Syrian, Jordanian and American negotiators had concluded ten rounds of talks. These negotiating sessions did not produce any substantial outcome. However, a number of developments within Israel and involving the Palestinians played a leading role in creating an environment for a major breakthrough. Firstly, the Labour Party regained power as a result of the June 1992 elections. Secondly, the new Israeli Prime Minister, Yitzhak Rabin, expressed his resolve to explore all the avenues for peace. Thirdly, the exclusive leadership of the PLO was seriously challenged by Hamas (the Islamic Resistance Movement) in the Occupied Territories. Hamas was an organization that pledged the destruction of the Jewish State and its replacement by an Islamic state. The Israelis now viewed the option of negotiating with the PLO as the more acceptable one.

Between January and August of 1993, the Israelis and the Palestinians met 14 times. In the first few rounds, the dialogue was conducted by individuals who did not represent officials on either side. However, the meaningful progress that was made in the ensuing sessions escalated the level of protocol and the significance of the issues discussed. The culmination of these rounds was the signing of the Declaration of Principles (DOP) on the front lawn of the White House on 13 September 1993, a day that changed the shape of the politics of the Middle East forever.

In general, this process is perceived by the Palestinians to be the beginning of the end – from interim self-rule in 'the Gaza-Jericho first' to the establishment of an independent Palestinian state, with Jerusalem as its capital. For the Israelis, this accord was to bring a series of diplomatic recognitions from a number of (if not all) Arab states, and negotiation of peace treaties with Syria, Jordan and Lebanon. Obviously, so many violent events and political upheavals have occurred since September 1993 that an adequate accounting is neither feasible for this chapter nor necessary.

The Israeli–Palestinian peace process continues to be marred by constant challenges and setbacks. For instance, one major issue is the personality of Yasser Arafat, who seems to have become so accustomed to the role of gun-toting revolutionary leader of a guerrilla organization that he appears quite ill-at-ease (and perhaps ill-suited) to play the more nuanced role of leader of a civilian, democratic administration. His autocratic style of decision-making and his pervasive cronyism, favouring those aides who were with him in Tunis, have caused considerable consternation among those who played a crucial role in planning and organizing the various aspects of the *Intifada* in the Occupied Territories long before the PLO even entered the negotiating process with Israel. Then there are the violent terrorist acts perpetrated by the followers of Hamas which are severely limiting the ability of Israeli officials to make major concessions to the PLO leading towards the extension of Palestinian self-rule in the Occupied Territories. The acute economic problems of the Palestinians living in the Occupied Territories demand immediate and massive assistance. However, very little remedial action has been forthcoming in this regard. The pervasive economic misery in the Occupied Territories might turn out to be the most significant reason for the derailment of the peace process.[2]

On the Syrian and the Lebanese fronts, the peace process has shown the least progress. The obvious linkage between any progress towards peace with Syria and Lebanon is not lost on the Israelis, since Syria is the occupying power of Lebanon. On the Jordanian front, the Israelis have most to cheer about, for they have signed a peace treaty with the government of King Hussein. All the apparent signs indicate that the peace between Jerusalem and Amman is likely to be a 'warm' one, as contrasted with a largely 'cold peace' between Israel and Egypt. The 'warm' and 'cold' characteristics of peace refer to the scope for trade, tourism and cultural exchanges between Jordan and Israel, as contrasted with the very meagre progress made between Israel and Egypt in these spheres, a point made earlier in this chapter.

The Gulf War also produced mixed results for the Palestinians. Saddam dragged the Palestinian issue into his condition for withdrawal from Kuwait so the Palestinians applauded his action. Yasser Arafat also made the blunder of meeting Saddam and was photographed giving him the traditional Arab hug and kiss. This symbolic endorsement of Saddam emanating from their meeting was not at all lost on the Gulf sheikhdoms. When Saddam's forces were beaten back from Kuwait, Palestinian support for his action could not escape the retaliatory measures. The Palestinian residents of Kuwait were expelled and money for the Palestinian cause contributed by the Gulf sheikhdoms also dried up fast. The Palestinian movement suffered one of its worst setbacks. The Bush Administration decided to initiate a multi-track dialogue between the Arabs and the Israelis that eventually became the beginning of the peace process between the Jewish State, the PLO, Jordan and Syria.

As the post-Cold War developments in the Middle East are put in perspective, there is no doubt whatsoever that the process leading up to the signing of the Declaration of Principles on 13 September 1993 was indeed highly significant. Of the four dimensions of the peace process –

Israeli–PLO, Syrian–Israeli, Jordanian–Israeli and Israeli–Lebanese – the most intractable one is that involving the Palestinians. This is not only the core of the Arab–Israeli conflict, but would also be the most dangerous dimension if it were to get off track. All the portents are ominous. The very incremental aspect of the PLO–Israeli peace process – as logical and realistic it appears to be – has become a lightning rod for controversy and charges of a 'sell-out'. No Israeli government could offer the PLO anything more than the government of Yitzhak Rabin has offered. Yet, from the Palestinian viewpoint, anything less than rapid progress toward the establishment of an independent Palestinian state is tantamount to the betrayal of the Palestinian cause.

Realistically speaking, a political environment conducive to the creation of a Palestinian state has been totally absent in the mid-1990s. What both sides expect, and indeed demand, from the other cannot be delivered by either the PLO or Israel. Arafat's side wants speedy progress towards the expansion of Palestinian self-rule, so that the PLO can proceed with the most difficult aspects of negotiations – i.e., the establishment of an independent Palestinian state and resolution of the future status of Jerusalem. Rabin's side expects, and indeed demands, that the PLO establish its authority and ruthlessly eliminate the ever-escalating, Hamas-related violence. This has become the litmus test for the sincerity and commitment of Yasser Arafat to the peace process. Yet, if Arafat becomes as heavy-handed in his dealings with Hamas and other religious extremists as the Israelis expect him to be, he is bound to undercut his fragile and shrinking political base. A politically weakened Arafat would be of no use to the Israelis, but he cannot be expected to extract major concessions from the Rabin government unless the latter can convince the Israeli electorate that peace with the Palestinians is indeed at hand. The realities of the Israeli political scene consistently frustrate such a hope.

One option for Arafat to pursue would be to broaden his coalition by incorporating the Hamas elements into the ruling circle. However, any such development might still not give him the kind of control he needs over the politically splintered Palestinian groups. Apart from considerations from the Palestinian viewpoint, on the Israeli side the time may be running out for the Labour government. The poisonous environment created by the escalating violence from both sides only promises to strengthen the hands of the Likud and Hamas hardliners. And, if the Israeli electorate decides to give the Likud politicians a chance to govern, then the peace process is destined to suffer yet another setback.

The implications of these developments for the Syrian–Israeli peace process do not appear promising either. Hafez Assad continues to prefer the maximalist approach of a complete Israeli withdrawal from the Golan Heights for a complete (or total) peace. It is worth noting here that as the PLO–Israel peace process becomes a victim of increasing violence within Israel, Yitzhak Rabin's government's ability to even come close to offering a complete withdrawal from the Golan Heights dwindles almost to nothing. As long as anything less than the complete withdrawal remains unacceptable to Hafez Assad, peace between Damascus and Jerusalem remains a distant possibility.

THE POST-COLD WAR REJECTIONISTS

The Islamic Republic of Iran has emerged as the leader of the New Rejectionist Front. As previously noted, the other participants are the Hizbollah Party of Lebanon and the Hamas of the Occupied Territories and Israel proper. It should be emphasized at the outset that this front – despite the fact that the word 'front' conveys some element of cohesion among its participants – is a very loose grouping. The consensus of interests of the members of the Front is based on their rejection of any cooperation or negotiations with Israel. All of them continue to view the Jewish State as an illegitimate entity that should be destroyed. All of them view any measure of cooperation with Israel as heretical to the cause of Islam. Whether they really believe in this line of thinking is not too significant, because their violent acts against Israel (even though there is no direct participation of Iran in such acts, only its endorsement) and its chief advocate – the United States – convey the fact that they view Israel and the United States as the 'enemies' of Islam. The three members of the Front may or may not be co-ordinating their policies and/or actions on a regular basis.

Iran

A clear understanding of the leadership of Iran can be developed only by examining it at three levels: ideological, strategic, and internal dynamic. Of these, the ideological level is the overarching one, since this is where the emphasis of the leader of the Islamic revolution, the late Ayatollah Ruhollah Khomeini, on Islamic internationalism becomes of extreme significance. The element of Islamic internationalism, as he perceived it, transcends the Iranian revolution, raising it beyond the limitations of being a merely Shiite phenomenon. It was important for Khomeini for this revolution be seen as a purely Islamic one, so that the chances of its emulation in the neighbouring areas (in the short run) and throughout the Muslim world (in the long term) remain high. In fact, Khomeini succeeded in this regard, because the exportability of this revolution to the countries of the Persian Gulf remains a potential reality and a threat even in the post-Cold War environment of the 1990s. Moreover, in North Africa the governments of Algeria and Egypt have come under increasing pressure from the Islamic groups. Regardless of the fact that both Egypt and Algeria are largely Sunni Muslim countries, the potential for the creation of an Islamic regime has been more of a reality since the Islamic revolution of Iran than it was previously. This emphasizes the precedent-setting aspects of the Iranian revolution for the Islamicist forces in Egypt and Algeria.

For the consumption of Shiites outside Iran, Iran has put a different twist on the ideological element. Iran's revolution was not only perceived as a Shiite phenomenon, but as the beginning of an era in which the underprivileged Shiite masses from Bahrain to Lebanon were going to be politicized and galvanized into demanding equitable treatment from the ruling elites in their respective countries. This galvanization is of the utmost significance in the Middle East. The politics of Lebanon will never be the same again because of the mobilization of the Shiites in that country. However, the credit for this goes largely to the late Imam Musa Sadr ('the vanished Imam') of Lebanon. The Islamic Republic later added fuel to the galvanization process, after the disappearance of Imam Sadr, who was reportedly assassinated by the agents of Muammar Qaddafi while he was visiting Libya in 1978.[3]

The leadership role of Iran not only focuses strategically on the overall Islamic aspect (as opposed to its Shiite element), but is also aimed at exploiting existing anti-establishment and anti-Western feelings in the Middle East. This argument could be taken too far and credit (or blame) could attributed to Iran for attempting to disrupt the political status quo. I do not believe that Iran possesses such an influence. Anti-establishment and anti-Western feelings, where they are present in one or more countries, emanate from their own political and economic realities. Iran might be able to inflame those feelings into greater turbulence, but it certainly cannot create them from without.[4]

At the strategic level of leadership, Iran is also interested in focusing on existing political conditions which are noticeably different from those in Iran. For instance, the political experience of the peoples of Central Asia, Algeria or Egypt is quite different from that of the Iranian masses. Yet all these countries have experienced colonial rule, and this has been identified as one of the significant reasons for their backwardness and economic distress. Since all of these countries are largely Muslim, the Islamic alternative can be very effectively emphasized by Iran as a panacea to all their problems.

In this regard, it is worth nothing that Iran has identified the Palestinian cause as one of its chief foreign policy concerns, and as an Islamic problem. In doing so, Iran was not at all constrained to have close ties with the PLO, even though it gave the PLO legitimacy by allowing that organization to open an embassy as the representative of the Palestinians in the immediate aftermath of the victory of the Iranian revolutionary forces.

However, the close relationship between Iran and the PLO did not last long for a number of reasons. Firstly, during the Iran–Iraq War, Iran expected the PLO to support its position in return for the Iranian support of that organization. Yasser Arafat's dilemma was complicated by the fact that the 'Arabs versus Persians' variable was successfully exploited by Iraq. Secondly, since the Gulf sheikhdoms were already afraid of the potential exportability of the Iranian revolution to their borders, they also became advocates of Saddam's propaganda, and put pressure on Arafat to support this war as an 'Arab cause'. Arafat yielded to the pressure from his Gulf paymasters. Thirdly, the entry of the PLO into Lebanon and its related attacks on Israel resulted in intermittent military reprisals from the Jewish State. The late 1970s and early 1980s also saw the politicization of the Shiites and the emergence in Lebanon of Hizbollah, a predominantly Shiite organization. Since the Iranian style of Islamic government was the archetype of what Hizbollah wanted to establish in Lebanon, the rift between Iran and PLO was bound to escalate, especially since the latter prided itself on its secular perspectives on government.

Since its expulsion from Lebanon and its finding a refuge in Tunisia, the PLO has been forced to renounce terrorism and accept the legitimacy of Israel. If this was not the final parting of the ways between Iran and the Palestine Liberation Organization, the signing of the DOP in September 1993 definitely was. The PLO now emerged in the eyes of Iranian leaders not only as a secular entity, but also as an organization which had committed the heresy of legitimizing the 'Zionist tyranny' over the subjugated Palestinians. Iran had to find an alternative to the PLO, an organization loyal to the Islamic aspects of the Palestinian Question. Hamas was such an organization.

The third level of the Iranian leadership of the Rejectionist Front may also be viewed as its grass-roots aspect. In the final analysis, whether Iran remains a revolutionary state or re-enters the ranks of conventional nation-states will have a lot to do with the dynamics of internal political manoeuvrings between the pragmatists and the hardliners. Even though President Ali Hashemi Rafsanjani, as the leader of the pragmatist forces, remains at the helm of government, the internal jockeying for power also continues in Iran. It is possible that Rafsanjani prefers an abandonment of the revolutionary (or in this instance, rejectionist) aspect of Iranian foreign policy in the Middle East. However, he is unable to put such a purported desire into practice because his government has been under constant pressure to be loyal to the revolutionary legacy of Khomeini. Moreover, given the fact that the economic performance of the Rafsanjani government has remained so poor, especially in the 1990s, it cannot afford to add further fuel to the continued rhetorical barrages of the hardliners by adopting moderate policies, either towards the peace process or towards the United States. One also has to keep in mind the fact that, given the lack of cohesiveness among Iran, Hizbollah and Hamas (especially between Iran and Hamas), any moderation on the part of Iran may not have much effect on the activities of Hamas.[5]

Hizbollah

The very establishment of Hizbollah in Lebanon is persuasive evidence of the popularity of Shiite activism, and a rejection of another powerful but conventional tradition of 'quietism' (i.e., quiet protest toward an unjust ruler). The genesis of this organization belongs to the religious activism of an Iranian cleric and an expatriate in Lebanon, Imam Musa Sadr, who was active long before the Iranian revolution became a reality. Musa Sadr brought with him the political activism that was conceived and nurtured during his formative years in the Iranian and Iraqi religious schools, and was very much influenced by his association with Khomeini and Ayatollah Mohammed Baqr Sadr – a leading Shiite cleric who was hanged by Saddam Hussein in 1980.[6] Musa Sadr's firebrand rhetoric was peppered with the 'Imamite language to demand that justice be meted out' to the Shiites who were at the very bottom of the economic heap in Lebanon. He fully understood that, as a first step towards galvanizing his people, he must politicize them and convey to them that they could improve their lot only by fighting to get what was rightly theirs. Instead of being referred to in the contemptuous phrase of the Lebanese polity as *Mitwalin*, he declared that the Shiites are *Rafidun*, 'the people of vengeance, the people who rebel against any expression of despotism'.[7]

Sadr founded the *Afwaj al-Muqawama al-Lubnaniyya* (which is better known by its acronym AMAL – Hope) – movement in 1975 as an organized effort to attain political equality for the Shiites. This was a major step towards the adoption of violence as a means of seeking justice by the *Mahrumin* or *Mustadafin* (the oppressed, i.e., the Shiites). AMAL also aimed at 'preserving the honour of the homeland [Lebanon] and containing Israeli attacks'.[8]

The Hizbollah emerged as a splinter group of AMAL after the disappearance of Musa Sadr. However, the objectives of this group were in complete harmony with the revolutionary objectives of the Islamic Republic of Iran. In the traditions of Musa Sadr and Khomeini, Hizbollah saw itself as a champion for the causes of the oppressed. It sought to create an Islamic republic in Lebanon independent of the East and the West. Originally, this Islamic republic was to follow the Iranian model of government under the *Vilayet al-Faqih* (i.e., the rule of the scholar of jurisprudence). However, this particular goal went through some noteworthy alteration, given the fact that Lebanon, unlike Iran, is a multi-religious state. A leading Lebanese Shiite cleric, Shaykh Mohammed Hussein Fadlallah, who is generally regarded as its chief theoretician or '*Murshid al-Ruhi* (spiritual guide)' even though he vehemently denies it, feels that an Islamic republic in Lebanon 'is a goal which will be achieved later rather than sooner, given the certain opposition of several communities in Lebanon and their powerful foreign supporters'.[9]

As regards Israel and a negotiated resolution of the Palestinian–Israeli conflict, Hizbollah's position becomes clear from the following statement:

> We strongly condemn all the plans for mediation between us and Israel and we consider the mediators [the United States] a hostile party because their mediation will only serve to acknowledge the legitimacy of the Zionist occupation of Palestine.... Islamic resistance must continue, grow and escalate, with God's help, and must receive from all Muslims in all parts of the world complete support, aid, backing and participation so that we may be able to uproot this cancerous germ and obliterate it from existence....[10]

After the Taif Accord of 1989, Hizbollah underwent a process of complex change and emerged as a political party. As such, it participated in the 1992 parliamentary elections. Even thus transformed, Hizbollah, according to one study, reflected the 'shifts' in Iranian foreign policy. This was in response to the ongoing struggle within the Iranian policy between the pragmatists (the Rafsanjani group) and the hardliners (the group led by Iran's famous radical, Ali Akbar Muhtashami). In a conference in Iran in October 1978, two factions of Hizbollah sided with their Iranian pragmatist and radical counterparts. The pragmatist group, led by Sayyid Abbas Musawi, Shaykh Subhi Tufaili, and Sayyid Hussein Musawi, argued for rapprochement with other religious and secular groups in Lebanon, thus reflecting the position of President Rafsanjani. The other group, led by

Sayyid Hasan Nasrallah, advocated the position of a 'perpetual Jihad' for Hizbollah. Hizbollah's decision to participate in the 1992 parliamentary elections in Lebanon is an indication that it may follow the pragmatist path more actively in the future, a process rather glibly referred to as the 'Lebanonization of Hizbollah'.[11]

However, given the uncertaintics related to the potential peace agreement between Syria and Israel, and the future of pragmatism in Iran, no one can state with any certainty which course the Hizbollah is likely to follow in the coming years. Regarding the peace process, it is highly unlikely that Hizbollah would make an about-face and accept the notion of compromise with Israel in the foreseeable future. If Syria signs a peace treaty with Israel, the latter will insist that Damascus place Hizbollah under its total control. The Syrian attitude regarding this issue and the peace process is inextricably linked to its ties with Iran, and with the dynamics of its own presence in Lebanon.

Hizbollah has been handled differently by Iran and Syria. Iranian and Syrian interests coincided regarding the Israeli withdrawal from Lebanon in the early 1980s. Syria did not want any external power challenging its hegemony in Lebanon. If the Iranian influence with the Shiites of Southern Lebanon and Hizbollah could have been used to force Israel out of Lebanon, the Syrians would not have preferred another option. In fact Hizbollah did play a crucial role in bringing about this reality. However, Iran also wanted to use Hizbollah to weaken the political power of the Maronite establishment in Lebanon. Obviously, Teheran had a zero-sum perspective on this issue. As Iran saw it, any loss of Maronite political power would result in the enhancement of the political status of the Shiites in Lebanon. Such enhancement would be reflected in a greater share of power for this group. Syria, on the other hand, pursued a more subtle policy in Lebanon. Hafez Assad, instead of favouring one group, person, or even organization at the expense of the others, preferred first and foremost to maintain a military balance among the various factions. Consequently, no group or person could become strong enough to threaten or challenge Syrian interests in Lebanon. On this issue, Iran appeared to demonstrate ample patience towards Syria. Perhaps Iran has understood that the demographic pressures – the large movements of the Maronites to France and other Western countries, along with high birthrates among Muslims – are eventually going to result in significantly strengthened political power for the Shiites in Lebanon, the Syrian balancing act notwithstanding.[12]

Both Syria and Iran have wanted to use the Hizbollah card in influencing the future dynamics of the peace process involving not only the Palestinians and Israel, but also Israel and Lebanon. Obviously, Syria has considerable advantage in this regard as a result of its proximity to both Israel and Lebanon, and also because it is an occupying force in Lebanon.

Hamas

The third rejectionist entity that will be discussed in this chapter is *Harakat al-Muquwwama al-Islamiyya* (the Islamic resistance movement) or Hamas (which also means 'enthusiasm' or 'zeal'), whose visibility became more pronounced with the signing of the DOP between the PLO and Israel. This organization was established at about the same time as the start of the *Intifada*, and is led by Sheikh Ahmad Ismail Yasin, who is currently in an Israeli jail.

Hamas is a spin-off from the Muslim Brotherhood of Egypt, which also has branches in Jordan and the Occupied Territories. It has a fundamental disagreement with the PLO over the nature of an independent Palestinian state. The PLO, mindful of the political pluralism and differences in religious background of its constituents, wants to establish a secular state. Hamas, while agreeing with the PLO on pan-Arabism, pursues the goal of creating an Islamic state. In this sense, Hamas opposes the Palestinian National Charter, with its predilection for secularism. The motto of Hamas is quite explicit in spelling out what it stands for. 'God is the goal, the Prophet is the model, the Koran is the constitution, Jihad is the path, and death on God's path is our most sublime aspiration.'[13] The renunciation of violence and acceptance of the existence of Israel by the PLO has only intensified the disagreements between it and Hamas, a relationship which was acutely competitive and fractious to begin with. The PLO's main support comes from the West Bank, while Hamas draws its political strength from the Gaza Strip. This might also be because the Gaza Strip is an area of abject poverty and is predominantly Muslim. The West Bank is a relatively prosperous area, and is also inhabited by educated Muslims and Christians who are receptive to the principle of secularism.[14]

Hamas has emerged 'in a context of disillusionment with the Palestinian secular political movements and with the frustrated hope of achieving salvation from Israeli occupation through them'.[15] The Islamic forces were originally actually encouraged to become politically active and visible by Israeli officials, hoping that this activism would weaken the PLO. The Israelis paid scant attention to the fact that, since there is no room for the notion of separation of church and state among Muslims, it would not be too long before the Muslim forces in the Occupied Territories focused their attention on political issues and the continued subjugation of their people, and turned on the Israeli authorities. What might have originally prompted the Israelis to pursue this policy was the Islamicists' concentration on charitable activities and religious education, and their abstention from terrorism. The Israelis did not misread the role of the Islamicists before the initiation of the *Intifada*. In fact, Hamas maintained a position that there was no point in promoting *jihad*-related activities. Instead, they focused on 'healing the Muslim soul'.[16]

Since Hamas was created in the highly charged and intensely activistic environment of the *Intifada*, it belied all the previous expectations Israeli officials had about the Islamicists of the Occupied Territories. As a movement, Hamas offered 'a special kind of activism that combined patriotism with moral purity and social action with the promise of divine grace'.[17] Its military wing, *Kataib Izzedin al-Qassam*,[18] has been responsible for carrying out violent attacks on Israeli targets. The covenant of Hamas of August 1988 declares the entire British Mandate of Palestine which ended in 1947 to be 'an Islamic trust inherited by Muslims'. It categorically rejects a negotiated settlement of the Palestinian-Israeli conflict. The only way to deal with Israel, according to this document, is by conducting a *jihad*. The territories thus liberated are to become an Islamic state, which, in turn, is just another step towards the eventual pan-Islamic union of all Muslims.[19]

According to two Israeli journalists, Ze'ef Schiff and Ehud Ya'ari, Sheikh Yasin offered something to a follower that Yasser Arafat could not. This was 'not just the redemption of the homeland but the salvation of his own troubled soul'. However, regarding Israel, the attitude of the Muslim Brotherhood and Hamas reflected a disturbing contrast. They 'gloried' in their expression of anti-Semitism and 'made the crude expression of Jew-hatred a common feature of their publications'.[20]

The legitimacy and popularity of Hamas among the Palestinian masses grew during the *Intifada* for a variety of reasons. Firstly, the religious orientation of this entity was one of the most crucial reasons, especially when one considers the widespread disillusionment with the secular leadership of all the other Palestinian organizations, including the Fatah faction of the PLO. Secondly, Hamas' ability to offer all sorts of social services and economic assistance, and its effectiveness even in settling personal disputes, enhanced the overall perception among the Palestinians that it genuinely cared for their well-being. Thirdly, and as a related factor, whatever measure of self-rule the Israelis had allowed earlier was suspended as the *Intifada*-related activities were intensified. Hamas was effective in filling this gap. Finally, Hamas was unhampered by the PLO's difficulties as an illegal entity facing logistical problems in receiving instructions and guidance from Tunis and other remote areas during the *Intifada*. Hamas was both visible and present in the Occupied Territories. The cumulative impact of these variables enabled Hamas to challenge the leadership status of the PLO. However, when Yasser Arafat signed the DOP with the Israelis, the rift between Hamas and the PLO intensified considerably. Hamas openly declared such an approach 'un-Islamic' and immoral.

THE NATURE OF INTERACTION AMONG THE REJECTIONISTS AND PROSPECTS FOR A CONTINUED PEACE

The rejectionists undoubtedly remain highly critical of the peace process. However, there remains the important question of how they are interacting to undermine the prospects for peace in the Middle East. If there is no effective interaction among them, then one cannot speak of a 'front'. If they are indeed interacting among themselves, then those who support the ongoing peace process must understand these interactions in order to undermine them.

It will be recalled that a multifaceted perspective of Iran's leadership was presented earlier in this chapter. By the same token, no straightforward statement can be made as an elaborate description of Iranian interests, for Iran's views regarding the peace process are intertwined with a rather complex web of regional and international interests. It is hard to believe that Iran has rejected the peace process purely for ideological reasons (Islamic or otherwise). Those who attribute an inordinate amount of significance to the idealistic notions of Iran's commitments to Islam tend to forget that this is the same country which traded weapons with both the United States and Israel during the so-called 'Iran-Contra Affair'. Khomeini, the patriarch of the Islamic revolution, was also very much alive then.

Iran's rejection of the peace process is intrinsically linked with the ongoing power struggle between the radicals and the pragmatists. As long as the pendulum of this struggle does not decisively swing in favour of the pragmatists (led by President Rafsanjani), Iran will continue to reject the peace process. And, given the fact that the pragmatists are not likely to improve their power position due to deteriorating economic conditions in Iran, Tehran is likely to continue its condemnation of the peace process. In fact, once Syria starts to make progress in its negotiations with Israel, Iranian–Syrian ties are likely to be strained. Even then, the future of Iran's ties with Syria will be influenced by the domestic power struggle between the pragmatists and the hardliners in Iran.

As Iran examines the intricacies of the Palestinian–Israeli peace negotiations, it does not feel that its own rejection of the peace process is based on faulty calculations. Unless significant progress is made by the Israelis and the PLO on this issue, Iran's continued condemnation should not be viewed as an irreversible position. Even the conservative monarchies are keeping their enthusiasm and support of this process at a low level, lest they be branded 'lackeys of the American–Zionist plot'. If the peace process gives definite signs of leading towards an independent Palestine, Iran is unlikely to be one of the last states to offer its approval.

The position of Hizbollah on the peace process is definitely going to be influenced by Iran, if or when the country changes its mind on this issue. In this respect, there is definite and regular interaction between Iran and Hizbollah. It should be remembered, however, that Hizbollah also has its own agenda with regard to Israel, namely, the dismantling of the so-called security zone and the disbanding of the Israel-backed militia, the South Lebanese Army (SLA), under 'General' Antoine Lahad. This whole issue is inextricably linked with Israel's negotiations with Syria and Lebanon. How far the government of Lebanon is likely to go in negotiating with Israel depends on what happens on the Israeli–Syrian negotiating front.

Israel will link any significant withdrawal from the Golan Heights with iron-clad Syrian guarantees to control future attacks by Hizbollah. In this sense, Hafez Assad is simultaneously riding two horses – Syria and Lebanon. In order to satisfy Israeli demands regarding Hizbollah, Assad might be forced to apply the 'Hama rule' in Lebanon.[21] This rule refers to the brutal suppression (and, it is even claimed, virtual elimination) of the Muslim Brotherhood by the Assad regime in the Hama region. However, Hizbollah, unlike the Muslim Brotherhood of Syria, has already emerged as a political party. As such, its behaviour is also likely to change once the Syrian–Israeli and Israeli–Lebanese peace process makes significant progress. Lest it be forgotten, another important variable in this regard is the future ability of the Israeli government to offer concessions to both Syria and Lebanon.

If pressed to identify the most crucial, intricate and delicate aspect of the Arab–Israeli conflict, the answer, most assuredly, has to be the relationship between the PLO and Israel. As previously noted, the PLO is the weakest of all the parties negotiating with Israel, yet it is also the most important. There are several aspects of the intricate Palestinian–Israeli negotiating process that deserve further consideration.

Firstly, two radical visions motivate the parties involved. It is not at all clear that the Israeli leadership has thought its way through the eventual outcome of its conflict with the Palestinians. If it had, would it eventually be willing to remove all the Jewish settlements? Would it, at some point in the future, be willing to transfer its sovereignty over Jerusalem to the PLO? Or are the Israelis hoping that the Palestinians can be persuaded to live under some sort of confederation with them, or with Jordan? No observer of the peace process can produce a clear picture of the perception of the Israeli leadership on this issue.[22] It is quite clear, however, what the Palestinians expect from the peace process. They want it to lead to the creation of an independent state, the removal of most (if not all) the Jewish settlements, and Jerusalem (either the whole city or part of it) as the capital. The intensity of emotion and religious fervour on both sides appear to be two of the greatest obstacles to the emergence of this solution, however. The religious Jews are likely to do their utmost to thwart its progress. Hamas has already declared its resolve to destroy the prospects for a negotiated solution.

Secondly, Rabin has linked any major progress in the negotiating process to the ability of Yasser Arafat to control (read 'crush') Hamas as a violent opposition group. In fact, he is on record as observing that Arafat would crush Hamas, without giving the Israel Supreme Court any say in this matter. In principle, Rabin was correctly interpreting Arafat's potential approach, for the Arab leaders have traditionally shown little compassion in stamping out political opposition. What is working against Rabin's expectations in this particular instance is the fact that Hamas' opposition to the peace process is especially popular in the Gaza region. In addition, Arafat has been afraid that his ruthless treatment of Hamas might trigger a civil war in the Occupied Territories. Consequently, the political futures of both Arafat and Rabin are closely tied to the future progress of the peace process. Any long-term stalling would escalate the chances of its unravelling, as the Rabin government's term of office approaches the electoral time of reckoning.

Thirdly, the issue of the Jewish settlements is, in my estimation, almost as explosive as the future status of Jerusalem. As far as the Palestinians are concerned, these must be removed. For a large number of Israelis, however, the settlements – especially those in the West Bank – are the manifestation of the return of the Jews to their Promised Land. Purely from the political perspective, however, such a removal would be regarded as the shrinking of the Jewish presence, a bad precedent whose potential implications for Israel could not even be contemplated as far the Jews are concerned. As one ponders the issue, one wonders whether the smaller Jewish settlements in the Gaza Strip are also attributed similar significance by the Israelis.

The fourth complication of the Israeli–PLO peace process concerns the ability of the Rabin government to offer political concessions. Yasser Arafat badly needs Israeli concessions in order to stem the tide of extremist opposition on the Palestinian side. Yet, as the violence perpetrated by the Hamas forces continues to escalate, the Rabin government is also likely to come under heavy pressure, not only from the hardline Likud party, but also from the Israeli voters to stop offering concessions to Arafat at the very least, or at worst, stop the negotiating process altogether. If either of these eventualities were to materialize, it would only boost the position of the Palestinian hardliners. Thus, both Rabin and Arafat need to make progress – one by offering concessions and the other by converting these concessions into a neutralization of the extremist forces.[23] Rabin's ability to maintain the negotiating momentum on the Palestinian front is bound to persuade Hafez Assad to initiate a Syrian–Israeli peace process. Any stalling of the peace negotiations with the Palestinians would only enable Assad to indulge in another round of 'I told you so'.

There is little doubt that Iran and Hamas have maintained contact, especially since both of them reject the peace process. I remain very unconvinced, however, that Hamas takes its political cues from Iran and/or Hizbollah. Hamas is primarily a Sunni entity. As such, any close association between it and Iran might be constrained by theological differences, for there is no theological basis for the acceptance of Khomeini's version of the *Vilayat-e-Faqih* among the Sunnis. When one observes the behaviour of Hizbollah and Hamas, however, one is struck by a particular similarity in their respective political programmes. Hizbollah has already participated in the Lebanese electoral process, and has emerged as more of a conventional political party. Hamas, on the other hand, is only contemplating and debating such a move. Even if Hamas were to follow Hizbollah's example – and the chances of such a development are good – I am not inclined to credit Iran for such a development. Hamas' political activities appear to be strongly focused on political developments within the Occupied Territories and its own competitive and antagonistic relationship with the PLO. At some point, the leaders of Hamas will be forced to give up their political inflexibility and opt for pragmatism. However, they will adopt a pragmatic approach only if the peace process between Israel and the PLO continues to make progress. Iran's own potential future acceptance or condoning of the peace process would have little bearing on Hamas' attitude.

A word should be said about the Israeli ability to offer concessions to Syria and Lebanon. The future of such potential is also tied to the dynamics of the peace process between the PLO and Israel. If the parties continue to extend the scope of their ongoing negotiations, Israeli public opinion might even allow Rabin to take bold measures in the form of a withdrawal from a large part of the Golan Heights. However, Rabin is likely to be looking for similar major concessions from Syria. But Assad is not known for his dramatic moves and theatrical gestures, unlike the late Anwar Sadat. So, even if the PLO–Israeli peace process were to show dramatic and promising improvement, only a willingness on the part of Hafez Assad to offer a 'comprehensive' peace to Israel would produce a corresponding Israeli withdrawal from the Golan Heights.

CONCLUSIONS

The interactions among the three protagonists of the Rejectionist Front do not appear to be terribly significant as regards the future of the peace process. Iran might endorse the peace process at some point in the future if (a) the pragmatists were to get the upper hand in the power struggle in that country's domestic political arena and (b) the PLO–Israeli peace process were to make steady progress towards the creation of an independent Palestine.

Hizbollah might be too bogged down in the domestic politics of Lebanon to continue to be a terrorist group in the future, provided that it continues to evolve as a conventional political party. As such, it might become receptive to a political give and take towards Israel. In the meantime, Iran's own attitude towards the peace process may continue to affect the political thinking of Hizbollah. Israeli policies towards the 'security zone' and the SLA would become a bargaining chip in future negotiations with Lebanon. However, any progress on this front is linked to the dynamics of future Syrian–Israeli peace negotiations. The potential incorporation of Hamas into the peace process has to be initiated by its own leadership. Iran would have little influence there.

NOTES

1. For a detailed background to the politics of Lebanon, see Wadi D. Haddad, *Lebanon: The Politics of Revolving Doors* (NY: Praeger Publishers, 1985).
2. For instance, see 'Supporters of Arafat in U.S. Say Financial Aids Is Too Slow, Limited', *The Washington Post*, 27 December, 1994.

3. For a good overview of Musa Sadr's role in politicizing the Shiites of Lebanon see Shimon Shapiro, 'The Imam Musa al Sadr: Father of the Shiite Resurgence in Lebanon', *The Jerusalem Quarterly*, Autumn 1987, pp. 121–44.
4. A careful student of this issue is always sceptical of accusations and counter-accusations. The Middle Eastern states are second to none in blaming foreign 'enemies' and 'conspirators' for the violent political upheavals that occur within their borders.
5. I am purposely ignoring the hardline factions of the PLO which are situated in Syria. They are under the tight control of Hafez Assad. They can make a lot of noise, but cannot launch any attacks on Israel, for Assad wants no military reprisals from the Jewish State. Once Syria starts serious negotiations with Israel, its role as a rejectionist is likely to be virtually eliminated by Assad, especially if Syria and Israel end up signing a peace treaty. It could be suggested that Hizbollah might also encounter a similar fate. I would argue that Hizbollah emerged as a political party in the 1990s. As such, its role might be somewhat altered if Assad ends up making peace with Israel. The likelihood of the elimination of Hizbollah from Lebanese politics is minimal at best. This might be a significant difference between Hizbollah and the hardline PLO factions of Syria.
6. A thoughtful discussion of the political philosophy of Baqr Sadr is to be found in Chibli Mallat's, 'Religious Militancy in Contemporary Iraq: Muhammad Baqr as-Sadr and the Sunni-Shia Paradigm', *Third World Quarterly*, April 1988, pp. 699–729.
7. Shapira, 'The Imam Musa al-Sadr', op. cit., p. 130.
8. Ibid., p. 135.
9. Martin Kramer, *The Moral Logic of Hizballah* (Tel Aviv, Israel: The Shiloah Institute, August 1987), p. 8.
10. From 'Hizbollah's Manifesto', in Uri Ran'anan, Robert Pfaltzgraff, Jr., Richard Schultz, Ernst Halperin, and Igor Lukes (eds), *Hydra of Carnage: The International Linkages of Terrorism and other Low-Intensity Operations* (Lexington, MA: Lexington, 1986), pp. 488–491.
11. A. Nizar Hamzeh, 'Lebanon's Hizbullah: From Islamic Revolution to Parliamentary Accommodation', *Third World Quarterly*, 1993, pp. 321–37.
12. A similar analysis of Syrian foreign policy is also present in Asad Abukhalil, 'Syria and the Shiites: Al Asad's Policy in Lebanon', *Third World Quarterly*, April 1990, pp. 1–20.
13. Ziad Abu-Amr, *Islamic Fundamentalism in the West Bank and Gaza: Muslim Brotherhood and Islamic Jihad* (Bloomington, IN: Indiana University Press, 1994), p. 81.
14. For an excellent treatment of the economic problems encountered by the residents of Gaza, see Sara M. Roy, 'Gaza: New Dynamics of Civic Disintegration', *Journal of Palestine Studies*, XXII, Summer, 1993, pp. 20–31.
15. Abu-Amr, op. cit., p. 66.
16. Ze'ef Schiff and Ehud Ya'ari, *Intifada, The Palestinian Uprising – Israel's Third Front* (edited and translated by Ina Friedman) (NY: Simon & Schuster, 1990), p. 224.
17. Schiff and Ya'ari, op. cit., p. 227.

18. Kataib Izzedin al-Qassam is a faction named after a Syrian-born preacher who came to Palestine in 1928, and became involved in armed struggle against both Britain, the Mandatory power of that time, and the Zionists who were struggling to establish their own state. He was killed by British forces in 1935. This wing reportedly operates independently of Hamas.
19. James P. Wooten, *Hamas: The Organization, Goals and Tactics of a Militant Palestinian Organization* (Washington, DC: Congressional Research Service, August 1993), p. 1.
20. Schiff and Ya'ari, op. cit., p. 227.
21. Thomas Friedman, 'Hama Rules', in *From Beirut to Jerusalem* (NY: Doubleday, 1989), p. 76–105.
22. A good example of this is the different visions of the eventual outcome of the peace process expressed by Israeli Prime Minister Yitzhak Rabin and Foreign Minister Shimon Peres. Rabin reportedly sees the peace process as eventually leading to a 'hermetic separation of Israel and the future Palestinian entity...'. Peres, on the other hand, perceives the outcome to be the creation of 'open borders' and economic cooperation. See 'Shimon Peres: The Unloved Visionary', *The Jerusalem Report*, 15 December 1994, pp. 11–16.
23. The point is that Arafat should be able to outmanoeuvre, not physically crush, the extremism of Hamas, for any physical suppression of extremist forces is likely to create a chain reaction, thus resulting in civil war among the Palestinians.

2 Kurdish Conflict in a Regional Perspective

Nader Entessar

INTRODUCTION

The purpose of this chapter is to analyze the Kurdish factor within the broader context of regional politics in the Middle East. The focus here is on relations between Iran and Turkey, with a secondary emphasis on Iraq. Relations between these three countries have been influenced by a variety of factors in recent decades, but the Kurdish factor has been the least understood of the variables which have shaped the contours of the political relationship between Iran, Turkey and Iraq. Given the increasing importance of the role of the Kurds in current and future conflicts in the Middle East, it is worth examining this somewhat neglected topic to see how it affects continuity and change in regional relations.

The processes of change and patterns of continuity in the foreign policies of the regional states can be examined within the context of the Kurdish conflict. The continuity variable is reflected in the fact that Iran, Turkey and Iraq have used their own Kurdish population as well as those of the neighbouring states in pursuit of their foreign policy objectives. As a consequence, the Kurds have, to various degrees, become victims of regional and international politics. The Gulf War, the establishment of a 'no-fly' zone in northern Iraq to protect the Kurds from military attacks by Iraqi forces and the subsequent creation of a Kurdish administration have brought about changes in regional variables affecting the Kurds. As will be discussed later, post-Gulf War developments have forced the principal states in the region to modify their foreign policies, at least in the short term, and to adjust their Kurdish policies accordingly.

In 1501, with the advent of the Shi'a Safavid dynasty in Iran, the Sunni Ottoman Empire saw Iran as an ideological and political challenge to its leadership of the Muslim world. Consequently, the Ottoman sultans sought to confront their new adversaries with the force of arms and threatened to crush the Shi'a state. The Ottoman sultans generally viewed the Persians as 'heathens' who blasphemed against Islam through their

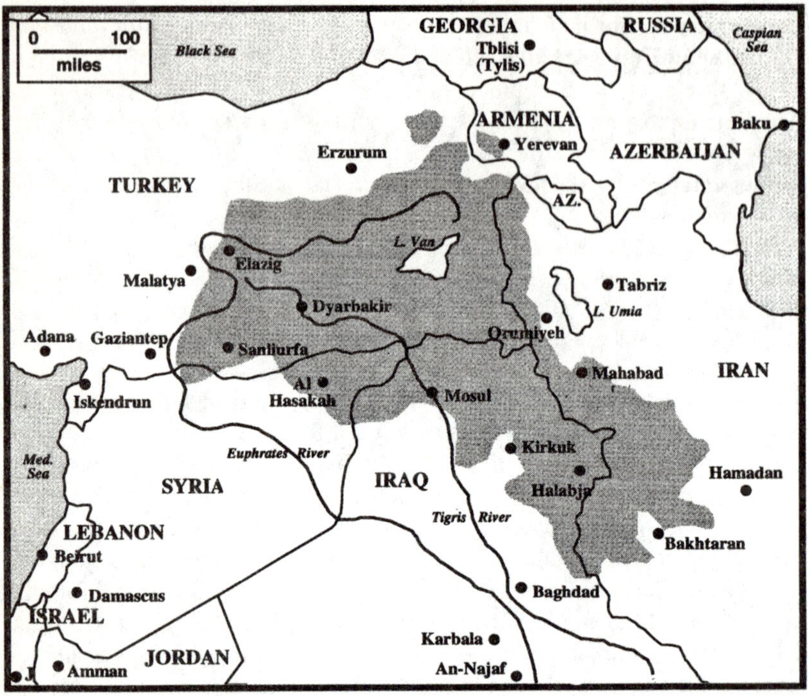

Map 2.1 Kurdish lands

conversion to Shi'ism under the Safavids. For example, the Ottoman Sultan Selim I in a vitriolic letter to Safavid king Shah Isma'il written in 1514, threatens his Iranian counterpart with death and exhorts other Muslims to take up arms for the 'destruction of heresy and impiety in thy person and the persons of those who follow thee'.[1] The ensuing centuries witnessed major wars and incessant territorial conflicts between these two rival Muslim entities.

With the defeat of the Ottoman Empire, its disintegration after World War I and the coming to power in Iran of Reza Khan (later Reza Shah, the first king of the Pahlavi dynasty), major improvements occurred in relations between the two rivals. Both Reza Shah and Mustafa Kemal Ataturk, the 'founder' of modern Turkey, embarked on the forceful secularization of their societies with varying degrees of success. Both endeavoured to establish strong central governments in their respective countries to accelerate the process of nation-building and westernization of the sociopolitical institutions. More important, Ataturk disavowed Turkey's Ottoman past, its territorial ambitions and hegemonic irredentism against its neighbours. Despite great improvements in relations between the two countries, the Kurdish issue remained a potential source of conflict between republican Turkey and the kingdom of Iran. This was particularly true in the 1920s when Kurdish revolts in Turkey were crushed by the Turkish army, forcing many Kurdish tribes to cross into Iran. The Turkish army's pursuit of the Kurds into Iran caused friction between Turkey and Iran, leading to charges and countercharges and the revival of some historical border disputes between the two neighbouring countries.

In the 1930s, the two states undertook several steps to resolve their disputes within the context of a broader security framework. The 1932 Frontier Treaty allowed Turkey and Iran to settle outstanding border claims, thus paving the way for a broader pact dealing with the long-festering Kurdish question. A more extensive agreement was that of the Saadabad Pact of 1937 between Turkey, Iran, Iraq and Afghanistan.[2] This agreement covered a broad range of security issues and called for 'non-interference, non-aggression, consultation on security affairs and arbitration of problems'.[3] Although the Saadabad Pact had no provisions for the use of collective force against foreign aggressors, it did include mechanisms through which Turkey, Iran and Iraq would coordinate their activities regarding cross-border Kurdish revolts and insurgencies. It also laid the groundwork for future regional co-operation between these states in the form of the Baghdad Pact (which became the Central Treaty Organization (CENTO) after Iraq's withdrawal from this grouping, following the overthrow of that country's Hashemite monarchy in 1958) and the Regional Co-operation for Development (RCD), which was an organization responsible mainly for promoting economic co-operation among its member states.

Although the Turks and the Persians have historically distrusted each other, Ankara's relations with Teheran remained remarkably cordial until the advent of the Islamic Republic in Iran. A number of factors helped bring about a mutuality of interests between Turkey and Iran. Anti-Sovietism was quite pronounced in the foreign policy postures of both countries, since each perceived Soviet expansionism as a major threat to its territorial integrity and national security interests in the region. The political and military ties they developed with the West as a hedge against the Soviet Union also brought about a commonality of interests between Ankara and Teheran and created the proper framework for the co-ordination of their regional activities with respect to Kurdish uprisings in the region. Furthermore, bilateral relations between Ankara and Teheran were strengthened as non-Arab Turkey and Iran saw themselves as a counterbalance to the Arab politics and policies of the region.

THE KURDISH REVOLT IN IRAQ IN THE 1970s: IRAN'S RESPONSE AND TURKISH CONCERNS

Notwithstanding border conflicts and differences over a range of foreign policy issues, Turkey, Iran and Iraq generally eschewed the temptation to use their 'Kurdish card' against each other's interests and adhered to the terms of the Saadabad Pact until the overthrow of the Iraqi monarchy. However, when Iraq became a republic in 1958 and a 'Pan-Arabist', anti-Western group seized power in Baghdad, the Kurdish card became a more attractive political and military weapon. This was particularly true in the case of Iran–Iraq relations.[4] The new Iraqi leader, Abdul Karim Qassem, sought to settle Iraq's own Kurdish problem by initiating peace talks with the Kurdish leader Mullah Mustafa Barzani. As a 'goodwill gesture', Qassem supplied some weapons and allowed the Kurdish fighters, or *peshmerga* ('those who face death'), to use Iraqi territory from which to launch attacks against targets inside Iran. Although Barzani's forays inside Iran were militarily insignificant and resulted in only minor disturbances in such border towns as Baneh and Marivan, they did open up a Pandora's box and eventually contributed to the shaping of the Shah's Kurdish policy. In fact, as I have argued elsewhere, Qassem's tactic of using the Kurds to destabilize the pro-Western Iranian regime backfired against Iraq in the early 1970s when the Shah, in conjunction with the United States and Israel, co-opted Mullah Mustafa Barzani into a scheme to destabilize the Iraqi regime.[5] With outside help and encouragement, Mullah Mustafa's *peshmerga* were able to fight the Iraqi forces and present a serious challenge to the viability of the Iraqi government.

Following Nasser's death in 1970 and the weakening of pan-Arabist sentiment in Cairo, Iraq's sense of vulnerability was heightened when Iran and Egypt began to forge closer links with each other. Iraq's sense of isolation became even more acute when the Shah managed to improve Iran's relations with Syria, another implacable 'pan-Arabist'. By mid-1974, Saddam Hussein, Iraq's Vice-President and *de facto* ruler, had grudgingly concluded that in order to break down Baghdad's isolation and defeat the Kurdish uprising on the political front, he needed to reach a *modus vivendi* with the Iranian government. King Hussein of Jordan, perhaps the only Arab leader who had maintained cordial relations with both the Shah and Saddam Hussein, played the role of a mediator in paving the way for an eventual Iranian–Iraqi rapprochement. During the 1974 Arab Summit meeting in Rabat, King Hussein managed to arrange a meeting between Iraqi representatives and an Iranian delegation that had travelled to Morocco to meet the Iraqis.[6] Officials from Teheran and Baghdad continued to hold meetings with each other until March 1975 through the efforts of such intermediaries as Algeria and Jordan.

In early 1975, the Soviet Union abruptly decided to curtail weapons shipments to Baghdad. As Saddam Hussein bitterly acknowledged, by the time he had decided to strike a deal with Iran, the Iraqi military possessed only three missiles and very few shells.[7] The Iranian government was in a position to push for the break-up of Iraq. However, the Shah did not view this possibility to be in the best interest of Teheran or Ankara, given the impact of such a policy on the Kurdish population in Iran and Turkey. It is not clear what prompted Moscow to withhold critically needed weapons from the Iraqi government at that time. The Soviets may have been disenchanted with the growing isolation of the Iraqi regime in the Arab world and hoped to bring about changes in the leadership or policies of the Iraqi government by withholding weapons from the Iraqi armed forces in their hour of need. Moscow may have calculated that the prolongation of the Kurdish crisis in Iraq and the related Iran–Iraq confrontation would have irreparably damaged Soviet chances of improving relations with Iran, a country with which they had hoped to develop economic ties and a country that was more important to Soviet geostrategic designs in the Persian Gulf than Iraq was. The Soviets may also have been worried about the implications of a Kurdish victory in Iraq for their own ethnic minorities in the Caucasus and Central Asia.

Mullah Mustafa Barzani was well aware of the efforts of various intermediaries to end the dangerous conflict between Iraq and Iran, and he was fearful that an eventual rapprochement between Teheran and Baghdad would seriously damage the Kurdish cause in Iraq. Consequently, in late February 1975, Barzani dispatched a high-level delegation to Egypt to express his concerns about developments on the diplomatic front between a militarily weakened Iraq and the Shah of Iran. The Kurdish delegation asked Egyptian President Anwar Sadat to use his influence and friendship with the Shah to preserve Kurdish interests in the event of an Iranian–Iraqi rapprochement. Sadat assured the Kurdish delegation that he knew of no negotiations between Teheran and Baghdad that would redound to the detriment of the Iraqi Kurds. As it turned out, President Sadat did not want to derail the sensitive negotiations between Iran and Iraq by publicly admitting their existence to Barzani's emissaries.

In March 1975, multilateral Arab efforts to bring about a settlement of the Iran–Iraq conflict bore fruit when Algerian President Houari Boumédienne arranged what was then viewed as an historic meeting between the Shah and Saddam Hussein during the Organization of Petroleum Exporting Countries' (OPEC) summit in Algiers. This meeting resulted in the signing of the Algiers Agreement on 6 March 1975. This agreement resulted, *inter alia*, in the termination of the Shah's support for the Kurdish uprising in Iraq, in return of Baghdad's concessions on a number of border adjustments between the two countries. These included Iraq's acceptance of the Thalweg Line, or mid-channel of the Shatt al-Arab (Arvand Rud as it is called by Iranians) as the boundary between Iran and Iraq. Since the Shatt al-Arab was Iraq's only major outlet to the Persian Gulf, the Iraqi regime had always insisted on total control of this river, claiming that Iraq's economic survival depended on total sovereignty over the Shatt al-Arab. Iran, on the other hand, had insisted that the waterway was crucial to its economy and navigation, and that international law had clearly recognized the Thalweg Line as the boundary between countries sharing a body of water such as the Shatt al-Arab.[8] Saddam Hussein's concession on this point was a bitter blow to the prestige of his regime, eventually forcing him to renounce the terms of the Algiers Agreement and invade Iran in September, 1980.

The Algiers Agreement was certainly a major blow to the Kurdish cause and to Mullah Mustafa's leadership. Within hours of the announcement of the Algiers Agreement, Baghdad launched a major offensive against the demoralized Kurdish *peshmerga* and eliminated any noticeable Kurdish resistance within a few weeks. Thousands of Iraqi Kurds sought refuge in Iran, and the Iraqi government began a policy of depopulating Kurdish villages and relocating their residents to other parts of the country. In the words of Iraqi dissident Samir al-Khalil (Kanan Makiya):

> Families of Kurds were bundled into army trucks and transported to large, hastily improvised camps or to Arab villages west of the Euphrates where they were settled in small groups.... [Iraqi] troops placed the [Kurdish] villages on trucks to be carried off at night in long caravans along sealed routes. Having reached their destinations families were supplied with a tent, and grouped in fives in so-called villages. Movement was prohibited except for official business. The men were assigned jobs at fixed pay.[9]

The Iraqi government also offered general amnesty to Kurds who wished to return to their villages from their refuge in Iran. However, upon arrival in their villages, some 85 per cent of them were rounded up by Iraqi forces and deported to the south-west desert region of the country. Estimates of the total number of Kurds affected by the Iraqi government's policy of deportation in the aftermath of Mullah Mustafa's defeat range from 50 000 to 350 000, depending on the source.[10] The Iraqi government obliquely acknowledged the population transfers, but justified them on grounds of national security, claiming that it needed to establish a ten-kilometre security belt along the Iranian border.[11]

Throughout the Iran–Iraq crisis of the 1970s, Turkey watched apprehensively from the sidelines as the Shah played his Kurdish card against the Iraqi regime and manipulated Mullah Mustafa Barzani and the Kurdish struggle to maximize Iran's political leverage against the Iraqi regime. Turkish authorities knew of the dangerous spill-over effects of the Shah's Kurdish regional power plays and feared the negative consequences of such moves on their own restive Kurdish population of twelve to fifteen million. When the Shah abruptly terminated his support of Mullah Mustafa and his *peshmerga*, Turkish leaders expressed a sigh of relief. At the same time, Ankara realized that the Shah would not 'shrink from playing the dangerous Kurdish card if it meant gaining leverage against Iraq, even if that move had consequences for Turkey'.[12] Notwithstanding this discomfiture, Turkish–Iranian relations did not suffer from the Shah's policy of orchestrating Mullah Mustafa's last revolt against the Iraqi regime.

THE IRANIAN REVOLUTION, THE IRAN–IRAQ WAR AND THE KURDS

The Iranian Revolution of 1978–79 brought about profound changes in Iran's foreign policy orientation affecting the country's relations with the

West as well as with its neighbours. As has been stated elsewhere, with the exception of a few Kurdish leaders who had benefited from their association with the Shah's regime, the vast majority of Iranian Kurds enthusiastically supported the Iranian Revolution, partly because of what they viewed as the Shah's betrayal of their cause.[13] The Iranian Kurds also realized that with the demise of the Pahlavi monarchy, they would have an unrivalled opportunity to exercise their right of self-determination in Iran. Both the Turkish and Iraqi governments followed the emergence of overt Kurdish nationalism in post-revolutionary Iran with some degree of apprehension. When it became evident that the Ayatollah Khomeini's objective of establishing a strong centralized Islamic state would clash with the goals of the autonomy-seeking Kurds, the fears of Ankara and Baghdad were substantially allayed with respect to the implications of Kurdish autonomy in Iran for their own Kurdish populations. In Khomeini's view, the demands of ethnic minorities for autonomy would be counterproductive and largely irrelevant in an Islamic environment:

> Sometimes the word minorities is used to refer to people such as the Kurds, Lurs, Turks, Persians, Baluchis, and such. These people should not be called minorities, because this term assumes that there is a difference between these brothers. In Islam, such a difference has no place at all. There is no difference between Muslims who speak different languages, for instance, the Arabs or the Persians. It is very probable that such problems have been created by those who do not wish the Muslim countries to be united.... They create the issues of nationalism, of pan-Arabism, pan-Turkism, and such isms, which are contrary to Islamic doctrines. Their plan is to destroy Islam and Islamic philosophy.[14]

Islamic Iran's concept of the role of nationalities in the country differed substantially from that of the avowedly secularist Turkey. In modern Turkey, the outline of the country's Kurdish policy was laid down by Mustafa Kemal Ataturk and has been followed by his successors. İsmet Inönü, a former Prime Minister and loyal Ataturk supporter, summarized the essence of the Kemalist Kurdish policy best when he said 'only the Turkish nation is entitled to claim ethnic and national rights in this country. No other element has any such right.'[15] Consequently, the Turkish government coined the term 'Mountain Turks' to refer to the country's Kurdish population. Numerous laws and regulations were published to outlaw the use of the Kurdish language and other expressions of Kurdish ethnicity in Turkey. It was not until September 1989 that the Kurdish government began to hint that some change was possible in Turkey's concept of Kurdish ethnicity and ethnic rights. In response to a question about the status of the Kurdish minority in Turkey, the then Prime Minister Turgut Özal stated that in its formative years, Republican Turkey had 'committed mistakes on this [Kurdish] matter', and that perhaps it was time to recognize the existence of a Kurdish minority in Turkey.[16] Events surrounding the Gulf War and the worldwide publicity given to the plight of the Kurdish refugees finally contributed to Turkey's repeal of the law outlawing the speaking of Kurdish on the streets. However, it is still illegal to speak Kurdish in official settings, at public gatherings and in court, and most of the cultural prohibitions still remain in place.[17] Both Iran and Iraq have repeatedly relied on these prohibitions to demonstrate to their own Kurds, as well as to the outside world, that the plight of the Kurds in Turkey is worse and in need of greater scrutiny than is the case in their respective countries. This also demonstrates that Islamic Iran is not averse to using its Kurdish card to restrain what it views as Turkish hegemonic designs in the region.

The Iran–Iraq War of 1980–88 again heightened the apprehension in Ankara about the possible use of the Kurdish card by the two antagonists and the implications thereof for Turkish security. Once the war started in September 1980, Iraq took the initiative in playing its Kurdish card as a strategic tool against a militarily disorganized and weak Iran. Ironically, this was akin to the strategy that the Shah had adopted earlier in undermining the Iraqi regime in the early 1970s. Infighting among various Kurdish groups made it easier for Saddam Hussein to use his Kurdish card. For example, at that time the two main Iraqi Kurdish parties, Jalal Talabani's Patriotic Union of Kurdistan (PUK) and the Kurdish Democratic Party (KDP) led by Mullah Mustafa Barzani's sons, Idris and Massoud, were locked in a fierce political battle to control the Kurdish movement in Iraq. Abdul Rahman Qassemlou, the leader of the Kurdish Democratic Party of Iran (KDPI), was engaged in his own struggle against the Iraqi KDP because the latter had accepted arms from the deposed Shah of Iran. In short, the absence of unity among the major Kurdish groups made it easier for Saddam Hussein to play one group off against another.

In January 1981, the Iraqi government established its first principal supply route to the forces of Qassemlou's KDPI near the cities of Nowdesheh and Qasr-e-Shirin. Securing Nowdesheh was Iraq's prime objective, as this city's strategic location would deny Iran the use of the Baghdad–Teheran highway. Since Nowdesheh was defended by only a small contingent of lightly-armed Iranian military and revolutionary guard (*pasdaran*) units, the Iraqis took the city and, with the KDPI's assistance, established an operational headquarters there. The KDPI's *peshmerga* were then able to use Nowdesheh to stage a three-month offensive against

Iranian forces, with some success.[18] In April, the KDPI's position *vis-à-vis* the Iranian forces was strengthened when the PUK, along with two Iranian opposition groups, the *Mojahedin-e Khalq* (People's Combatants) and the *Fadaiyan-e Khalq* (People's Sacrificers) joined together in a loose tactical alliance and fought the Iranian forces throughout the Kurdish province of Iran. Bolstered by weapons and ammunition supplied by Iraq or captured from military depots inside Kurdistan, they were able to force the *pasdaran* units out of major cities in Iranian Kurdistan, including Sanandaj, the provincial capital and an important military outpost.

The principal goal of the KDPI was to establish 'liberated Kurdish zones' in various parts of Iranian Kurdistan from which it would launch further operations against the Iranian forces. However, by early 1982, the tide began to turn against the KDPI and Iraq as the Iranians launched a series of major counter-offensives against the Iraqi forces in the north, forcing them to retreat from captured Iranian territory. Once the bulk of the Iraqi forces were outside Iran, Iranian ground forces under the command of Colonel Sayyad Shirazi launched a series of devastating attacks against the isolated KDPI bases. Colonel Shirazi was one of the Iran–Iraq War's most innovative military strategists, responsible for many Iranian successes on the battlefield against Iraq during the early phases of the war. Shirazi adopted a simple yet effective strategy against the KDPI. He first forced Qassemlou's forces into spreading themselves thin and then encircled the overstretched Kurdish *peshmerga*, inflicting heavy casualties on them. After this, the KDPI was no more than a marginal factor in the Iran–Iraq War.

Having neutralized Iraq's Kurdish advantage, the Islamic Republic of Iran began to play its own Kurdish card against Saddam Hussein's forces. By 1983, the Islamic Republic had managed to acquire the support of both Barzani's KDP and the PUK in a united Kurdish front against the Iraqi regime. As Saddam Hussein began to feel vulnerable to the prospect of a potentially destabilizing Iranian–Kurdish alliance on the northern front, he sought to open up a secret channel of negotiation with the Kurds by offering them incentives and promising them greater autonomy in their internal affairs. At the same time, the Iraqi government was coming under heavy pressure from Ankara to control Kurdish activities along the border regions with Turkey. Turkey had claimed that the border areas under the control of the KDP were porous and a danger to its security. Ankara had further charged that the KDP had allowed Turkey's principal anti-government Kurdish guerrilla group, the Kurdish Workers (PKK), to use Iraqi territory from which to launch military operations inside Turkey.

Both Ankara and Baghdad were also concerned about possible Kurdish attacks and sabotage against a strategic pipeline that connected the Kirkuk oil-fields to Iskenderun in Turkey. This pipeline, which transported one million barrels of oil per day, supplied a third of Turkey's oil needs and paid Ankara over US$300 million in rental fees. Because of the strategic importance of the Kirkuk–Iskenderun oil pipeline, neither Ankara nor Baghdad could afford damage to it. They therefore signed two agreements in 1981 and 1984 to allow Turkish troops to enter Iraqi territory in pursuit of Kurdish guerrillas. Ankara was also fearful that an Iranian victory in the Iran–Iraq War would inevitably lead to the disintegration of Iraq and the establishment of a Kurdish state or autonomous region with negative consequences for the Kurdish regions of Turkey. Ankara concluded that to prevent such a possibility, an outright Iranian military victory over Iraq must be prevented, and the KDP should not be allowed to strengthen its ties with Teheran. For their part, the Kurds, particularly the KDP, needed to strengthen their alliance with Iran in order to counter this new military threat.

To increase the pressure on Baghdad, the Iranian government issued a number of threats against the Kirkuk–Iskenderun pipeline, claiming that it was a legitimate target in wartime. Iraqi forces had already targeted and destroyed several major Iranian oil installations, including the giant refinery in Abadan. Turkey, however, insisted that it would view any Iranian or Iranian-supported Kurdish attack on this pipeline as an attack on Turkish interests and a hostile act against Turkey itself. Ankara also threatened to cut its lucrative trade ties with Iran if Teheran did not desist from aiding anti-Iraq Kurdish groups. The right-wing Turkish press even speculated that Iran's ultimate objective in aiding the Kurds was to seize the Kirkuk oilfields.[19] Other Turkish sources postulated that the United States was encouraging Turkey to capture Kirkuk and its oilfields before Iraq was fractured and to deny Iran a military victory in its war with Iraq.[20]

By late 1986, the Turkish forces had increased their incursions into Iraq, and the Turkish air force had stepped up its bombing of several Kurdish villages in northern Iraq which were suspected of harbouring PKK guerrillas. The Iranian government was particularly upset about the timing of Turkish attacks against the Iraqi Kurds because Teheran was preparing to launch a major offensive against Iraqi targets in collaboration with KDP. In December 1986, the Islamic Republic organized a meeting of anti-Saddam Hussein groups in Teheran to stress Iran's commitment to the territorial integrity of Iraq, in order to reduce tensions with Turkey and alleviate Ankara's fears of alleged Iranian territorial ambitions against Iraq. However, Khamenei, the then President and current *faqih*, or spiritual leader, of the

Islamic Republic, stated that Iran would not hesitate to challenge another country's intervention in Iraq's internal affairs. Prime Minister Mussavi echoed the same sentiment when he warned other countries not to revive old territorial claims against Iraq.[21] Although neither Khamenei nor Mussavi mentioned Turkey by name, it was clear that they were addressing their comments to Turkish officials. The crisis between Turkey and Iran came to a head in August 1987 when Turkish border officials arrested ninety-five members of an elite unit of the Iranian *pasdaran* and charged them with attempted sabotage of the Kirkuk–Iskenderun pipeline. Although the Turkish government did not produce any evidence for its charges and the crisis was eventually defused through diplomatic negotiations, this episode clearly demonstrated the potential role of the Kurdish factor in future Turkish–Iranian confrontations.

The last major Iranian–Kurdish offensive on the northern front was launched in March 1988. By this time, the United States was heavily biased in favour of Iraqi war aims and had lent logistical support to Baghdad by supporting the re-flagging of Kuwaiti oil tankers and escorting those of the Gulf Arab allies of Saddam Hussein. By attracting direct and indirect American support for his war efforts, Saddam Hussein managed to internationalize the war, thus making it costlier for the Islamic Republic to pursue the conflict on the southern battlefields. Although Saddam Hussein was unable to exploit his advantage in manpower and weaponry against the Iranian–Kurdish forces in the north, by June 1988 he was able to capitalize on outside support in order to recapture much of the Iraqi land from the Iranian forces. The Iranian press sought to portray these defeats as tactical battlefield retreats, but it was clear to most people that Iran was no longer able to fight the Iraqi forces and their American and Arab allies.[22] On 18 July, 1988, the Islamic Republic announced its acceptance of UN Security Council Resolution 598, bringing the Iran–Iraq War to an end.

When the Iran–Iraq War ended, the Iraqi regime accelerated its attacks on Kurdish villages, which included the use of chemical weapons. It is beyond the scope of this chapter to discuss Iraq's use of chemicals against its Kurdish population or the wholesale extermination of Kurdish villages conducted throughout the 1970s and 1980s by the Iraqi regime. For our purpose, it is important to note the reactions of Turkey and Iran to Iraqi policies in this regard within the vortex of Ankara–Teheran–Baghdad's changing relationship in the aftermath of the Iran–Iraq War. As Kurdish refugees began to enter Turkey to avoid certain death or persecution in Iraq, the Turkish government initially supported Baghdad's claim that chemical weapons had not been used against the Kurds. Turkey was mostly concerned about repatriating Kurdish refugees to Iraq and did not want to encourage the Iraqi Kurds to seek sanctuary inside Turkey. Nor did Ankara want to give Saddam Hussein an excuse to renege on his US$2 billion debts to Turkey by joining the anti-Iraq coalition or doing anything to jeopardize its lucrative trade with Iraq. Iran, on the other hand, was anxious to put international pressure on Iraq to withdraw from Iranian territory and implement all the provisions of the UN Security Council resolution terminating the Iran–Iraq War. In particular, the Islamic Republic gave full publicity to the Iraqi use of poison gas against its Kurdish population.

In September 1988, Teheran invited representatives of the UN High Commissioner for Refugees (UNHCR) and the International Committee of the Red Cross to visit Kurdish refugee camps in the Iranian province of West Azerbaijan and obtain eyewitness reports of Baghdad's use of chemical weapons against Kurdish civilians. At the same time, a two-person UNHCR team toured Kurdish refugee camps in south-eastern Turkey to collect data on the reported use of Iraqi chemical weapons against the Kurds. In both cases, the visiting teams concluded that they saw no evidence to substantiate the refugees' claim in this regard. On the other hand, independent international human rights bodies lent credence to the Kurdish claims. For example, in an appeal to the UN, Amnesty International condemned Baghdad's reliance on chemical weapons as part of a 'systematic and deliberate policy by the Iraqi government to eliminate large numbers of Kurds'.[23] It was not, however, until after Iraq's invasion of Kuwait that Western governments and international organizations joined in a chorus of condemnation of Iraq and its use of chemical weapons against the Kurds.

THE KURDISH FACTOR IN THE POST-GULF WAR ERA

The regional balance of power and strategic alliances changed dramatically in the aftermath of Iraq's August 1990 invasion of Kuwait. After occupying Kuwait, Saddam Hussein revived the old Iraqi claim to Kuwait and declared the conquered country to be Iraq's nineteenth province. The eventual massive deployment of American air, naval and ground forces as part of a multi-national force to fight Iraq in Operation Desert Storm placed Turkey and Iran in a quandary. Given Turkey's lucrative economic ties with Iraq and the *modus vivendi* Ankara had reached with Baghdad regarding the containment of Kurdish issues, Turkey could have been deterred from drastically changing its policies toward Iraq. On the other hand, as Iraq's neighbour and a major regional power, Turkey could not have been expected to soft-pedal Iraq's annexation of Kuwait and acquiesce to a major change in the regional power configuration.

Ankara's initial response to Iraq's invasion of Kuwait was a 'traditional Kemalist reaction – that is to say Turkey reacted with extreme caution, with a reluctance to become embroiled in an intra-Arab dispute....'[24] In this vein, a plethora of Turkish officials issued mild statements deploring Iraq's invasion of Kuwait and expressing the hope that Baghdad would soon withdraw from Kuwait. With the adoption of UN Security Council Resolution 661 on 6 August 1990, which called on all countries to boycott all goods of Iraqi origin, pressure was mounted on Ankara to shut down its two oil pipelines to Iraq and join the economic embargo against Baghdad. As the events unfolded at a fast pace and over 500 000 American air, naval and ground forces assembled in the region in preparation for an eventual war against Iraq, the traditional incremental Kemalist response to the Gulf crisis was no longer a viable option for Turkey. By agreeing to halt all economic ties with Iraq, Turkey momentarily removed itself from the centre of the impending storm.

Between August and December 1990, a number of Turkish officials and prominent private citizens visited Baghdad in order to try to smooth Turkish–Iraqi relations in the aftermath of Ankara's economic sanctions against its erstwhile major trading partner. Among the more prominent Turkish individuals who visited Baghdad and held talks with Saddam Hussein or other high-level Iraqi officials were former Prime Minister Bülent Ecevit, the leader of the Social Democratic Populist Party, Erdal Inönü and the head of the Islamic-leaning Welfare Party, Necmettin Erbakan. These visits proved futile and paved the way for President Özal to strengthen Turkey's commitment to the goals of the US-led anti-Iraq coalition forces. In a controversial move, Özal also granted permission to the United States to use the Incirlik air base in south-eastern Turkey from which to launch attacks against Iraqi targets whenever it decided to do so. By the time the war against Iraq started in January 1991, Turkey was already a major participant in the conflict.[25]

Iran's initial reaction to the crisis in the Persian Gulf generated by Saddam Hussein's invasion of Kuwait was somewhat ambivalent. Unlike Turkey, Iran had no qualms about condemning Iraq's annexation of Kuwait in the strongest terms. In fact, the Islamic Republic felt that its policies during the Iran–Iraq War and its uncompromising stance towards Saddam Hussein had now been vindicated. On the other hand, Teheran did not welcome the stationing of a large contingent of American troops so close to its own borders and security zones. The 'radicals' and their allies in the ruling hierarchy took advantage of the stationing of a large number of American troops on Saudi soil to bolster their position against their more pragmatic counterparts both inside and outside of governing circles. Ayatollah Khamenei, who was gradually moving to the radicals' position on foreign policy issues, expressed his concern about the consequences of Western military deployment in the Persian Gulf region in the following words:

> This region's security is the business of this region's nations. You [Americans] are buyers of the oil belonging to these nations, so you had best line up outside and refrain from interfering in their affairs.... If you see the region as insecure today, then you are responsible. It was you who armed Iraq and you who encouraged [Saddam Hussein] to feel strong and attack Kuwait.... If you had not helped [Saddam Hussein] as much as you did..., then the region would not be facing this insecurity.... Utter shame on those governments which allow aggressive America to come here in pursuit of its own interests.[26]

Ayatollah Khamenei's serious concern about this issue was echoed by a number of deputies in the *majlis* (parliament) who were associated with the radical faction of the ruling hierarchy. Their condemnation of the Western forces' build-up in the Arabian peninsula became more vociferous after Saddam Hussein's desperate bid for Iranian support for his policies and after he offered unilateral concessions to the Islamic Republic on the Shatt al-Arab boundary dispute.

The 'pragmatists' in the ruling hierarchy, however, remained suspicious of Iraqi overtures towards Iran and their position on the Western military build-up in Saudi Arabia remained cautious. They remained in touch with Kuwait's ousted royal family, and according to one report, kept the Kuwaitis abreast of Iraq's 'peace overtures' towards Iran.[27] The two leading pragmatists, President Ali Akbar Hashemi Rafsanjani and Foreign Minister Ali Akbar Velayati, continued to pursue several avenues for the peaceful settlement of the crisis. Through close contacts with Turkey and Syria, two key Muslim members of the anti-Iraq coalition, they stayed abreast of the unfolding developments in the Gulf crisis.

Although the 'pragmatists' continued to subscribe publicly to the official government policy of neutrality and portrayed the crisis as a conflict between two equally guilty aggressors, it was evident that they sought to take advantage of this window of opportunity in order to re-establish Iran's credentials as a responsible and key player in regional affairs. In a meeting with a group of Teheran University students shortly before the onset of the air war against Iraq, Foreign Minister Velayati stated that since Saddam Hussein was unwilling to leave Kuwait peacefully, the presence of foreign troops in Saudi Arabia might be justified so long as those troops were stationed there for limited security purposes.[28] This was a clear departure from the previous public statements of Iranian officials on the Gulf crisis, and it signalled at least the temporary ascendancy of the 'pragmatists' in the foreign policy domain.

Perhaps both Turkey and Iran were convinced by then that the Kuwaiti crisis would lead to war and another inevitable Kurdish refugee crisis. The devastating lightning Iraqi military defeat was followed by US appeals to the Iraqi population to revolt against Saddam Hussein's government. The CIA-run Voice of Free Iraq, which operated from Jeddah, Saudi Arabia, had been encouraging a Kurdish uprising for several weeks. As a result, the Iraqi Kurds believed that they would receive assistance from the United States if they led an uprising against the Iraqi regime.[29] After some initial success, the Kurds succeeded in gaining control of some cities in northern Iraq. However, the Iraqi forces soon regrouped and drove back the Kurdish *peshmergas* by attacking their positions from air and land. With no help from the outside, the Kurdish villages were once more devastated and another mass exodus of Kurdish refugees to Turkey and Iran began while these two countries were still grappling with the Kurdish refugee issues associated with the Iran–Iraq War.

On the political and diplomatic fronts, both Massoud Barzani and Jalal Talabani continued to negotiate with Saddam Hussein to achieve the elusive autonomy the Iraqi Kurds had been demanding for so many years. Ankara was somewhat supportive of these negotiations, as it was not pleased with the influx of over 500 000 Kurdish refugees into Turkey. Iran, for its part, was more apprehensive about the Kurdish overtures to the Iraqi regime. The principal reason for Iran's objections was that Teheran felt that the Kurds would be obligated to join the Iraqi army to fight the Shi'as in southern Iraq in exchange for concessions they might obtain from Saddam Hussein in Kurdistan. Teheran was also intent on exploiting the close collaboration between Baghdad and the Iraqi-based Iranian opposition *Mojahedin-e Khalq* to its advantage by enticing the Iraqi Kurdish *peshmerga* to attack *Mojahedin* units inside Iraq. The Iranian cause was helped initially by purported eyewitness reports of *Mojahedin* participation on the side of the Iraqis against the Kurds. According to the British journalist and veteran Middle East analyst David Hirst, in one particular case the Kurdish forces trapped fifty-seven *Mojahedin* troops who were accused of aiding the Iraqi soldiers inside a school, and shot them to death.[30]

A SAFE HAVEN AND KURDISH AUTONOMY IN NORTHERN IRAQ

The tragedy of Kurdish refugees fleeing Iraqi forces and the implications of the refugees into Turkey prompted President Özal to suggest the establishment of a 'safe haven' inside Iraq to protect the Kurds from Iraqi reprisals and encourage Kurdish refugees to return home. With the support of British Prime Minister John Major, the United States took the lead in establishing such a zone north of the 36th parallel. The United States then warned Iraq not to fly fixed-wing aeroplanes or helicopters in this zone. Over 8000 American, British and French troops occupied the zone in order to enforce the no-fly rules and aid in the resettlement of returning refugees. Several thousand additional Western troops were also stationed on Turkish soil to help maintain the integrity of the Kurdish 'safe haven' and deter Iraqi military incursions north of the 36th parallel. This undertaking, which functioned under the name of Operation Poised Hammer, was supported by President Özal and successive Turkish administrations. The Turkish parliament also extended the terms of this arrangement several times, despite some misgivings about the long-term effect of Turkish collaboration with Western powers against neighbouring Iraq.

Iran, on the other hand, consistently opposed Western operations inside Iraq and questioned the legality of the *de facto* partition of Iraq by unilateral action of the West. Iran was also fearful that the no-fly zone could be used by the United States to threaten Iran's territorial integrity in the future or might simply become a safe enclave for a variety of anti-Iranian opposition forces, including the KDPI *peshmerga*. The Iranian authorities asserted that their intelligence sources had obtained information regarding a plan by the United States to use the KDPI forces to destabilize the border regions in the northwest.[31] In March 1993, the Iranian government began a series of bombing raids against the KDPI and its supporters inside the no-fly zone in Iraq. The bombings were repeated in April and May, inflicting heavy damage on the KDPI forces.[32] Iranian attacks against the Kurds opposing their regime have been routinely condemned by the KDPI as a violation of the regulations in the no-fly zone and an 'insult' to the Americans and their allies by the Islamic Republic.[33] The KDPI also asserted that the Iranian incursions inside Iraq were a violation of the terms of UN Security Council Resolution 598, which set guidelines to end the Iran-Iraq War and established a ceasefire between the two belligerents in that war.[34] At the Sixth Plenum of the Central Committee of the KDPI, Iranian forays inside Iraqi Kurdistan and the methods to be adopted to combat them received special attention.[35]

The KDPI's strategy in highlighting Iranian incursions inside Iraq was partly designed to compel Turkey to put pressure on Iran to modify its position. The KDPI also began printing laudatory articles in its publications about Turkey and its Kurdish policy. For example, in an article published in *Kurdistan*, the official organ of the KDPI's Central Committee, the late Turkish President Turgut Özal was eulogized as a great statesman who took major steps to reduce oppression against the Kurds in Turkey and recognize their national rights.[36] In a similar vein, when Abdullah Öcalan of the PKK announced a unilateral ceasefire to coincide with the Kurdish New Year in March 1993, the KDPI expressed the hope that the PKK might have finally entered a new era in its unmitigated opposition to the Kemalist system in Turkey and that it had developed a 'more realistic' assessment of the conditions of the Kurds in Turkey.[37]

So far, Ankara seems to have adopted a cautious attitude as far as identifying with the plight of the KDPI is concerned, while at the same time giving them some support as a counterbalance to the alleged Iranian assistance to the PKK *peshmerga*. The Iranian policy of bombing the border regions has been aimed ostensibly at signalling to the Iraqi Kurdish authorities that they should safeguard the border regions or else risk the livelihoods of the Kurdish farmers and other Kurds involved in lucrative trade with Iran. Teheran has even offered to arm Iraqi Kurdish guards who are willing to guarantee the safety of the border zones and prevent the KDPI forces from launching attacks into Iranian Kurdistan from their bases inside Iraq. This strategy may already have had some success as thousands of the KDPI supporters have been moved away from the 350-mile Kurdish area along the Iranian border.[38]

The Kurdish factor in Turkish–Iranian relations became even more prominent after the establishment of a *de facto* Kurdish state in the 'safe haven' Kurdish zone in northern Iraq. On 19 May 1992, free parliamentary and presidential elections were held for the first time in Iraqi Kurdistan; some one million Kurds participated. The two major Kurdish political parties, the KDP and PUK, dominated the elections, with the KDP receiving 45.26 per cent of the votes and the PUK 43.81 per cent.[39] Although these elections resulted in the institutionalization of the dominance of the KDP and PUK in the emerging Kurdish political entity, the closeness of the votes obtained by each of these parties did not result in the election of a president, which would have been possible in a more decisive election. Under Western protection, the Kurdish zone soon developed many of the rudimentary attributes of a sovereign nation-state without the official recognition of other states and international bodies that is needed for it to be recognized under international law as a sovereign country. For example, in addition to the Kurdish parliament, a national police force and a unified army have been established as important integral parts of the embryonic Kurdish state. However, neither the West, at least for the time being, nor Turkey, Iran or other Arab countries have favoured the establishment of an independent Kurdish state in Iraq.[40] The Iraqi

Kurds are quite mindful of these objections and have not yet formally pushed for the recognition of their state as a sovereign entity.

The Kurdish government of northern Iraq has made a number of overtures to Turkey, and, to a lesser extent, to the Islamic Republic of Iran in order to receive their support, or at least their acquiescence, concerning developments in Iraqi Kurdistan. Ironically, this has resulted in closer cooperation between Iran and Turkey while at the same time increasing suspicions about the ultimate goals of each country in its new dealings with the emerging Kurdish state. Iran, Turkey and Syria have held meetings at the ministerial level to discuss how they could coordinate their responses to developments in Iraqi Kurdistan. For example, in their 12 February 1993 meeting in Damascus and their 7 June 1993 gathering in Teheran, the foreign ministers of the three countries issued a declaration reaffirming their 'unwavering commitment to the territorial integrity of Iraq' and warning of the 'grave consequences' for regional peace and stability if Iraq is formally partitioned.[41] At the conclusion of the tripartite meeting in June, Turkish Foreign Minister Hikmet Çetin divulged that the three countries were particularly determined to fight 'terrorism collectively and individually' for the sake of peace in the region.[42]

Turkey and Iran have also established a more formal arrangement to deal with the Kurdish problems along their borders as well as the border regions of Iraqi Kurdistan. Turkish–Iranian security meetings have been held at interior, defence and foreign ministry levels and have dealt with a broad range of issues, but particularly with the Kurdish issues of concern to both countries. At the sixth Turkish–Iranian security meeting, held in Teheran in September 1993, both sides acknowledged that due to the topography of their border regions, they might not able to control Kurdish activities at all times, and the existence of such activities should not be construed as having the blessing of either of the two governments.[43] Nevertheless, it seems that both Teheran and Ankara have allowed military incursions into each other's territories in 'hot pursuit' of the *peshmerga* of the PKK and KDPI. For example, according to the Turkish daily *Milliyet*, in late May and early June 1993, Turkish troops entered Iran from the Saray district with the full knowledge of the Iranian authorities and launched a major operation against the PKK forces and their sanctuaries inside Iranian Kurdistan. The two countries then mounted a joint operation against the KDPI forces.[44] Although Iran remained silent about these operations, the Turkish media reported on the existence of a wide-ranging agreement between Teheran and Ankara on this matter. The Istanbul daily *Hurriyet* reported that the neighbouring provinces of West Azerbaijan in Iran and Hakkari in Turkey had signed an agreement on matters relating to trade and joint security.[45] These and similar agreements are indicative of the emergence of a unified Turkish–Iranian position on security issues along their borders and the coordination of their efforts to contain Kurdish uprisings in their respective regions.

Notwithstanding the convergence of Turkish–Iranian interests in establishing security and calm along their Kurdish-inhabited border regions, Ankara and Teheran have developed somewhat divergent policies towards the fledgling Kurdish state in northern Iraq. While Turkey has sought to co-opt the major Iraqi Kurdish parties and forge closer links with them, Iran has remained suspicious of both the ultimate goals of the Kurdish government and Turkish motives in the region. Even before the establishment of a Kurdish government in Iraq, PUK leader Jalal Talabani, in a surprise announcement from Turkey, proposed that Ankara take a more active role in solving the Iraqi Kurdish problem and denounced the PKK and its leader Abdullah Öcalan for continuing to carry on the Kurdish struggle against the Turkish state.[46] Iran has identified several developments that have compelled the Islamic Republic to view with some apprehension the increasingly close ties between Turkey and the Kurdish government in Iraq.

First, Teheran is fearful that Turkey will seek either directly or indirectly to control the oilfields of northern Iraq, thus altering the balance of power in the region. Although the newly republican Turkey officially renounced its claim to the Ottoman territory of Mosul in northern Iraq in 1926, some ultranationalist elements in Turkey revived the notion of the Turkish control of that region in the aftermath of the Gulf War. Today, Turkish claims to Mosul are not simply based on former Ottoman control of the area. Rather, the fact that the Mosul area is inhabited by some 500 000 Turkmen, a Turkic minority, may give Ankara an incentive to seek the control of the Kurdish oil region on the pretext of defending the rights of the Turkmen. Graham Fuller contends that the Iraqi Turkmen feel that they are 'harshly oppressed by Baghdad and the Kurds, but consider themselves abandoned even by Turkey over the years. Not without significance, the oil resources of [the Kirkuk area] produced 1.5 million barrels per day in 1990, a very important factor to be considered in any future Kurdish–Iraqi negotiations over the status of Kurdistan.'[47] The revival of Turkish claims to the oil-rich parts of Iraqi Kurdistan have received extensive coverage in the Iranian media, and some observers have contended that Turkey will eventually be forced to abandon its 'opportunistic and adventurist' territorial designs in Iraqi Kurdistan because of their negative consequences for the stability of Turkey's own Kurdish regions.[48]

Iran has also objected to the collaborative efforts of Turkey and the Iraqi Kurdish forces against the PKK *peshmerga*. On 4 October 1992,

Iraqi Kurds launched a major operation against the PKK, ostensibly to push them back into Turkey and terminate the operations against the Turkish state from Iraqi Kurdistan. A few days later, Turkey launched a full-scale military operation, in tandem with the Iraqi Kurds, against the PKK. This operation, which had the full support of Massoud Barzani and Jalal Talabani, was the most important manifestation of the emergence of a new alliance of convenience between Turkey and the government of Iraqi Kurdistan. In the October operation, some 10 000 Iraqi Kurdish forces took part in attacking their brethren from Turkey, eventually forcing some 5000 to 10 000 PKK *peshmerga* to surrender to them or flee to Iran and Syria.[49] Talabani sought to justify this Kurdish–Turkish military cooperation by claiming that the PKK leader Abdullah Öcalan was 'a madman leading his people into catastrophe [and that] Islamic fundamentalist Iran is supporting a Marxist-Leninist party [PKK]'[50] to thwart the realization of Kurdish goals in northern Iraq. Even before the onset of this major Turkish–Iraqi Kurdish joint operation against the PKK, the Iranian media had warned of this eventuality and had severely criticized Barzani and Talabani for their 'reckless' policies at the expense of the Kurdish people. The following illustrates the type of criticism that appeared in Iranian print media:

> The submissive attitude of the leaders of the Iraqi Kurds towards Turkey in recent months has shocked people the world over. These Kurdish leaders [Barzani and Talabani] openly discuss their desire to join northern Iraq with Turkey in some fashion. While the Kemalist Turkey has had a long history of genocide and mass murder against the Kurds, these gentlemen [Barzani and Talabani] are proud to publicly admit their admiration for the Turkish state and are even proud of holding Turkish passports. Could this about face have something to do with the lucrative business the Iraqi Kurdish leaders have established with Turkey and through which they have enriched their personal coffers at the expense of the larger Kurdish interests?[51]

After several months of acrimonious charges and countercharges, the Kurdish authorities sought to defuse tensions with Iran. In early 1993, the Kurdish National Congress sent a letter to the Iranian *majlis* expressing the desire of the Kurdish authorities to cooperate with Iran. The letter focused on Iran's concerns about the establishment of a Kurdish federated state in Iraqi Kurdistan. It stated that such a state was not a prelude to the dismemberment of Iraq; rather it was an essential ingredient in the creation of a more democratic and peaceful Iraq that would be no threat to its neighbours.[52] In conclusion, the letter stated that Iraqi Kurdish authorities understood Iran's security concerns and would do their utmost not to jeopardize Iran's interests.

Later in the summer of 1993, a military and political delegation visited Iraqi Kurdistan and held talks with Kurdish leaders. This marked the first high-level meeting between Iranian officials and Barzani and Talabani on Iraqi Kurdish soil. The Iraqi Kurds reportedly promised to keep the anti-Islamic Republic KDPI *peshmerga* away from the border regions and not allow their territory to be used for KDPI attacks against Iranian positions. The Iranian delegates, in turn, promised to expand their ties with the Iraqi Kurds and to look into the possibility of allowing the opening of a representative office of Iraqi Kurds in Iran.[53]

Despite these overtures, major policy differences still separate the Turkish, Kurdish and Iranian positions in the region. In particular, Iran has yet to accept the Kurdish and Turkish position that the principal purpose of the American presence in Iraqi Kurdistan is to deter Iraq from launching another offensive against its Kurdish population. Iranian press reports have hinted that the American military-civilian presence in the city of Zakho in northern Iraq is intended to facilitate anti-Iranian insurgency and to aid the Baghdad-based *Mojahedin-e Khalq* and the KDPI guerrillas in their 'terrorist' operations inside Iranian territory.[54] These charges, irrespective of their veracity, will undoubtedly have a negative impact on Iranian policy decisions regarding Iraqi Kurdistan and its *de facto* government.

CONCLUSION AND PROSPECTS FOR THE FUTURE

The Iran–Iraq War, the Gulf War against Iraq and the establishment of an autonomous Kurdish administration in northern Iraq have reaffirmed continuity in relations between Ankara and Teheran while, at the same time, engendering new vistas of opportunities for changes in the configuration of regional power. New orientations in Turkey's foreign policy towards the Middle East and Ankara's assertive policy in Central Asia and the Caucasus may cause serious problems with Iran, which has historical, cultural and security interests in these regions. Although I do not share Graham Fuller's assessment that Ankara's relations with Teheran 'seem almost certainly headed for serious deterioration and even confrontation in the next decade',[55] Turkish–Iranian competition in Central Asia and the Caucasus and their policies toward Iraq and Iraqi Kurdistan will undoubtedly affect the shape and content of Turkish–Iranian relations into the twenty-first century. The policies of Ankara and Teheran with regard to these issues are fluid and remain subject to other factors. Conflict between

Turkey's avowed secularism and Western orientation and Iran's profound Islamic orientations will also continue to play a decisive role in determining the shape of Turkish–Iranian relations in the near future.

The Turkish press and, to a lesser extent, the Turkish government have frequently accused Iran of undermining Turkish interests by supporting anti-secular Islamic forces in Turkey. The murder on 24 January 1993 of the leading secularist Turkish journalist, Uğur Mumcu, demonstrates the potential for conflict between Turkey and Iran over charges of Iranian complicity with the Turkish Islamicists who claimed responsibility for Mumcu's assassination. Although the Iranian authorities have steadfastedly denied any involvement in Mumcu's murder, or the assassination of four other secularist authors by Turkish Islamicists which preceded Mumcu's killing, anti-Iranian sentiments have grown in Turkey. According to the Istanbul daily *Sabah*, Foreign Minister Hikmet Cetin presented Iran with a dossier concerning the involvement of certain circles in Iran in anti-Kemalist Islamic militancy, but Teheran did not respond to these charges.[56] Instead, Iran claimed that certain secularist Kurdish newspapers and political and military figures, in collaboration with the US Central Intelligence Agency, are intent on spreading false rumours to poison Turkish–Iranian relations.[57]

In general, several high-level Turkish and Iranian officials have sought to downplay these acrimonious charges and have instead tried to rely on quiet diplomacy to deal with the rise of Islamic militant groups in Turkey and the alleged Iranian role in fanning the flames of Islamic revivalism in that country. While then-Prime Minister Suleyman Demirel hinted at some Iranian involvement, his government refrained from directly accusing the Iranian government of aiding and abetting 'Islamic terrorism' in Turkey. Interior Minister İsmet Sezgin also absolved the Iranian government of any involvement in sponsoring Mumcu's killing.[58] In fact, a joint Iranian–Turkish committee has now been established for the purpose of investigating and apprehending individuals accused of committing 'terrorist acts' against each state. The implications of the rise of Islamic revivalism for the security of the Kurdish regions of Turkey has been a subject of concern for Ankara. For example, in the south-eastern city of Batman, clashes have occurred on a regular basis between Kurdish nationalists and the 'Iran-inspired' Islamic Hizbollah. Some analysts have attributed the growing of Hizbollah in Batman and other south-eastern cities to Islamic elements in the Turkish army and police who have sought to foster 'Islamic Fundamentalism as a weapon to be used against [secular] Kurdish nationalism'.[59] The intra-Kurdish battles between the PKK and the Hizbollah, as well as the struggle of these two groups against the Turkish army, may certainly add a new and hitherto unexplored dimension to the Kurdish question in Turkey and Turkish-Iranian relations.

The situation in Iranian Kurdistan will also affect regional Kurdish issues. The KDPI, as the major Kurdish group, has been waging an intermittent guerrilla war against the Islamic Republic since 1979. The level of opposition in Iranian Kurdistan to the policies of the Islamic Republic has also increased in recent years. This discontent was reflected in the Iranian presidential election of mid-1993 when President Rafsanjani received only 34.17 per cent of the votes cast in the Kurdish province compared to 55.38 per cent for his major opponent, Ahmad Tavakoli. In fact, Kurdistan was the only province in which Rafsanjani did not receive either the majority or the plurality of votes. In view of the fact that Tavakoli was an obscure candidate, Kurdish support for him was not so much an affirmation of his candidacy as a rejection of the policies of the central government in Teheran by Iranian Kurds.[60]

Turkey, as well as Iraq, was able to exploit the discontent among some sectors of the Iranian Kurdish population by exacerbating tensions between the KDPI and the Islamic Republic. The KDPI, like its counterparts in Iraq, has sent positive signals to Turkey to try to win Ankara's support for its cause. For example, in an article comparing Iran with Turkey, the KDPI asserted: 'Turkey is a country in which religion and politics are separated. No one is persecuted in Turkey because of his/her religious views and no one is denied basic rights in that country. This is not the case in Iran where religious intolerance and political oppression rule supreme.'[61] Turkey has not yet fully played its Kurdish card in this respect, but if relations between Ankara and Teheran deteriorate, Turkey can conceivably add a new twist to the Kurdish conundrum in the Middle East.

Finally, the future status of the Kurdish administration in northern Iraq and the prospects for the establishment of an independent Kurdish state will have a major impact on the foreign policies of Iran, Turkey and Iraq. Although unforeseen changes in global politics might bring about dramatic transformations in the region's geopolitics that would allow the creation of an independent Kurdish state, such factors do not currently favour it. None of the countries of the area with a substantial Kurdish population wants the creation of such a state, as this might lead to the further disintegration or disequilibrium of the whole area. Furthermore, it is not clear whether the Kurdish administration in northern Iraq can maintain its current independence when the US and Turkish military shield is no longer present. In addition, Iran and Turkey have strengthened and normalized their security arrangements, and have effectively coordinated their Kurdish policies.

Kurdish infighting in 1993 and 1994 has highlighted the fragile nature of the Kurdish regional government. In particular, military clashes between the two major governing Kurdish parties, the KDP and PUK, have severely shaken the unity of purpose that was present at the formation and early stages of the Iraqi–Kurdish administration. In short, the long-term viability of an autonomous or independent Kurdish state is compromised by both external obstacles and internal divisions that have affected Kurdistan for many decades.

NOTES

1. Quoted in Ruhollah K. Ramazani, *The Foreign Policy of Iran: A Developing Nation in World Affairs, 1500–1941* (Charlottesville: University Press of Virginia, 1966), p. 17.
2. For details, see ibid., pp. 258–76.
3. Graham E. Fuller, *The 'Center of the Universe': The Geopolitics of Iran*, (Boulder, CO: Westview Press, 1991), p. 210.
4. Nader Entessar, *Kurdish Ethnonationalism* (Boulder, CO: Lynne Rienner Publishers, 1992), pp. 116–17.
5. Ibid., pp. 117–24. Also, see Michael M. Gunter, *The Kurds of Iraq: Tragedy and Hope* (New York: St. Martin's Press, 1992), pp. 25–31, and Edmund Ghareeb, *The Kurdish Question in Iraq* (Syracuse, NY: Syracuse University Press, 1981), pp. 142–5.
6. Chris Kutschera, *Le mouvement national kurde* (Paris: Flammarion, 1979), pp. 322–3.
7. Christine Moss Helms, *Iraq: Eastern Flank of the Arab World*, (Washington, DC: Brookings Institution, 1984), p. 150.
8. For a detailed analysis of the Iranian position on the Shatt al-Arab dispute, see Nasser Farshadgar, *Nezam-e Hoqooqi-e Rudhay-e Bainolmelali va Arvand Rud* (The Legal Systems Concerning International Rivers and Arvand Rud), Teheran: Institute for Political and International Studies, 1989. For an Iraqi position, see Tareq Y. Ismael, *Iraq and Iran: Roots of Conflict* (Syracuse, NY: Syracuse University Press, 1982).
9. Samir al-Khalil, *Republic of Fear: The Inside Story of Saddam's Iraq* (New York: Pantheon Books, 1990), p. 24.
10. Ibid.
11. Nader Entessar, *Kurdish Ethnonationalism*, p. 127.
12. Fuat Borovali, 'Iran and Turkey: Permanent Revolution or Islamism in One Country?' in Miron Rezun (ed), *Iran at the Crossroads: Global Relations in a Turbulent Decade* (Boulder, CO: Westview Press, 1990), p. 84. Also, see his 'Kurdish Insurgencies, the Gulf War, and Turkey's Changing Role', *Conflict Quarterly*, vol. 7, no. 4, Fall 1987, pp. 29–45.
13. Nader Entessar, 'The Kurds in Post-Revolutionary Iran and Iraq', *Third World Quarterly*, vol. 6, no. 4, October 1984, p. 923.

14. Quoted in David Menashri, 'Khomeini's Policy Toward Ethnic and Religious Minorities', in Milton J. Esman and Itamar Rabinovich (eds), *Ethnicity, Pluralism, and the State in the Middle East* (Ithaca, NY: Cornell University Press, 1988), p. 217.
15. Quoted in Kendal [Nezan], 'Kurdistan in Turkey', in Gérard Chaliand (ed), *People Without a Country: The Kurds and Kurdistan*, translated by Michael Pallis (London: Zed Press, 1980), p. 65.
16. 'Ozal Puts Up Brave Performance in a Strasbourg – But Brussels Still Says "No"', *Briefings*, 21 October 1989, p. 4.
17. See Helsinki Watch, *Kurds of Turkey: Killings, Disappearances and Torture* (New York: Human Rights Watch, 1993).
18. Nader Entessar, 'The Kurdish Mosaic of Discord', *Third World Quarterly*, vol. 11, no. 4, October 1989, p. 95, and Edgar O'Ballance, *The Gulf War* (London: Brassey's 1988), pp. 133–4.
19. See, for example, *Tercuman*, 5 November 1986.
20. *Milliyet*, 17 November 1986.
21. *Ettela'at*, 12 January 1987, and *Kayhan*, 13 January 1987.
22. *Kayhan*, 3 and 5 June 1988, and *Ettela'at*, 3 and 4 June 1988.
23. *Amnesty Action*, September–October 1988, p. 1.
24. Philip Robins, 'Turkish Policy and the Gulf Crisis: Adventurist or Dynamic?' in Clement H. Dodd (ed.), *Turkish Foreign Policy: New Prospects* (Cambridgeshire, UK: Eothen Press, 1992), p. 72.
25. For a succinct description of Turkey's changing role during the Gulf War of 1991, see ibid., pp. 72–80.
26. *Iran Times*, 21 September 1990.
27. *International Herald Tribune*, 21 March 1991.
28. *Iran Times*, 11 January 1991.
29. Ibid., 12 April 1991.
30. *Guardian Weekly*, 28 April 1991.
31. *Kayhan Havai*, 17 February 1993.
32. *Iran Times*, 26 March 1993 and 30 April 1993.
33. *Kurdistan* (Organ of the Central Committee of the Kurdish Democratic Party of Iran), no. 195, March 1993, p. 2.
34. Ibid., no. 198, June 1993, p. 9 and no. 200, August 1993, pp. 1 and 5–7.
35. For details, see ibid., no. 198, June 1993, p. 9.
36. Ibid., no. 196, April 1994, pp. 9 and 12.
37. Ibid., pp. 8–9.
38. *Iran Times*, 17 September 1993.
39. For details, see 'Elections in Iraqi Kurdistan', Kurdish Institute (Paris), *Information and Liaison Bulletin*, no. 86, May 1992, pp. 1–3 and 9–12.
40. For a succinct description of the prospects for an independent Kurdish state, see James M. Prince, 'A Kurdish State in Iraq?' *Current History*, vol. 92, no. 570, January 1993, pp. 17–22; Robert Olson, 'The Creation of a Kurdish State in the 1990s?' *Journal of South Asian and Middle Eastern Studies*, vol. 15, no. 4, Summer 1992, pp. 1–25, and Michael M. Gunter, 'A *de facto* Kurdish State in Northern Iraq' *Third World Quarterly*, vol. 14, no. 2, 1993, pp. 295–319. For a discussion of international legal principles and Kurdish self-determination, see Nader Entessar, *Kurdish Ethnonationalism*, pp. 161–9.

41. *Iran Times*, 19 February 1993; *Kayhan*, 8 June 1993, and *Jomhoori-e Eslami*, 8 June 1993.
42. 'New Turko-Irano-Syrian Meeting', Kurdish Institute (Paris), *Information and Liaison Bulletin*, no. 99, June 1993, p. 3.
43. *Kayhan Havai*, 8 September 1993.
44. *Milliyet*, 8 June 1993.
45. *Hürriyet*, 27 May 1993.
46. *Iran Times*, 5 July 1991.
47. Graham E. Fuller, 'Turkey's New Eastern Orientation', in Graham E. Fuller, Ian O. Lesser, with Paul B. Henze and J. F. Brown, *Turkey's New Geopolitics: From the Balkans to Western China* Boulder, CO: Westview Press, 1993), p. 60.
48. For a good example of this type of analysis, see Mohammad Nuri, 'Kurdistan-e Araq va Esterateji-e Mantaqei-e Amrika' (The Iraqi Kurdistan and America's Regional Strategy), *Kayhan Havai*, 25 August 1993, p. 22.
49. Hugh Pope, 'Digging Into Iraq', *Middle East International*, no. 437, 6 November 1992, p. 4, and *New York Times*, 7 October 1992.
50. For a critical report on the collaboration of Iraqi Kurdish forces with the Turkish military against the PKK, see Vera Beaudin Saeedpour, 'A Conflict of Interests', *Kurdish Life*, no. 4, Fall 1992, pp. 1–5.
51. B. Rabie, 'Dar Kurdistan-e Araq Che Migozarad?' (What Is Happening in Iraqi Kurdistan?), *Kayhan Havai*, 9 September 1992, p. 22.
52. *Iran Times*, 15 January 1993.
53. Ibid., 23 July 1993, and *Salam*, 14 July 1993.
54. *Kayhan Havai*, 21 and 28 July 1993.
55. Graham E. Fuller, *Turkey Faces East: New Orientations Towards the Middle East and the Old Soviet Union*, Santa Monica, CA: Rand Corporation, R-4232-AF/A, 1992, p. vii.
56. *Sabah*, 25 February 1993.
57. *Ettela'at*, 27 February 1993, and *Iran Times*, 12 March 1993.
58. *Kayhan Havai*, 10 February 1993, and *Christian Science Monitor*, 11 February 1993.
59. Hugh Pope, 'Conflict Over Killings', *Middle East International*, no. 444, 19 February 1993, p. 12.
60. For a brief analysis of the KDPI's views on the 1993 Iranian presidential election, see *Kurdistan*, no. 199, July 1993, p. 8.
61. *Kurdistan*, no. 200, August 1993, p. 15.

Part II New Dimensions of Historical Conflicts

3 Iran, the Persian Gulf and the Post-Cold War Order

M. E. Ahrari, Brigid Starkey and Nader Entessar

INTRODUCTION

Defying those who declared it a pariah, the Islamic Republic of Iran re-emerged as an international power in the 1990s. This is partly due to the military defeat of its nemesis, Iraq, during the 1991 Gulf War. But, on a more substantial basis, the re-emergence of Iran as a pivotal regional player is the fulfillment of its natural role in south-west Asia. The maintenance of Iran's pre-eminence in the Gulf was a keystone of the policy of Shah Mohammad Reza Pahlavi as well as of his successor, the Islamic Republic. In the post-Cold War era, the stakes for regional influence are higher than ever, as the politically-defined Middle East and the culturally-defined Muslim world have explicitly begun their extensions into the Caucasus and Central Asia.

Yet, the Islamic Republic of Iran remains a dangerous enigma to its Gulf neighbours, as well to those striving for balance in the region. Whereas Iran and Saudi Arabia shared the status of 'twin pillars' of the American-designed Middle Eastern security regime in the 1970s, post-revolutionary Iran has been continuously at odds with Washington and Riyadh over the nature of its foreign policy goals. Leaders of both nations have portrayed Iran as a major threat and source of instability in the region, especially after the destruction of much of Iraq's military capability. This shared perception became the basis of the US decision to continue large-scale arms sales to Saudi Arabia. Iran, for its part, views the alliance between the United States and Saudi Arabia as a major source of concern and a direct challenge to its national security interests, thus prompting the Islamic Republic to engage in its own military build-up.

The current relationship between the three is dominated not by the significant common ground which exists between them,[1] but by the hostility and suspicion which the United States continues to have for the post-revolutionary Iranian state which is now well into its second decade of leadership. Leaders in Teheran must share the responsibility for the nature of this relationship which continues to be destructive. Whenever a more moderate American policy seems possible, anti-establishment figures in Iran issue calls for assassinations and throw up roadblocks to regional peace efforts.

The security landscape of the Persian Gulf continues to be heavily influenced by this ideological feud. For the Europeans and the Japanese, the Islamic Republic has clearly regained its pre-revolutionary status as a vital trading partner and a regional power that cannot be ignored. This perception seems dominant in Ankara, Islamabad and Moscow as well. It also has many advocates in the capitals of the smaller Gulf nations. It is a perception that the United States has lobbied hard to alter and one which Teheran itself calls into question with its periodic reversions to confrontationalism.

Is the Islamic Republic poised to fully re-enter the international scene? Or is it a dangerous renegade state which threatens the core principles of that system? This chapter suggests that there is no definitive answer as yet. Rather, Iran continues to stand at a crossroads. It faces some nations which continue to try to actively engage it in constructive international business and diplomacy. It faces others which feel it is reprehensible to do business openly with a regime whose internal and external policies have frequently been deemed unethical and even criminal. Ultimately, the future course taken by Teheran may well be determined by which side will prove the stronger and by the internal dynamics of a struggle for dominance that is still being played out.

FROM REGIONAL POLICEMAN TO IDEOLOGICAL ZEALOT: IRAN DURING THE COLD WAR ERA

The strategic significance of Iran in the Persian Gulf has been recognized by all the principal protagonists on the world stage for most of the twentieth century. The former Soviet Union coveted Iran's northern territory in the 1940s, engendering the first Soviet-American post-war crisis. During the Cold War period, both Moscow and Washington sought to have good political relations with Iran. Iran, for its part, was able to exploit the rivalry between the two superpowers and at times benefit from this situation. However, after engineering a *coup d'état* against the nationalist Iranian Prime Minister Mohammad Mossadegh in 1953 and bringing the Shah back to power, the United States managed to gain the upper hand in the superpower rivalry and establish significant political, economic and military ties to Iran.[2] While the Shah never forgot the role America had played in his return to power, the perception that he was beholden to Washington for his throne was very unpopular in Iran. It became very clear during the tumultuous revolutionary periods of late 1978 and early 1979 that, despite his efforts, the Shah had failed to establish an independent image for himself in the eyes of most Iranians. The Cold War may have prolonged the Shah's rule but it could not establish the regime's legitimacy.

Internationally, Shah Mohammad Reza Pahlavi followed a classic realist course. In the context of Cold War politics, Iran attained a pivotal role in American strategic designs, capitalizing on what had long been a dangerous vulnerability – its long common border with the Soviet Union. The strategic importance of the Shah's Iran to the United States was clearly indicated in the 1970s when the 'Nixon Doctrine' used Iran as a regional policeman. Iran's role was to provide the muscle to back Saudi Arabia's wealth in what Nixon and Kissinger deemed the 'twin pillars' policy. To bolster his new status, the Shah was given *carte blanche* to purchase the most sophisticated weaponry in the US arsenal.

Teheran quickly became the envy of its long-time regional rivals. Saudi Arabia had to accept that it could not claim 'twin' or equal weight when it came to population size, military and economic infrastructure or technical sophistication. Iraq found itself at a distinct disadvantage as the beneficiary of the 'other' superpower. Moscow, for reasons of its own, never sought to arm Iraq to the level required to challenge Iran's preeminence in the Gulf.

Not surprisingly, the Shah was not content to rest on the laurels of deterrence. He adopted an active posture in the Persian Gulf sub-region, within the increasingly influential Organization of Petroleum Exporting Countries (OPEC), and let it be known that he was beginning to look towards the Indian Ocean in his quest for enhanced 'regional' influence.[3]

In the end, it seems clear that the Shah failed to 'sell' his foreign policy to his own people as an independent one. He had hoped to counter the negative image of his close security relationship with the US by acquiring the biggest and best military equipment available. In making this trade-off, the Shah lost sight of the most fundamental tenet of Iranian foreign policy, namely, the need to maintain independence in a nation scarred by repeated great-power intervention.[4]

For a number of reasons, the revolution that brought down the Shah has been one of the most significant developments in the modern history of the Middle East. It established the first Islamic government in the post-colonial Middle East. Although both Pakistan and Saudi Arabia claim to be Islamic states, they have been ruled by either monarchies or military and have certainly lacked the popular legitimacy that the Islamic Republic of Iran could claim in its formative stage. It is only recently that Pakistan has begun experimenting with democracy, though the army still plays a crucial role in its politics.

In addition, the establishment of the Islamic Republic initiated an era during which Iranian perspectives on the nature of the political order in the Persian Gulf underwent radical transformations. Under the Islamic Republic's founder and spiritual leader, Ayatollah Ruhollah Khomeini, Iran ceased to be a dependent state in the Cold War. In fact, Khomeini's rhetoric depicted both superpowers as 'evil' and exploiters of the Muslim world. According to Khomeini, it was 'incumbent on all Muslims to vigorously oppose the superpowers and rescue the oppressed people from their suffocating clutches'.[5] The language of politics and political discourse underwent major changes in post-revolutionary Iran. The Islamic Republic utilized a new litmus test for the legitimacy of ruling elites and regimes in the region. It was not necessarily their adherence to Islam but what Iran viewed as their 'subservient ties' to the United States that became the basis for the judgement of their legitimacy. The pro-US Arab regimes were given intermittent warnings that their rule would be ended when their people rose up against the 'usurpers of power' in their countries.[6] In other words, the example set by the Iranian revolution would inspire other Muslims to overthrow their own political systems and replace them with Islamic forms of government. This was how Iran's revolution was supposed to have been 'exported' to other countries in the region. In Khomeini's words, 'Our revolution is not limited to the boundaries of Iran. Economic and political difficulties should not compel our officials to forgo the principal task of exporting our lofty Islamic revolutionary goals.... If the lackeys of the United States accuse us of expansionism, so be it. In fact, we will welcome their accusations against us. We are determined to eradicate the corrupt symbols of capitalism, communism and Zionism from our midst.... The true meaning of the export of our revolution is to awaken the Muslims and their governments so that they can change themselves and not allow their precious resources to be plundered by anti-Muslim outsiders'.[7]

The Islamic revolution converted Iran into an unconventional state, a potential destabilizer of the status quo, and a spoiler of the then existing world order. The conventional nation-states did not know how to deal with Iran. The Gulf sheikhdoms were frightened of the spillover effects of the Iranian revolution. Iraq was befuddled and angry over Khomeini's public exhortations to the Iraqi people to overthrow Saddam Hussein's regime. The United States – the 'Great Satan' – bore the brunt of the fury of the

Iranian revolutionary upheaval through the hostage crisis. The Soviet Union, even though it cautiously welcomed the end of the Shah's pro-US regime, could find no basis for close ties with Iran. After the Soviet invasion of Afghanistan in 1979, Moscow had little chance of establishing cordial relations with an Iran that was highly condemnatory of the superpower domination of the Muslim world.

In the 1980s, the Islamic government of Iran was clearly interested in establishing something akin to an Islamic sub-system in the Persian Gulf. This was to safeguard the gains of the Revolution and to allow the nascent Islamic Republic to formalize its institutions. However, the method it chose to use to achieve its objectives was hardly a prudent one. The threat of exportability of the Islamic Revolution to the neighbouring states was inherently self-defeating. The Arab sheikhdoms, most of which were weak and fragile, had long championed the political status quo and hence were reluctant to become part of a sub-system which Iran would inevitably come to dominate. They had a variety of options, which they exercised throughout the 1980s. Their first concrete response to the Iranian Revolution was the creation in 1981 of the Gulf Cooperation Council (GCC). This was a grouping of the conservative Gulf regimes of Saudi Arabia, Kuwait, Bahrain, Qatar, Oman and the United Arab Emirates. The ostensible *raison d'être* of this organization was to provide collective security for the Arab peninsular states in the area. Faced with their most dramatic threat – the Iran–Iraq War – Saudi Arabia and Kuwait actively supported Iraq. Saddam Hussein's regime was viewed as the lesser of two evils. At the same time, GCC policy maintained that all conflicts in the Persian Gulf should be resolved without the interference of outside powers. This policy was in harmony with Khomeini's insistence on excluding both superpowers from the affairs of the region. The GCC members were always aware, however, that in a worst-case scenario, they could rely on the intervention of the United States.

The Iran-Iraq War had a logic (or illogic) of its own. Both Saudi Arabia and Kuwait continued to be the targets of harsh Iranian rhetoric for their assistance to Saddam Hussein's attacks on ships bound for Iran. Teheran viewed the behaviour of its Gulf neighbours as an act of war and subsequently began to target some Kuwaiti-bound ships. In 1987, Kuwait asked both superpowers to make their presence known in the Gulf. The long-standing zero-sum relationship between Washington and Moscow was triggered once again, despite the fact that the Soviet Union was then in the midst of cataclysmic internal changes.

The opportunity for Washington to flex its military muscles against Teheran was too good to pass up. Still smarting from the 444-day Hostage

Crisis, as well as its own 'arms for hostages' fiasco, the Reagan Administration moved to put this 'renegade' state in its place. It succeeded in this objective not only by destroying a significant portion of the outgunned and out-manned Iranian navy, but also by enabling Iraq to gain the upper hand in the last and most important phase of the Iran–Iraq War.[8] The Islamic Republic's decision to accept the UN-sponsored ceasefire in July 1988 was an important victory for Washington in the ongoing confrontation between the United States and Iran.

Another significant event in the ushering in of a new era in post-revolutionary Iranian foreign affairs was the death of Ayatollah Khomeini and the ensuing opportunity for the Iranian leadership to seriously weigh the value of the isolationist international stance it had been taking, over one which accepted the reality of 'interdependence'.

In fact, three indicators point to the fact that pragmatism had begun to overcome ideological principles by the late 1980s, positioning Iran back on the edge of international respectability in the post-Cold War era. These were (1) muted responses to international crises involving the loss of Iranian lives; (2) a return to seeking solutions to international crises within multilateral organizations, including the United Nations, the Non-aligned Movement and the Economic Cooperation Organization; and (3) a return to a traditional Iranian foreign policy strategy – playing the great powers off one another.[9] Muted responses, made through official channels, greeted the 1987 Saudi–Iranian Hajj Crisis, the 1988 USS *Vincennes*–Iran Air airbus incident, and the aforementioned 1988–89 Tanker War in the Gulf. Official Iranian responses to these events were not violent, but included boycotts, appeals to the United Nations and the International Civil Aviation Authority, and a personal visit by President Rafsanjani to the Soviet Union, following the death of Khomeini in 1989. Revolutionary credentials were being kept intact in less costly ways by this point. Even the 1988 Salman Rushdie Crisis was one such revolutionary engram. Iranian involvement came only after disturbances in India, London and other locations had signalled the 'Islamicization' of the issue.[10] The seizure of this opportunity to create a full-blown diplomatic crisis fits well with Precht's evaluation of the regime's general strategy at that point: 'to maintain fidelity to the revolution's ideals while protecting the country through pragmatism'.[11] Ironically, although the United States has persisted in labelling Iranian foreign policy confrontational and radical in the 1990s, President Rafsanjani actually remains locked in an internal struggle to promote a pragmatic but independent approach. Much of Teheran's confrontational behaviour comes in apparent response to US challenges to the legitimacy of the post-revolutionary regime.

FORGING AN INDEPENDENT FOREIGN POLICY: POST-COLD WAR IRAN

The American humiliation over its misreading of the Shah's stability now works against all instincts to reinterpret Iranian international intentions. This state of affairs is not helped by the Clinton Administration's recycling of key foreign policy makers from the Carter Administration (most notably, current Secretary of State Warren Christopher, who was badly burned by the Hostage Crisis). US leaders have repeatedly asked their European, Japanese and Russian counterparts to stop trading with the Islamic Republic, including arms deals. However, the rehabilitation of Iran is considered to be well underway by Bonn, Tokyo and Moscow, where economic realism clearly transcends ideological factors, including human-rights-based arguments.

For their part, Saudi Arabia and the smaller Gulf nations find themselves trapped between the temptation to try to engage Teheran constructively in regional politics and economics and their inclination to abide by the lessons of recent history regarding sinister Iranian motives in the sub-region. There is conflicting evidence of Iranian intentions, as the Islamic Republic's international politics continue to be dangerously ambivalent.

There are conflicting assessments as to whether internal competition for influence over foreign policy has increased or decreased since the election of a much more conservative *Majlis* (parliament) in April of 1992. Some observers characterize the mood as highly contentious when it comes to questions of rapprochement with the United States and further economic liberalization within Iran.[12] Others see relative harmony in the overall approach, including the scope of the military build-up and the country's claims to Abu Musa and the Lesser Tunbs.[13]

There are two main areas which must be examined for evidence of intentions and motivations in this decision-making environment which is, in any case, still severely factionalized.

1. How Does 'Islamic Internationalism' Interact with Traditional National Self-Interest in Iranian Foreign Policy?

In the 'heady' days of the Hostage Crisis, as the revolution unfolded in Iran, the Ayatollah Khomeini, who was in the ascendant, talked of the need to 'export' Iran's revolution to other parts of the Persian Gulf sub-region.[14] Whether this export effort was intended to be a violently subversive one or an export by example continues to be the subject of contention. When revolutionary fervour met Islamic internationalism, the result was the foreign policy equivalent of Thermidor. There were attempts to influence political events in Saudi Arabia, Iraq, Kuwait, Bahrain and Egypt, as exhortations to rebel went out over Teheran Radio.[15] An effort was also made to politicize the Hajj, and Revolutionary Guards were despatched to Lebanon to support the then-nascent Lebanese Hizbollah and the Islamic Amal movements.[16]

Suspicions about Iranian foreign policy tactics, based on these activities which were most prevalent in the immediate aftermath of the revolution, continue to work against acceptance of the regime in Teheran. Periodic episodes of 'violent diplomacy', targeted against external powers operating in the Middle East, are also very damaging to the Islamic Republic's international reputation.[17]

Despite Khomeini's clarification that use of a sword should not be necessary and that what he was supporting was the export of the message of Islam, the perception that Teheran was attempting to foment revolution around the region has remained a popular one in the 1990s.[18] It is lent credence by the political infighting in Teheran, which leads 'hardliners' to resort periodically to Islamic internationalist rhetoric, albeit mostly for domestic consumption. Nervousness in the international community over an alleged Teheran-inspired African-Islamic connection has arisen in the wake of Iranian support of anti-establishment Islamicist movements in Algeria, Egypt and Sudan. There are also allegations of Iranian support for Hamas in the Palestinian territories.

Yet, on balance, it seems clear that geopolitical pragmatism does prevail over ideology in the post-Cold War foreign relations of the Islamic Republic. It is when national interest is well-served by playing up the Islamic dimension of its international relations that Teheran causes the most consternation. While Saudi Arabia and Iran generally refrained from attacking each other on religious grounds in the 1990s, there is still heated competition between the two for politico-religious power in the Muslim world. This is not really a matter of Shiite-Wahabi doctrinal differences, as is often asserted. The real competition involves strategic concerns. Who will or ought to have an upper hand in the strategic affairs of the Persian Gulf? And, which state would (or should) emerge as the superior economic and military power? These are questions with which the late Shah also had to deal.

Non-Arab Iran has always faced an uphill battle in its efforts to assume leadership of the Gulf region. This certainly remains true under the current regime. Despite numerous efforts to convince the smaller Gulf nations of its good intentions following the death of Khomeini, the Islamic Republic is still – at best – the mediator of last resort for the smaller Gulf sheikhdoms. In the aftermath of the Gulf War, Iran was once again excluded from the collective security arrangements being worked out in the Arab capitals.

The 'GCC plus two' or Damascus Agreement was particularly infuriating to Teheran. It has been designed to bring the Arab states of Egypt and Syria into cooperation with the GCC states as a deterrent against further Iraqi aggression. Predictably, intra-Arab rivalry caused the rapid demise of this plan, providing Iran with an opportunity to push further for its own inclusion in the GCC security arrangement. Despite widespread resistance to this idea – in Riyadh, Cairo and Washington – some of the smaller sheikhdoms expressed periodic support for Iranian inclusion. Even the al-Saud family has had to admit that it is difficult to imagine a lasting security arrangement for the region that might not somehow include Iranian interests.

In the post-Cold War Middle East, competition for influence now embraces Turkey, as well as Iran and Saudi Arabia. The redefined Middle East includes Azerbaijan and the five independent Central Asian Muslim republics of Kazakhstan, Kyrgyzstan, Tajikistan, Uzbekistan and Turkmenistan. One of the most significant aspects of the politics of these new nations is that as they develop their national identities, Islamic perspectives compete with secular ones for institutional influence. All three nations – Iran, Saudi Arabia and Turkey – could play important roles in the unfolding of events; Iran because of its proximity to these countries and its 'radical model' of political change, Saudi Arabia because of its significance as a Sunni state and the birthplace of Islam, and Turkey because of its proximity and its favour in the West as a model of the secular development path.

This 'Islamic' dimension of Central Asian politics continues to be a source of anxiety in both Washington and Moscow. Of particular concern are the advantages which the Islamic Republic brings to the 'competition'. Iran enjoys a certain advantage in Central Asia and the Caucasus. It has deep historical and cultural ties with the area. The cities of Samarkand and Bokhara, located in today's Uzbekistan, have been the cradle of some of the most memorable classical Persian literature. Large Iranian migrant communities have carried this cultural torch for several centuries.[19] In the contemporary era, Iran can provide economic assistance in kind and some financial aid. Iran is also a natural channel for the transport of Central Asian goods to the rest of the world.

Yet, in mitigation of the theory of a potentially bloody competition for the newly-emerging countries is the fact that Iran has joined with Turkey in the establishment of the Economic Cooperation Organization (ECO). It has used this forum to promote – not Islamic internationalism – but regional economic coordination of a decidedly neo-realist bent. The ideological component of Iranian foreign policy still seems to be relegated to more remote areas – Africa, in particular. National self-interest in its current economically determined mode continues its ascendancy in Iran's relations with its immediate neighbours in the post-Cold War era.

2. What Is Teheran's Agenda Regarding Military Preparedness?

Post-revolutionary Iran has found itself locked in a spiralling arms race, not unlike that which preoccupied the Shah during his reign. The stakes have been even higher, however, as the Revolution severely damaged Iran's military capability and demoralized and decimated its highly trained manpower. It was this weakened condition which Saddam Hussein sought to exploit when he launched the full-scale invasion of Iran in 1980, touching off the eight-year war. This protracted conflict was particularly perilous for the Iranian military because its hardware lifeline to the United States had been cut, forcing it to rely on weapons purchased from the Warsaw Pact nations, the People's Republic of China and various other secondary and tertiary sources.

While Iran's security position in the Gulf improved significantly with the allied coalition's defeat of Saddam Hussein in the 1990–91 Gulf War, its insecurity in its own sub-region persists. The continuing rule of Saddam Hussein is regarded as a threat by Iran, but so is the potential fragmentation of Iraq. Furthermore, in the aftermath of the Gulf War, the United States has further committed itself to arming Saudi Arabia and its GCC partners, in response to the explicit threat from Baghdad and what is considered an ever-present implicit threat from Teheran. Between 1980 and 1988, Iraq, Saudi Arabia, Kuwait, Bahrain and the UAE had either contracted to purchase or deployed some of the world's most advanced military aircraft. These included AWACS, F-15s, F-16s, F-18s, Hawk 200s, Mirage F-1s, Mirage 2000s, Tornadoes, MiG-25s, MiG-29s, SU-24s and SU-25s.[20] Following Operation Desert Storm, the United States announced an agreement to sell Riyadh an additional US$21 billion worth of several categories of advanced weapons, including F-15C and F-15D fighter planes, TOW and Hellfire missiles, Apache helicopters and M-1A2 and M-60A3 tanks. In addition, the smaller Gulf sheikhdoms all concluded bilateral military and security agreements with the United States in the aftermath of the Gulf War.[21]

Not surprisingly, the view from Teheran is that the southern Gulf nations have crossed the line from deterrent to confrontational behaviour.

The Rafsanjani regime responded with a reported US$10 billion plan to enhance its army, air defence, air and naval equipment.[22] Though the design and scope of this expansion effort remain vague, the Islamic Republic has managed to add some sophisticated weaponry to its arsenal, including MiG-29s, SU-24s, F-6 and F-7 fighter jets, SCUD C ground-to-ground missiles and Kilo-class diesel submarines.[23] Interested observers are further concerned about the post-revolutionary regime's efforts to pick up where the Shah left off with an indigenous weapons procurement programme. The initial work of enabling Iran to emerge as a major military power was done by the Shah's government when it embarked upon a programme of sustained and large-scale industrialization as a substitute for imports in 1970.[24] As an integral part of this programme, the Shah's government signed production assembly agreements with seven major defence contractors in the United States and Great Britain, covering an unprecedented amount of technology transfer, including nuclear technology, to Iran. A number of joint ventures between major American defence companies and Iran eventually produced military hardware of a different level of sophistication.[25] Since 1989, some of these programmes have been revived by the Rafsanjani government, the major exception being that Iran is now relying on military joint ventures with the CIS. The reverse engineering techniques developed by the Chinese are now reportedly being utilized by the Iranians to make spare parts for F-4s and F-14s. Iran's ambitions also include manufacturing indigenous fighter aircraft and main battle tanks.

Teheran also acquired dozens of Iraqi military aircraft during the 1991 Gulf War when Iraqi pilots decided to seek asylum by flying their planes to Iran. The Islamic Republic decided to keep these aircraft, possibly as partial payment of war reparations.

Iran's revolutionary leaders developed a fascination with the acquisition of missile technology during the war against Iraq. According to one study, during both the 'war of cities' and the 'tanker war', the Iranian leadership became convinced of the psychological advantages of possessing large inventories of missiles.[26] Since then, Iran is reported to have developed a huge inventory of missiles from a variety of sources. From China it purchased *Oghab* tactical artillery rockets, the C-801 (somewhat comparable with French Exocet missiles) and the R-17/SCUD-B missiles. In addition, the Chinese sold the following technologies to Iran: technology for 130-kilometre-range *Iran* 130 missiles, facilities to indigenously produce 1000-kilometre SRBMs, the Tonder-68, 100–125-kilometre SRBMs, transfer of M-class missile technology to produce 600-kilometre range missiles and infrastructures to produce HY-2 Silkworm anti-ship and M-class missiles. Iran also contracted with North Korea to produce

Mod-B versions of missiles, and signed a joint production agreement with Syria to produce SCUD Mod-C missiles using North Korean technology. A number of SRBMs have also been supplied to Iran by the former Soviet Union.[27]

Iran's purchase of three Russian-built Kilo-class submarines was given prominence in the Western media. The United States unsuccessfully sought to persuade President Boris Yeltsin not to go through with this deal. The general thinking in the United States was that through the acquisition of these submarines, Iran would emerge as the dominant naval power in the Persian Gulf, and that it would enhance its capability to control the strategic Straits of Hormuz. Although Iran has so far deployed two Kilo-class submarines, and the introduction of submarines can be viewed as an escalation of the regional arms race in the Persian Gulf, these submarines still would not allow Iran to develop the best-equipped regional navy. As a Middle East arms expert has correctly noted, 'with the delivery of the first submarine to the Iranian navy, Saudi Arabia announced the second phase of its Al-Sawari contract with France (worth US$4 billion) for the delivery of three more upgraded Lafayette-class frigates (armed with anti-ship and anti-aircraft missiles, torpedo tubes and anti-submarine warfare helicopters). When this deal is completed, Saudi Arabia will have the most powerful navy in the Gulf, with seven frigates, four US-supplied Badr-class corvettes, nine US-supplied Siddiq-class missile attack vessels and dozens of supply ships, torpedo boats and minesweepers. Iran, on the other hand, was reported to have, in 1993, two submarines, three ageing destroyers, five frigates, 10 missile craft and fewer than five mine-warfare vessels.'[28] If the US naval presence in the Gulf is added to this equation, the balance of power is further tipped against Iran.

In short, Iranian efforts, significant as they are in the post-Cold War era, are still dwarfed by the combined efforts of the southern Gulf nations. US allies in the region spent a combined US$48 billion on defence in 1993,[29] compared to Iran's US$1 billion.

CONCLUSION: ASSESSING THE ISLAMIC REPUBLIC'S POSITION IN THE POST-COLD WAR INTERNATIONAL SYSTEM

As has been shown, the motivations and intentions of the Islamic Republic in the post-Cold War era remain difficult to determine. Those who continue to be sceptical of Iran's ability to fully rejoin the international system emphasize the Islamic component of its foreign policy. They talk of Iran's desire to subvert the prevailing system with a violent and confrontational

'Islamic bloc'. On the other side, there are many nations – in Africa, Asia, Europe, and the Americas – that have re-engaged in relations with Teheran on both an economic and a political basis.

Whether Iran's behaviour is viewed as sinister and threatening or as a reaction to provocation from Baghdad, Washington, Riyadh and Cairo determines perceptions of its military intentions. Despite differing viewpoints on Teheran's security posture, its re-emergence into the international economic system is now indisputable. Even the United States has slowly improved its trade relations with the Islamic Republic to the point that in the first half of 1994, it stood as one of Iran's largest trading partners.

To those who accept Iran's economic importance but continue to deny or reject its importance to the security landscape of the Gulf, a warning should be sounded. Iran is too strategically significant to be excluded from any lasting security arrangements in the region. In fact, logic compels one to conclude that only by including Iran in future regional security arrangements would the United States and other great powers be able to stabilize the Persian Gulf. The inclusion of Iran would most likely lead to a de-escalation of the arms build-up in the region. No matter how much Saudi Arabia spends on building up its military capabilities, it cannot single-handedly maintain the security of the Gulf. Arms purchases alone do not turn a country into a military power. On the basis of economic and military self-sufficiency, trained manpower and infrastructure, Iran remains the dominant force in the Gulf. So, why not build the political stakes for Iran to become part of an all-inclusive regional security system?

It would be imprudent to ignore the ideological and confrontational aspects of Iranian foreign policy which still exist. However, they must be recognized for what they are. They represent one of the remaining vestiges of the Revolution. The economic successes and failures of the Islamic regime will ultimately determine whether Iran will fully re-emerge as a traditional political force or whether it will marginalize itself and join the ranks of 'pariah' states outside the international system. As long as the domestic struggle for power continues between the so-called 'secular' and 'religious' elements,[30] President Rafsanjani will be forced to play both sides of the fence. It is a potential tragedy that the United States is still unable to recognize the need to support his efforts to normalize his foreign policy.

For every Abu Musa-style confrontational incident, the Iran of the post-Cold War era has also adopted a conciliatory posture. Mediation in Tajikistan's civil war and neutrality in the Yemeni internal conflict represent two such policies. It is crucial, as the United States continues to lead re-definition of the post-Cold War international system, that Iran's efforts at traditional *realpolitik* should not be misinterpreted as aberrant behaviour. Efforts to develop nuclear capability on the part of Iran, Iraq and many other states are admittedly frightening. What must be remembered, however, is that the force of the deterrent capability of these weapons is a lesson that these states have learned from the five permanent members of the UN Security Council. Emulation has always been a cornerstone of the international behaviour of states and should not be forgotten in the American rush to label Iran as a pariah.

NOTES

1. All three nations have an interest in maintaining the free flow of Middle Eastern oil – particularly the US and Iran; all have an interest in maintaining the territorial integrity of Iraq, while ensuring that Saddam Hussein does not regain his previous level of power; all have common interests in Bosnia and Afghanistan. *The Evolution of Clinton's Policy Toward Iran* (Washington, DC: Forum on American-Iranian Relations, 1993).
2. The literature on the subject of the 1953 coup is extensive. For example, see Mark J. Gasiorowski. *US Foreign Policy and the Shah: Building a Client State in Iran* (Ithaca, NY: Cornell University Press, 1991), pp. 57–84; Kermit Roosevelt, *Countercoup: The Struggle for the Control of Iran* (New York: McGraw-Hill, 1979); and Richard W. Cottam, *Iran and the United States: A Cold War Case Study* (Pittsburgh, PA: University of Pittsburgh Press, 1988), pp. 103–9 and 116–17.
3. Policies during the activist period included the November 1971 invasion of the islands of Abu Musa and the Greater and Lesser Tunbs – a power play that was recently repeated by the leaders of the Islamic Republic; a 'hawkish' stance in OPEC, pushing for intermittent price escalations, much to the dismay of the US and Saudi Arabia; and a foray into the protracted Indo-Pakistani conflict in an effort to challenge Soviet influence in that part of the world.
4. Iran's fear of outside intervention has been compared to Soviet fears of invasion following the world wars. See R. K. Ramazani, *The Foreign Policy of Iran 1500–1941: A Developing Nation in World Affairs* (Charlottesville, VA: University Press of Virginia, 1966).
5. *Ayeen-e Enqelab-e Islami: Gozide-e az Andishe va Ara-e Imam Khomeini* (Principles of the Islamic Revolution: Selections from Imam Khomeini's Thoughts and Edicts) (Teheran: Organization for the Collection and Publication of Imam Khomeini's Writings, 1994), p. 391.
6. For a succinct analysis of the impact of Iran's revolution on the Gulf Arab countries, see David E. Long, 'The Impact of the Iranian Revolution on the Arabian Peninsula and the Gulf States', in John L. Esposito (ed.), *The Iranian Revolution: Its Global Impact* (Miami: Florida International

University Press, 1990), pp. 100–15. For an analysis of the Islamic dimensions of Iran's foreign policy, see Shireen T. Hunter, *Iran and the World: Continuity in a Revolutionary Decade* (Bloomington, IN: Indiana University Press, 1990), pp. 36–45, and Mahmood Sariolghalam, 'Conceptual Sources of Post-Revolutionary Iranian Behavior Toward the Arab World', in Hooshang Amirahmadi and Nader Entessar (eds), *Iran and the Arab World* (New York: St. Martin's Press, 1993), pp. 19–27.

7. *Ayeen-e Enqelab-e Islami*, op. cit. pp. 414–16.
8. For recent studies of the role of the United States in arming Iraq and bolstering Saddam Hussein's war objectives, see Alan Friedman, *Spider's Web: The Secret History of How the White House Illegally Armed Iraq* (New York: Bantam Books, 1993), pp. 131–271; Bruce W. Jentleson, *With Friends Like These: Reagan, Bush and Saddam* (New York: W. W. Norton, 1994), pp. 31–68; William W. Hartung, *And Weapons for All* (New York: HarperCollins, 1994), pp. 222–47; Nader Entessar, 'Superpowers and Persian Gulf Security: The Iranian Perspective', *Third World Quarterly*, vol. 10, no. 4, October 1988, pp. 1427–51, and Murray Waas and Craig Unger, 'In the Loop: Bush's Secret Mission', *The New Yorker*, 2 November 1992, pp. 64–83.
9. Even before the death of Khomeini, and apparently with his blessing, Khamenei and Rafsanjani had begun to talk about interdependence and a new 'open door' foreign policy. See R. K. Ramazani, 'Revolutionary Iran's Open Door Policy', *Harvard International Review*, January 1987, pp. 11–15.
10. Brigid A. Starkey, 'The Islamic Republic of Iran as Crisis Actor: The Persian Gulf Crisis of 1990–91'. Presented at the Annual Meeting of the International Studies Association, Atlanta, Georgia, 1992.
11. Henry Precht, 'Ayatollah Realpolitik', *Foreign Policy* 70, Spring 1988, pp. 109–28.
12. See Bahman Baktiari, 'Iran's Political System', *US–Iran Review*, February 1994, pp. 6–15; and Dan Ramirez, 'The Faithful Opposition: Religious Resistance to Rafsanjani's Reforms', *Harvard International Review*, Summer 1994, Vol. XVI, No. 3, pp. 42–75.
13. See Kenneth Katzman, *US–Iran Review*, op. cit., p. 4.
14. See James A. Bill, 'Resurgent Islam in the Persian Gulf', *Foreign Affairs* 63 (1), 1984, pp. 108–27 for more details on this era.
15. See Cheryl Benard and Zalmay Khalizad, *The Government of God: Iran's Islamic Republic* (New York: Columbia University Press, 1984).
16. Ibid.
17. See Alex von Dornach, 'Iran's Violent Diplomacy,' *Survival*, vol. 30, 1988, pp. 250–330 for a discussion of violent diplomacy, which he describes as a strategy that includes actual violence such as assassinations, bombings, beatings and kidnappings, as well as intimidation through the use of threats of violence.
18. Kenneth Katzman notes in his article, 'Rafsanjani and His Opponents', *US–Iran Review*, November 1993, p. 5 that 'US Ambassador to the United Nations Madeleine Albright said [in September 1993] the United States had growing indications of an emerging alliance between Iran, Sudan and Somali warlord Mohammad Farah Aideed'.

19. For a good summary of the historical and cultural links between Iran and Central Asia, see Mohammad Assemi, 'Bord va Bakhtaye Ma dar een Haftad Sal' (Our Wins and Losses During the Past Seventy Years), *Par Monthly Journal*, Vol. 7, no. 2, March 1992, pp. 1–17.
20. Anoushirvan Ehteshami, 'Iranian Rearmament Strategy under President Rafsanjani', *Jane's Intelligence Review*, July 1992, pp. 312–15.
21. See Anthony Cordesman, *After the Storm: The Changing Military Balance in the Middle East* (Boulder, CO: Westview Press, 1993)
22. Cordesman, op. cit., discusses this unsubstantiated rumour on p. 401.
23. See Mohammad Faour, *The Arab World after Desert Storm* (Washington, DC: United States Institute of Peace, 1993), p. 88.
24. 'Iran Builds its Strength', *Jane's Defence Weekly*, February 1992, pp. 158–9.
25. Ibid, p. 158.
26. Gordon Jacobs and Tim McCarthy, 'China's Missile Sales – Few Changes for the Future', *Jane's Intelligence Review*, December 1992, pp. 559–63.
27. Jacobs and McCarthy, op. cit., and Joseph Bermudez, Jr, 'Ballistic Missiles in the Third World – Iran's Medium Range Missiles', *Jane's Intelligence Review*, April 1992, pp. 147–52.
28. Anoushirvan Ehteshami, 'Iran's National Strategy: Striving for Regional Parity or Supremacy?' *International Defence Review*, vol. 27, no. 4, April 1994, p. 37.
29. *US–Iran Review*, November 1993, p. 3.
30. Ramirez uses these terms in 'The Faithful Opposition', op. cit., p. 42.

4 Islam as a Source of Continuity and Change in the Middle East

M. E. Ahrari

Islam plays an extraordinarily significant role in the fractious politics of the Middle East. Since the Prophet Muhammad was also a statesman, a diplomat, and a soldier, there emerged a powerful tradition of emulating his example, whereby rulers in the Middle East also claimed to be 'defenders of the faith'. Even the Umayyad rulers – whose religious credentials were questionable largely because the founder of this dynasty, Muawiya, came to power by fighting a battle with Ali (the fourth Caliph of Islam, cousin and son-in-law of the Prophet), and by denying the right of Caliphate to his son, Hassan, strongly proclaimed their leadership of Islam.

When the Ottoman empire disintegrated after being the 'sick man of Europe' for so long, and was replaced by the modern state of Turkey, Kemal Ataturk, its founder, renounced the historical tradition of the intermingling of religion and politics. In its place, he adopted the Western concept of a secular state. Since then, Turkey has been a state run by a secular government.[1] But secularism in the post-World War II Middle East has had a mixed record of success. Most republican states that also espoused Arab nationalism – such as Egypt, Iraq and Syria – also remained openly secular. Iraq adopted Islamic symbols during the Gulf conflict of 1990–91. It is hard to believe, however, that Saddam Hussein – a lifelong secular Ba'thist – has really had a change of heart about Islam. For other Muslim countries – both within and outside the Middle East – secularism is largely viewed as a Western notion adopted by the ruling elites since independence. In no other Muslim country – with the arguable exception of Turkey[2] – has secularism been accepted by the population at large as a political or governmental framework. Even in Egypt, where there have been intermittent debates over 'secularism versus Islam' and where a secular government is in power, it appears in 1993 that the advocates of secularism are fighting a losing battle. More important, in Egypt, the government has kept a confusing role of remaining close to certain 'moderate' Islamic groups who are clearly opposed to secularism. For instance, Sheikh Mohammed al-Ghazali – an Islamic cleric with close ties to the government of Egypt – when asked whether people advocating secular views should be punished, said that 'they should die'.[3] He was testifying during the trial of certain Islamicists who were accused of assassinating Farag Fodah, one of Egypt's well-known writers.

This essay elaborates on the role of Islam in Middle Eastern politics, and discusses a number of questions in this context. What role is Islam likely to play in the future politics of the countries of this region? Is the notion of Islamic government a feasible one? Is the notion of Islamic government applicable to the polities of Middle Eastern countries in the 1990s and beyond? Finally, is the conflict related to Islam resolvable?

PERSPECTIVES ON ISLAMIC GOVERNMENT

The major political role of Islam in all Middle Eastern countries revolves around the issue of whether a country is being run by an Islamic government. But exactly what constitutes an Islamic government is a question that has defied precise answers. Of course, one can look at the prototype of Islamic government of 623 CE when the Prophet ruled Medina. Even though the 'Constitution of Medina' became the basis for Islamic government among the Islamicist groups today, it should be noted that it remains only a very basic outline.

The Prophet ruled for less than ten years before his death in 632 CE. His constitution distinguishes the Muslims of Medina as a distinct community (*Ummah*), which is significant because Muslims, regardless of their geographic location, universally subscribe to this point. Moreover, the notion of *Ummah* is at the heart of the international aspect of Islam. The Medina Constitution also establishes the general code of behaviour among believers, and a *modus vivendi* between believers and non-believers. The Constitution of Medina appoints the Prophet as the arbiter of conflicts between individuals.[4] It is worth noting, however, that the primacy of the Prophet as the arbiter emerges from the belief that he had 'the best knowledge of what God's decision would be ....'[5]

When one looks for the evolution of an 'administrative state' in the days of the Prophet, one finds quite a few rudiments of it, but not much beyond that. As Rafiq Zakaria writes:

> Despite the strong moral base that the Prophet had given to his state, it could not meet all the requirements of the times. There was no

> organized secretariat, no regular police force, no established courts of justice. Also there was only a volunteer army. He repeatedly impressed upon the people – both the Muslims and the non-Muslims – that they were to maintain law and order by themselves and guard the security of the state. *It was only the commanding presence of the Prophet and the devotion he inspired in his followers which enabled the government of the day to be run smoothly and effectively.*[6]

Another principle of Islamic government that was practised by the Prophet was that of consultation. On matters of government, and even on personal issues, he often consulted those who were either socially prominent or whose advice he valued. But even on this issue, his position as the Messenger of God (*rasul allah*) was a powerful source of his legitimacy.

If one is viewing this tradition for its precedent-setting value, its role is rather limited, however. In fact, during the rule of the second of the Caliphs (i.e., the *Rashidun* or the 'rightly-guided ones') Umar Ibn al-Khattab, the tradition of consultation resurfaced with much vigour. However, given his authoritarian personality, Umar did not invariably abide by the advice that he had received from the Companions on important matters of governance,[7] and he often did not even bother to consult them. One can assume that as the Prophet relied on his authority and insight as the Messenger of God, Umar might have relied on the authority and insight that he had gained as one of the closest confidants of the Prophet. It should be noted, however – as his biographer tells us – that even when Umar did not consult with others, or when he ignored the advice offered him on state matters, his behaviour was guided by a zeal to serve the best interests of Islam and the Islamic state.

Another important aspect of Islamic government stemming from the Constitution of Medina was the guarantee of life and property for non-Muslims. In fact, this document declares the Jews (the Banu Awf and other Jewish tribes) as 'a community (*ummah*) along with the believers'. It goes on to state 'To the Jews their religion (*din*) and to the Muslims their religion. (This applies) both to their clients and to themselves, with the exception of anyone who has done wrong or acted treacherously; he brings evil only on himself and on his household.'[8]

The administrative aspect of Islamic government developed more extensively during the rule of Caliph Umar. Describing the role of this Caliph as the 'architect of the Islamic state', Zakaria notes:

> No aspects of [the Islamic state's] functions escaped his attention. The consultative council, provincial autonomy, military organization, independent judiciary, land reforms, regulation of commerce and trade,

> supply of goods and services to the people, safeguarding of weights and measures, the institution of a fiscal system, or protection of the rights and interests of the non-Muslims – all these came under his care and were fondly nourished by him.[9]

At the end of the Umar Caliphate, Islam faced internal disputes under the rule of his successor, Uthman Ibn Affan. This conflict exploded into the first major crisis of the Islamic state during the rule of Ali Ibn Abu Talib, Uthman's successor and son-in-law and a cousin of the Prophet. In fact, the issue of Ali's succession became a permanent source of conflict among Muslims, dividing them into two groups, the Sunnis and the Shiites.

The intense conflict during the rule of Ali, which resulted in his assassination, eventually culminated in the rule by Musawiya Ibn Abi Sufiyan, the founder of the Umayyad dynasty. The establishment of this dynastic rule created a tradition that the world of Islam has never really shed. Even today, three Arab countries – Saudi Arabia, Jordan and Morocco – are ruled by kings of three dynasties, the Saudi, the Hashemite and the Alawi dynasties, respectively.

The rulers of the Umayyad dynasty remained suspect because the dynasty was founded through the shedding of blood of the Prophet's closest relatives. Moreover, the Umayyad rulers, with the exception of Umar II, were more motivated by their hunger for personal power and glory than by their Islamic zeal.

The succeeding dynasty, the Abbassids, based its claim to the caliphate on descendancy from the Prophet because its founder, Abul Abbas Al-Saffah, was related to the Prophet's uncle al-Abbas. This dynasty was followed by yet another dynasty, that of the Ottomans. Even though they were not even Arabs, the Ottoman rulers called themselves Caliphs by virtue of their role as 'defenders of faith'.

In this dynastic rule, one loses the sense of exactly what constituted an Islamic government. Was it the city-state that prevailed during the days of the Prophet, or its more developed version that emerged during the rule of Caliph Umar? The Islamic order that prevailed during the days of Umar comes close to being labelled as the type of order that would be emulated by contemporary Islamicist groups. Even the governing style of Umar – not his authoritarianism but his predilection for innovation in the art of governance and interpretation of the Quran and Sunnah – might also become a source of emulation. But this observation requires some explanation.

The tradition of innovation by itself remained as one of the chief sources of acute controversy in the world of Islam. How far should a ruler go before his innovation (*Tajdid*) might be labelled as *Bid'a* (heresy)? On this question, the orthodox school has established a powerful tradition that goes back to its founding father, Imam Ahmad Ibn Hanbal. This school was the least tolerant of deviation from Quran and the Sunnah of the Prophet. The Islamic modernists, on the other hand, would be quite receptive to innovation. Thus, it is obvious that the precise nature of Islamic government is an issue on which there is little agreement even among the Sunni groups. We have not even begun to examine the Shiite version of Islamic government – a subject beyond the scope of this study, but whose most recent manifestation is what Ayatollah Ruhollah Khomeini has termed *Vilayat-e-Faqih*, which roughly translated means 'rule of the clergy'.

The history of the Middle East has been bound up with Islam ever since its inception. In this sense, Islam was and continues to be extremely relevant to the future political dynamics of that area. Moreover, when one examines the various historical crises in the Middle East since the advent of Islam, one is struck by the fact that every major crisis resulted in the emergence of one or more Islamicist groups who argued that the reason underlying their plight was the refusal of the ruling elite to remain faithful to Muslim orthodoxy. What is important here is a powerful historical tradition that underscores the relevance of Islam for the believers. In this sense also, Islam has remained extremely relevant to Middle East politics.

There is another variable that has remained largely neglected. The role of Islam as the last of the three monotheistic religions gives it a sense of finality and invincibility among its believers which non-Muslims do not really understand. Social scientists of all ideological persuasions, when examining the contemporary Islamic resurgence in the Middle East, frequently point out that the Islamicists – especially the radical element – are turning toward Islam out of frustration with modernization. Such an explanation was prevalent during the days of the Cold War when it was said that the masses in Third World countries were turning to Communism out of frustration at the failure of the ruling elites to fulfill their expectations (the so-called explanation of 'failure of rising expectations'). Now the same explanation is being casually applied to the escalating violence related to Islam in Algeria or Egypt.

For the believers, the ultimate victory of Islam is promised in the Quran and by the Prophet. After all, Muslims believe that their religion is for all of humanity, is 'eternally true', and is 'to supersede all previous revelations'.[10] For Muslims of all generations:

> With the full articulation of the message of Muhammad in a universal community obedient to divine command, what was significant in history

> came to an end. History could have no more lessons to teach, if there was change it could only be for the worse, and the worse could only be cured, not by creating something new but by *renewing* what had once existed.[11]

So, even if an Islamic government in Iran or elsewhere were to be overthrown, it would not be a defeat for Islam. Rather, it would be interpreted as a temporary setback, only to be overcome at a later date. Alternatively, a defeat of an Islamic government may also be interpreted as the result of a lack of total commitment on the part of the ruling elite to adhere to the true principles of Islam.

Even though the precise nature of Islamic government remains obscure at best, its establishment serves as the chief motivating factor underlying the political activities of all Islamicist groups in the Middle East. Its creation in one country is not likely to stabilize it in the short run, for the problems of Middle Eastern societies are not likely to go away just because such societies have succeeded in creating an Islamic government. In an increasingly uncertain world, in which the abilities of governments to resolve the economic miseries of their masses is diminishing, the creation of an Islamic government emerges as a source of hope and salvation for the believers from both their temporal and spiritual problems.

THE FEASIBILITY OF ISLAMIC GOVERNMENT

Any discussion of the feasibility of an Islamic government in any Muslim country today should begin by asking whether such a government would be composed of elected officials. The Middle East has no tradition of democracy. A long history of dynastic rule has established a powerful tradition of authoritarianism. Consequently, all the governments in the contemporary Middle East practice varying degrees of authoritarianism, in which political dissent is either barely tolerated or ruthlessly suppressed. But these observations beg the question of how compatible Islam and democracy are as political arrangements.

Before entering into this discussion, let me list some very general but significant principles of democracy. As a system of government, democracy aims at promoting representation, which in turn is the relationship between the few leaders and many followers. Democracy is about electoral accountability, which is the ability of voters to oust those elected leaders who do not achieve the policy goals of the majority. Finally, at the heart of democracy is the principle of majority rule and minority rights. In addition, according to

Robert A. Dahl, 'an ideal democratic process would satisfy five criteria'. These are (1) equality in voting; (2) effective participation (i.e. it should be representative of all sectors of the population); (3) enlightened understanding (i.e. 'democracy must be a marketplace of ideas'); (4) final control over the agenda (i.e. 'citizens should have the collective right to control government's agenda'); and (5) inclusion (i.e. 'the government must include and extend rights to all those subject to its laws').[12]

If representation is viewed as an arrangement aimed at promoting the common good or public welfare, Islam as a religion and as a political system is in harmony with this objective. However, representation in democracy means that the leaders are elected by their constituents. From this perspective, the precedents set by the four caliphs who succeeded the Prophet can be labelled as anything but democratic in nature. The First Caliph, Abu Bakr, was chosen by the prominent Companions of the Prophet. Thus, it was an elitist exercise. Accession to power by the second Caliph Umar did not even follow this procedure. He was the personal choice of Abu Bakr. The selection of Uthman, the third Caliph of Islam, was brought about as a result of arbitration, another elitist exercise. The fourth Caliph, Ali, also came to power through a similar, albeit a more contentious, process. Since then, Islam has had an unending series of dynastic rulers. So, precedence for representation in a strict democratic sense was never really established, much less nurtured, in the history of Islamic rule in the Middle East and North Africa.

Moreover, when one examines the evolution of political thinking in various dynasties, Muslim scholars remained more preoccupied with obedience to rulers and with the prevalence of order than with anything else. The process of selection of a ruler itself was not an issue of primary significance. For instance, al-Ghazali emphasized the religious role of a ruler, in which he should be obeyed. 'Who he (the ruler) is, and how he is chosen are important but logically secondary', he noted.[13] Another Islamic thinker, al-Mawardi, stated that the function of a Caliph was 'to maintain [religious] orthodoxy, execute legal decisions, [and] protect frontiers of Islam…'. However, he was quite explicit in stating that people should stop being obedient to a Caliph 'if he is immoral'.[14] One can surmise that the very nature of dynastic rule necessitated the primacy of obedience, which, in turn, led to general order and stability.

But for Rashid Rida, the head of a Muslim state or caliph is the elected leader of all Muslims. Rida does not share the inordinate preoccupation of al-Mawardi and al-Ghazali for obedience to a ruler. His position is that the Caliph 'should be obeyed only to the extent that his decisions conform to the principles of Islam, and have a bearing on public interest'. He goes on to add that 'the community, through its representatives, has the right to challenge his decisions whenever these are seen to contravene those principles'.[15]

Nor should one ignore the tradition of *shura* (consultation), the practice of which dates back to the days of the Prophet. This tradition comes close to representation, though not strictly in terms of what it means from the perspective of democratic theory. However, as previously noted, even though the Prophet practised it frequently, *Shura* was not adhered to with any regularity by his successors. In fact, Rashid Rida takes the position that democracy is ensured for Muslims 'once the government implements the principle of *Shura*, or consultations between the ruler and the ruled, and the provisions laid down by the jurisconsults on the right to resist injustice … .'[16]

The second characteristic of democracy, electoral accountability, has to be examined by taking apart these phrases. Obviously, leaders in the Islamic Middle East were not (and still are not) elected. However, just because they are not elected does not necessarily mean that, somehow, they are not accountable. The tradition of accountability was very much present during the rule of the four successors to the Prophet. But the establishment of dynastic rule served as a death-knell to this tradition. Nevertheless, from the perspective of Islamic orthodoxy, a just ruler is, or ought to be, accountable to the ruled. It should be noted at the same time that the Islamic Ulama (clerics) have played an important role in diluting the significance of accountability.

The third sub-principle of democracy – majority rule – receives mixed treatment in Islam. There is a famous *hadith* in which the Prophet says that his people would never agree in an error. This may be regarded as an ultimate compliment to the wisdom of the majority. However, at the same time, laws contrary to Islam may not be (or ought not to be) passed just because that is the will of the majority at any time.

Democratic theory mentions the notion of the 'tyranny of the majority' in a different context. It underscores the principle of protection of minority rights, without which the rule of the majority becomes tyranny. The tyranny of majority in Islam would be the passage by a majority of laws that are contrary to Islamic precepts. That is not acceptable. As long as it is understood that such actions will not be tolerated in a Muslim state, Islam would have no objection to majority rule. Similarly, Islam has no quarrel with the subprinciple of minority rights. In fact, the protection of religious minorities, as previously noted, was guaranteed in the Constitution of Medina. Moreover, Islamic rulers have maintained a powerful tradition of protecting religious minorities throughout the course of history.

Even in the five criteria for democracy alluded to by Robert Dahl, one would find ample room for agreement between Islam and democracy. From the perspective of Islamic theology, there is nothing against the principle of one person, one vote. On this issue one might put forward the fact that women are denied the right to vote in Saudi Arabia or Kuwait. The denial of this right to women has no basis in Islam. It merely stems from the anachronistic perspective of conservative monarchies for political reasons. By the same token, the notion of effective participation will find little argument from Islam.

The third criterion of democracy, enlightened understanding – despite the fact that it is so imprecise – deserves some scrutiny. This phrase underscores the availability of a variety of sources of information in a society – including information about all religions or even against religions – and the freedom of an individual to read and use it for the development of his/her understanding of the world at large. Western democracies emphasize and cherish this freedom. Islam has a rather restricted view of enlightenment. An individual is free to read all sorts of information, but not information that is contrary to Islam. In fact, there is little room for any criticism of Islam. In this regard, it is interesting to note that the use of *kalam* (i.e., the use of rational discourse to study Islam), which is an integral aspect of enlightened understanding, caused considerable controversy in Sunni Islam. The Hanbali and some of the Shafiis were opposed to it. Al-Ghazali, who was a master of *ashari kalam*, opposed its use by persons of ordinary intellect. His position was that 'It should not ... be practised by those whose faith might be troubled by it.... It was a matter only for specialists, working independently outside the schools.'[17] The fourth and fifth criteria of ideal democracy – final control over the agenda and inclusion – do not come into conflict with Islam.

There is a powerful cultural and political opposition to unorthodox views and to what Majid Khadduri labels as 'free thinking' in the Middle East. Undoubtedly, freedom to hold and propagate such views is indeed an essential aspect of enlightened understanding. Khadduri notes:

> Today, the fate of free thinkers in the Arab world is not much better than in the past; most of those who hold unorthodox views have been reluctant to speak openly because of state censorship and traditional intolerance towards innovations. Association with Western free thought brought them under attack by orthodox thinkers first for their views and then as denounced traitors to their culture, which made their position even more difficult. State censorship, often invoked under popular pressures, does not always result in imprisonment or execution, though popular commotion may reach a high pitch reminiscent of past centuries. Nonetheless, the impact of free thought on current religious and political thought has proved to be far-reaching.[18]

One other important aspect of any discussion of Islam and democracy should also be mentioned. It has been often stated that while democracy promotes popular sovereignty, Islam underscores the sovereignty of God. Abul Ala Maududi, one of the foremost thinkers of Islamic thought, rejected democracy because it promotes sovereignty of the people. He regarded this principle as contrary to the principle of sovereignty of God that is promoted by Islam. In fact, Maududi went to the extent of equating democracy with *shirk* (polytheism or blasphemy). Elaborating on the issue of freedom to legislate any laws, which is an important aspect of democracy, Maududi argued that this freedom is restricted by God in Islam.[19] Fazlur-Rahman, another noted Muslim scholar, rejects Maududi's argument. He writes that sovereign 'as a political term ... denotes that definite and defined factor (or factors) in a society to which rightfully belongs coercive force in order to obtain obedience to its will'. In this sense, writes Rahman, 'it is absolutely obvious that God is not sovereign ... that only people can be and are sovereign, since only to them belongs ultimate coercive force...'. Rahman points out that even though the Quran describes God as the most Supreme Judge, it is 'making no reference to political sovereignty whatever. It does not even refer to legal sovereignty.' What the Quran asks Muslims, as Rahman quite correctly points out, is to decide matters in accordance with the holy book, and at other times they 'should decide matters in accordance with justice and equity'.[20]

Despite a number of points of incompatibility, ample agreement is found between Islam and democracy. Both emphasize participation, accountability of rulers to the ruled, the rule of the majority (with certain caveats by Islam), and minority rights. The issue of representation is, by and large, in harmony with Islam, despite the fact that there is no tradition of elected rulers in Islamic history. However, the absence of such a tradition does not mean that present or future rulers cannot or should not be elected. There is no theological disagreement on this point. The major problem between Islam and democracy stems from the principle of secularism, which is at the heart of the liberal democracies that prevail in many Western countries.

ISLAM vs. SECULARISM: A PERMANENT CHASM?

Western insistence on separation of church and state as a precondition for democracy leads one to reiterate the question about secularism that was raised earlier in this study: is the conflict between Islam and secularism resolvable?

Since secularization was brought about in Europe after a long conflict between church and state, it has been frequently and ardently argued that if Middle Eastern countries were to incorporate secularism, somehow, they would become democratic and stable. Little attention is paid to the fact that since Islam has been very much part and parcel of politics throughout the course of the history of that region, it is well nigh impossible to create such a reality now. More important, since such a separation was not made in the days of the Prophet, it is hard to imagine that it could be brought about in any Middle Eastern country without causing a great upheaval. One has only to be reminded of the significance of the Prophet's tradition and his own behaviour as they are seen by Muslims all over the world, and have been seen through the ages. By the same token, the types of pressure the government of President Hosni Mubarak is under should be examined. Of course, the inept performance of his government in reducing the acute economic disparities in Egypt is largely responsible for that country's internal troubles. But an additional factor is the wrath of Islamicist forces who consider the secular character of the Egyptian government as anti-Islamic.

The most serious problem which the issue of secularism faces in the Middle East today is definitional. What exactly does one mean by a secular state? Donald Smith offers a very useful definition, namely a state 'which guarantees individual and corporate freedom of religion, deals with the individual as a citizen, irrespective of his religion, is not constitutionally connected to a particular religion nor does it seem either to promote or interfere with religion'.[21] *The Oxford English Dictionary's* description of secularism should also be considered, since it offers a good basis for discussion. According to this source, secularism 'represents the doctrine that morality should be based solely in regard to the well-being of mankind in the present life, to the exclusion of all considerations drawn from belief in God or in the future state'.[22]

Majid Khadduri goes to the roots of this controversy when he writes:

> Ever since the Kemalist regime took action to separate the state from religion – an action often referred to as 'secularization of Islam' – (which indeed was inspired by a Western movement for a separation of church from state) – the term 'secularization' has acquired in the Arab world a connotation of undermining religion. Thus any secular proposal intended to reform an Islamic institution has been rejected on the ground that it aimed at the 'secularization of Islam.'[23]

Muslims have not forgotten that the Kemalist move to abolish the caliphate in 1924 was intended to secularize Turkey, an action that caused considerable consternation and violence.

Even though the notion of secularism has found some support among Muslim scholars, by and large it has remained a repugnant ideology. In fact, one of the Arabic words for secularism is *la diniyya*, which literally means 'without religion'. One major source of support for secularism comes from Abid Al Raziq, an Egyptian.[24] Raziq put forward two major arguments. Firstly, he claimed that the caliphate is not inherent in Islam and is therefore not necessary. Secondly, he argued for the separation of church and state, which is the essence of secularism. Raziq's argument regarding the caliphate was that the Prophet exercised it out of necessity, 'but his action should not be taken to imply that he attempted to found a state or that it was part of his religious mission, a mission which was "prophetic" not "temporal"'.[25]

Concerning the issue of separation of church and state, Raziq's view was that 'Quranic legislation relating to civil matters did not call for the association of religious with civil authorities.'[26] Raziq further noted that the Prophet explicitly told his Companions that on temporal matters he was not immune from error, and that while rules relating to spiritual life were unchangeable, those regarding temporal affairs 'should be regarded as secular and subject to change by the state and in accordance with society's needs'.[27]

Another noteworthy case for secularism is Rafiq Zakaria's book *Struggle within Islam*. Zakaria is an accomplished Muslim politician in India. One can fairly argue that a substantial aspect of his political accomplishment stems from the fact that he became a public practitioner of secularism in India during that country's struggle for freedom. As he is a lifelong secularist, his book is as much an argument for secularism as it is a historical record of struggle within Islam. Zakaria's plea for secularism takes the route of the narration of Islam's tolerant attitude toward non-Muslims. He writes:

> The general attitude towards non-Muslims is contained in [Quranic] verses which are unencumbered by any such context. There is, for instance, the oft-repeated dictum: There is no compulsion in religion (2:256), which has been elaborated in many other verses in the Quran and forms the basis of secularism in Islam.[28]

While Raziq's claim – that 'Quranic legislation relating to civil matters did not call for the association of religious with civil authorities' – may be considered valid, he certainly ignores the relevance of the Prophet's practices and tradition, and, equally important, the governmental practices that were implemented during the rule of the Caliph Umar. These traditions clearly established a stable link between religion and politics. But Zakaria's argument in using the above-mentioned Quranic verse as justification for secularism remains at best highly tenuous and questionable.

When one contrasts the Arabic phrase *la diniyya* with Smith's above-mentioned definition of a secular state, one gets the distinct impression that these two descriptions could not pertain to the same phrase – secularism. But, more often than not, reality is what we perceive it to be, and the Muslim perception of secularism is that, somehow, the phrase is anti-Islamic in nature. Abul Ala Maududi condemned it in the strongest possible terms. Dr Mohammad Iqbal, an Islamic poet and philosopher who is regarded as the father of the concept of Pakistan as a Muslim state, described a government that is devoid of religion as 'tyranny' and 'heresy'. The reader has only to recall the response of Sheikh al-Ghazali mentioned in the beginning of this essay – that the people advocating secular views should die.

The common perception in Muslim countries as a whole is that secularism regards religion as contentious – less than pure – and that it should not even be part of any public discourse. Another aspect of the Muslim perception of secularism is reflected in the *Oxford Dictionary* definition. While the secular criterion of morality in any country underscores the well-being of mankind in the present life, the Islamic criterion of morality is focused on the hereafter. Everything a Muslim does in this life is to ensure that God is pleased with him/her in the eternal life that follows death. Even though such an emphasis does not negate the well-being of mankind in this life, Islam forbids a Muslim from becoming obsessed with it. The Islamic perspective in this regard is that excessive emphasis on well-being in the present life leads to an obsession with materialism and material well-being. The danger is that this will become an end in itself. Secularism de-emphasizes, indeed discourages, any judgement drawn from belief in God. On the contrary, the entire frame of reference of Islam revolves around not only believing in one God, but also incorporating the lifestyle of the Prophet into the lives of individuals as much as possible. In Islam, a legitimate and good government is judged by its commitment to *Sharia* (Islamic law), whereas secularism not only attempts to exclude religion from political life, but also uses an entirely different set of criteria for judging the legitimacy of a government.

For these reasons, secularism in its totality may never be acceptable to most Muslim countries. European colonialism and the post-colonial emergence of nation-states in the Middle East initiated the tradition of the secular state in that region. The secular governments of Turkey and Iran under the Pahlavis did not create desirable examples for others to emulate. The emergence of Turkey also coincided with the abolition of the

Caliphate, a development that caused a considerable shock to the Muslim psyche. The secular Turkish state has not played a major role in the political history of the Middle East since World War II, except in the Gulf War of 1991. It seems that Turkey has spent much of its time seeking acceptance and recognition as a Western state from the recalcitrant Europeans, who still perceive it to be a Middle Eastern nation. When the Muslim republics of Central Asia became independent as a result of the breakup of the Soviet Union, Washington hoped that Turkey would lure those countries into refraining from adopting an Islamic model of government by offering its own secular model as an alternative. The jury is still out on how successful Turkey is likely to be in this regard.

Iran, the other state that adopted a secular type of government, returned to the Islamic fold as a result of a bloody revolution. The rest of the Muslim states in the Middle East – monarchies as well as republics – are experiencing a growing challenge as they try to define the role of government that is acceptable from the perspective of Islam. Islam, on the other hand, remains the ultimate source of legitimacy in that region and it has been so for the past 1400 years. Even Nasser's pan-Arabism, which emerged as a powerful emotive and secular concept of unity among Arabs after the 1950s, could not replace Islam. Nasser was also forced to seek an arguable justification for his Arab socialism by describing it as an integral aspect of Islam. Most recently, Saddam Hussein, a life-long adherent of secular Ba'thist nationalism, adopted Islamic symbols, even if only for purely pragmatic reasons, in the wake of Operation Desert Storm. It is either through their genuine commitment to Islam, or by practising its outward manifestations and applying its major symbols that governments throughout the entire history of Islam have stabilized themselves in the Middle East.

So, the chasm between Islam and secularism appears not only to be a permanent one, but also seems to be widening. In the post-World War II era, a number of the newly independent states in the Middle East adopted secularism to acquire credentials of modernity and its attendant promise. By doing so, they unwittingly (or even perhaps wittingly) attempted to distance themselves from Islam, thereby accepting the European argument that only by giving up the 'archaic' worldview and lifestyle of Islam could they enjoy the technological and cultural advances of the twentieth century world. In the 1990s, with a largely miserable record of economic progress, a number of them are under growing pressure to seek 'Islam as a solution'. This slogan may or may not be transformed in the near future into concrete solutions to the socio-economic problems faced by a great many of them. However, many of these governments will continue to face increasing challenges from within to abandon secularism.

THE NATURE OF CONFLICT IN THE MIDDLE EAST

The essence of conflict within the nation-states of the Middle East revolves around the ability of the governments to remain in power by allowing little popular participation, and their resistance to the introduction of change in the style of governance. From the perspective of the population – or at least those groups which are intent on bringing about political change – these governments are elitist, distant from the people, corrupt, un-Islamic in some instances, unwilling to change, and determined to sustain the questionable (and in some cases outright illegitimate) status quo.

Viewing the same situation from the perspective of Middle Eastern governments, political order is of the utmost significance. Countries like Egypt, Algeria, Syria and Tunisia – even though regarded as secular by the West – do not consider themselves any less committed to Islam than do the other Middle Eastern countries. What they object to is yielding to the demands of religious extremists or radical Islamicists.

In a country like Saudi Arabia, there is no question about the commitment of the government to Islam. The brunt of the argument of the critics of the Saudi dynasty is that it is presiding over a very closed system, where there is no room for political dissent, no matter how constructive. By the same token, the Saudi government steadfastly refuses to make itself receptive to any suggestions of changing the political status quo. Even the practice of *shura* is a sham, since members of the consultative council rubber stamp all political decisions of the regime. Similar arguments are equally applicable to other peninsular sheikhdoms.

Thus, the most intractable conflict within Middle Eastern countries boils down to the questionable-to-shaky legitimacy of the political regimes, or to a chronic shortage of legitimacy. The implanting of a sense of legitimacy, according to David Easton, 'is probably the single most effective device for regulating the flow of diffuse support in favour of both authorities and of the regime'. He goes on to note that:

> the most stable support will derive from the conviction on the part of the member that it is right and proper for him to accept and obey the authorities and to abide by the requirements of the regime. It reflects the fact that in some vague or explicit way he sees these objects as conforming to his own moral principles, his own sense of what is right and proper in the political sphere. The strength of support implicit in this attitude derives from the fact that it is not contingent on specific inducements or rewards of any kind, except in the very long run.[29]

Ted Gurr is more precise when he writes that regimes are legitimate 'to the extent that their citizens regard them as proper and deserving of support'.[30]

In a democracy, governmental legitimacy is established through a process of 'constitutionalism', which is a principle of limited government on the basis of a written or unwritten constitution.[31] Constitutionalism also provides for an institutional framework of government and establishes the scope of power, responsibility, and the process of election of government officials, etc. In the final analysis, the legitimacy of a government stems from the fact that its very existence revolves around a constitution.

In Arab politics, the most important aspect of what Easton refers to as 'right and proper' stems from the citizens' perception of how Islamic a government really is. This variable becomes especially significant when a government is also perceived as un-Islamic, inept at resolving economic problems and politically corrupt. The last two charges apply to almost all Middle Eastern countries, excluding only the rich oil sheikhdoms. Even there, it is the availability of oil revenues – not the effective governance of the ruling groups – that is postponing the emergence of serious challenges to their rule.

In Arab politics, Islam has also remained the chief source of constitutionalism, the details of which are the least precise and most controversial in the sense that no two groups are likely to agree on all its essentials. A government can become legitimate when it is committed to *Sharia*. But how are the leaders to be selected? As we have seen, on this issue there is no clear-cut precedent. That question is yet another aspect of conflict over the selection of rulers. Under dynastic rule, leadership selection was based on the bloodline. Consequently, since there never emerged a tradition of democratically elected leaders, the process of leadership selection in the contemporary era has also remained undemocratic.

Islamic tradition points to the creation of a strong executive. Early in its history, Islam produced a series of strong leaders – the Prophet himself, his four successors, kings of various dynasties – and in the contemporary era, dictators and kings. There has been an overwhelming tradition of powerful executives whose effectiveness is measured by their ability to impose a personal style of rule.

As Adeed Dawisha points out, in a democracy political leaders obtain their legitimacy from the overall legitimacy of the political system of which they are an integral part. In Arab politics, on the other hand, legitimacy of the political system stems from the personal legitimacy of a ruler.[32] This personal legitimacy, in turn, emanates from one or more major accomplishments of that ruler. Examples include Nasser's stand during the Suez crisis of 1956, Sadat's decision to go to war with Israel in 1973, Hafez Assad's decision to reject the compromise reached between Lebanon and Israel in 1982, Saddam's 'victory' in the Iran–Iraq war, etc. The tribal nature of Arab societies has also necessitated this reliance on strong leadership.

As one probes further to identify the specifics of Islamic constitutionalism, one quickly runs out of characteristics beyond adherence to *shariyah* and reliance on a strong executive. Even though there has been a tradition of an independent judiciary in Islam, the presence of a strong executive – especially in the contemporary context – has made it virtually impossible for a strong and independent judiciary to emerge. Similarly, a strong legislature cannot emerge in the presence of a strong executive, especially when there are no constitutional constraints on the power and responsibilities of such an executive in the Middle East.

Even though there is no Islamic basis for the denial of political dissent or for the absence of avenues of participation, the prevalence of authoritarian rule in the Arab world has deprived the masses of participation in the political system. They do not have any right to criticize or express political grievances, except through clandestine political organizations. Almost all of them are living in political systems in which the coercive apparatus of the government, known as the security apparatus, is highly developed, and in some instances, brutally effective in suppressing political dissent.

An unfortunate aspect of Middle Eastern history is that Islam has been used, both by rulers and religious scholars, to justify absolute rule. It has been a long-standing tradition to equate subservience and loyalty (if not acquiescence) to a ruler with subservience to God and the Prophet. It is prudent to state that this sort of justification is also responsible for the prevailing authoritarianism in the twentieth century.[33] But this role of Islam works as a two-edged sword in that Islam has also become an avenue through which clandestine political protests against the contemporary governments are expressed. However, the most ironic part of the rhetoric of the Islamicist organizations is that they promise to follow the same path of authoritarianism that they are currently trying to bring to an end, if or when they gain political power in a country. Iran's example is not a happy one, since its record of suppression of political dissent and human rights is well documented and deservedly condemned.

What we are witnessing in the Middle East is the unhappiness of political dissenters or Islamic reform groups with the present style and nature of government in different countries. These groups are using Islam to measure the performance of these governments and labelling them un-Islamic, partly because they are accused of economic incompetence, rampant corruption and, more importantly, because they are not adhering to the *Sharia*. An equally important aspect of these protests stems from the fact that these governments are highly authoritarian; and this trait, along with their purported violation of *Sharia*, make them illegitimate in the eyes of the Islamicist groups. However, the very style of violent protest adopted by these groups and, more importantly, their failure to put forth an alternative blueprint for government, make them least acceptable to the population at large. The Algerian Islamicists – FIS – might have been an exception to this charge, since at one time they promised to remain faithful to democracy. However, since they have not even been given a chance to come to power, no one can state with certainty whether they would have kept their promise. The violent nature of continuing political clashes between the FIS and the Algerian military junta is edging that country closer to a major disaster. The performance of Islamicist radicals in Egypt is no better. There is that same absence of a blueprint for an Islamic government, in conjunction with increasing terrorism against the politically corrupt and economically inept government of President Hosni Mubarak.

QUO HINC RUIMUS?

A number of major points emerge from the preceding discussion. First, the centrality of Islam for Middle Eastern politics has remained unchanged for the past 1400 years, and it is not likely to change in the distant future. Secondly, there is no general agreement among Islamicist groups as to the exact nature of Islamic government, nor does it seem that such an agreement is warranted. Each country can determine its own model, as long as the centrality of Islam is the basis of such an agreement. Saudi Arabia, Pakistan and Iran have determined their own models of Islamic government. Of these, the Saudi model may be most problematic, for monarchy is quite antithetical to all the notions of egalitarianism that have been so consistently emphasized by Islam. Even the puritanical Wahabi tradition of Saudi Arabia serves a very limited purpose, because ample interpretation of the Quran and *Sharia* is warranted for running a complex state in an equally complex world politics. The innovations introduced during the rule of Caliph Umar serve as an excellent precedent for the consideration of Islamicist groups throughout the Middle East.

Thirdly, the doctrines of separation of church and state and secularism are most likely to be discarded by Muslims all over the world since they are generally perceived as un-Islamic, if not anti-Islamic. What worked in the West – i.e., separation of church and state and the attendant secularism – is not likely to work in the Middle East. Middle Eastern countries are an integral part of the Islamic world, and they ought to develop in harmony with Islam if that region is to remain stable.

Given the fact that Islam has remained at the heart of Middle Eastern politics, all the countries of that region will be forced to face the issue of how Islamic they really are. For the West, this question may be archaic or even anachronistic. But such phrases are only applicable when one applies Western values to the politics of Middle East. For a great number of Muslims, it is vital that their respective governments remain loyal to Islam. However, a majority of these people also do not necessarily want to go back to the days of the Prophet on matters of contemporary political and economic concerns.

The greatest problem faced by all Middle Eastern countries is the prevalence of authoritarianism as practised by the monarchies as well as the republican states. Ibn Khaldun correctly notes that the caliphate declined into kingship, thereby assigning an excessive primacy to the political role of rulers. This outcome was never intended by the Prophet or his successors. This tradition, when it remained unchallenged through the course of centuries, resulted in a diffusion of the political and religious roles of a ruler, thereby demanding acquiescence from the ruled on issues of religion as well as politics. This tradition is at the root of the emergence of authoritarianism in the post-World War II politics of the region. It is difficult for me to envision Islam and political authoritarianism co-existing in the Middle East in the coming years. Authoritarian governments since World War II have remained in power by establishing a powerful security apparatus, whose sole purpose has been to stifle dissent. Such a governmental ploy has only postponed their demise. When the end came, it was always a bloody one. The Iraqi Revolution of 1958 and the Iranian Revolution of 1978–79 are two such examples. One cannot rule out similar cataclysmic and violent changes in Iraq, Syria and Libya in coming years.

What Middle Eastern countries need is a system of government that blends democracy with Islam. An Islamic democracy would be an arrangement in which there was ample scope for a strong executive, but where the legislature must also be assertive. No one can state with certainty that conflict related to Islam in the Middle East will be resolved in the foreseeable future. Governmental legitimacy in that region appears to face three types of challenge: religious, political and economic. Of these, the religious aspect may be resolved if a regime adopts some sort of Islamic government. The next two challenges are typical of those faced by all Third World countries. By resolving the religious aspect of their legitimacy, governments in the Middle East may be able to focus on resolving the equally obdurate political and economic problems without getting distracted by the religious groups.

NOTES

1. I recognize the fact that the Turkish constitution labels Turkey as a secular state. My position is that the mere fact that Turkey's government is secular does not make that country a secular state. After all, it is a state in which Muslims are in a majority. It is possible, though not probable, that the majority may change its mind about the constitution of the country.
2. Even in the case of Turkey, it is highly questionable whether secularism has really permeated the whole society. There is no doubt, however, that it is a well-entrenched notion among the ruling groups, especially the armed forces.
3. Youssef M. Ibrahim, 'Egypt Fights Militant Islam With More of the Same', *The New York Times*, 18 August 1993.
4. On this point Montgomery Watt writes, 'The referring of disputes to Muhammad is closely connected with the recognition of him as prophet. The wording of the Constitution is that disputes are to be referred to *God and to Muhammad*'. Watt, *Muhammad at Medina* (Oxford: Clarendon Press, 1956), p. 229.
5. Watt, op. cit., p. 230.
6. Rafiq Zakaria, *The Struggle within Islam: The Conflict between Religion and Politics* (London: Penguin Books, 1989), p. 31. Emphasis added.
7. These were individuals who had known the Prophet, and, through their acquaintance with him, were considered as persons of great religious insight and devotion. There were about 10 000 of them at the time of the death of the Prophet of Islam.
8. Watt, op. cit., p. 223.
9. Zakaria, op. cit., p. 59.
10. One *hadith* (saying of the Prophet) goes, 'Other prophets before me were sent only to their peoples, I have been sent to all humanity.' This and previous quotes in the paragraph are from Albert Hourani, 'The Islamic State', in Hourani, *Arabic Thought in the Liberal Age* (London: Oxford University Press, 1962), pp. 1–24.
11. Ibid., p. 8, emphasis added.
12. This discussion is extracted from Robert L. Lineberry, *Government in America* (Fourth edn) (Glenview, IL: Scott, Foresman/Little, Brown series on political science, 1989), pp. 40–1.
13. Hourani, *Arabic Thought in the Liberal Age*, op. cit., p. 13.
14. Ibid., p. 10.
15. Hamid Enayat, *Modern Islamic Political Thought* (Austin, TX: University of Texas Press, 1982), p. 81.

16. Ibid., p. 77.
17. Albert Hourani, *A History of the Arab Peoples* (Cambridge, MA: Harvard University Press, 1991), pp. 167–8.
18. Majid Khadduri, 'Free Thought and Secularism' in Khadduri, *Political Trends in the Arab World* (Baltimore, MD: Johns Hopkins Press, 1970), pp. 212–52.
19. S. Abul Ala Maududi, *The Political Theory of Islam* (Lahore, India: n.d.), pp. 29–30.
20. Fazlur-Rahman, 'The Islamic Concept of State', in John J. Donohue and John L. Esposito, *Islam in Transition* (New York: Oxford University Press), pp. 261–71.
21. As cited in Zakaria, op. cit., p. 20.
22. Ibid.
23. Khadduri, op. cit., p. 213.
24. The word which is commonly used to describe secularism, however, is *ilmaniyya-duniyawiyya*. In this phrase, one has to keep in mind the pejorative aspect of the *duniyawiyya*, which can be taken as an obsession with materialism. Another phrase to describe secularism is *addahriyya*, which also denotes an absence of belief in God.
25. Khadduri, op. cit., p. 217.
26. Ibid.
27. Ibid., Also Leonard Binder, *Islamic Liberalism: A Critique of Development Ideologies* (Chicago, IL: The University of Chicago Press, 1988), pp. 128–69.
28. Zakaria, op. cit., p. 35.
29. David Easton, *A System Analysis of Political Life* (New York: Wiley, 1965), p. 278.
30. Ted R. Gurr, *Why Men Rebel* (Princeton, NJ: Princeton University Press, 1970), pp. 183–5.
31. Jack C. Plano and Milton Greenberg, *The American Political Dictionary* (Sixth edn) (NY: Holt, Rinehart & Winston, 1982), p. 6.
32. Adeed Dawisha, 'Power, Participation, and the Dilemma of Legitimacy in the Arab World' (Washington, DC: Smithsonian Institution, 1986).
33. Also see Michael Hudson's observation that 'In terms of doctrine, it [Islam] has been interpreted to justify virtually absolute rule....' *Arab Politics: The Search for Legitimacy* (New Haven, CT: Yale University Press, 1977), p. 91.

5 Assessing Prospects for Democracy in the Middle East

James H. Noyes

Despite the great differences in development among the states of the Middle East region, there is a common note of heightened political expectation running through it. The Cold War's passing coupled with the dwindling credibility of Arab military options against Israel has shifted attention more to failures of governance, to corrupt bureaucracies, and to endlessly unfulfilled promises by the old ruling groups for better living standards and more political expression. The primary question is whether this ferment suggests real and positive change in the offing or whether it means turbulence merely within authoritarian continuity. Old issues are resurfacing. After World War II, how could progress towards democracy accommodate communist, Ba'thist and other power monopolists; yet if these represented significant popular political expression, how could they be excluded by democracy's advocates? Today, similar questions are presented in a different form by radical Islamists who have forced greater authoritarianism on governments professing democratic aspiration. If Islamicists alone appear capable of rallying a long inert populace into a viable political opposition, can one democratize without them?

Furthermore, the basic concept of the nation-state is once again being subjected to serious challenge. Earlier Pan-Arabism, expressed in Nasserism and Ba'thism, insisted on sweeping away the old Europe-designed states in favour of one great Arab nation. In part, this emphasis was utopian, but it was also a realistic defence against the dangers of division among Arab leaders and of that process igniting the powerful forces of separatism present within each state. Ultimately, of course, the utopianism was revealed not only as impractical, but as a tool of statecraft cynically employed by leaders, from Nasser down to Saddam Hussein and Iran's mullahs. Today, the radical Islamists create a challenge to the state as a secular concept subject to man-made laws. Impetus to this is given by the leaders of Iran's Revolution who employ Pan-Islamism as a nationalist tool with which to weaken ties among Arab states as well as their Western links.

The dangers of separatism that so preoccupied the leaders of the post-colonial era have erupted again. Lebanon's unity still hangs by a thread. Post-'Desert Storm' Iraq amply displays the potential for state disintegration that menaces the region and invites Western analysts to confuse the impetus for political pluralism in a democratic format with simple communal separatism. Despite the Iranian Revolution's pretensions to universality, the ugly communal repressions integral to the movement emphasize that country's potential for disintegration.

This study surveys a necessarily limited sample of states in an effort to identify a few common elements in political evolution and their inhibitors. The first essential is the recognition that the most powerful movements at work, while often drawing upon ancient origins, were actually formed in the colonial period and retain a xenophobic and embittered core from that experience and from earlier foreign intrusions. Because this poses particular problems for Western policy and for democratic prospects in the region history demands first attention.

The historian Amin Maalouf notes, 'The people of the Prophet lost control of their own destiny as early as the ninth century. Their leaders were practically all foreigners.'[1] He observes that the Crusades revealed this weakness. The leaders of the struggle against the crusaders were Turks like Zangi, Nur al-din, Qutuz, Baybars and Qalawun, Armenians like al-Afdal or Kurds like Shirkuh, Saladin and al-Kamil; many warriors from the steppes frequently joined the ranks of the military rulers despite their lack of ties to Arab or Mediterranean culture. Thus, despite the contemporary Arab glorification of these rulers, Maalouf sees the reality of an Arab world, 'Dominated, oppressed and derided, aliens in their own land ... unable to continue to cultivate the cultural blossoms that had begun to flower in the seventh century'.[2]

Although Arab civilization was in many ways more advanced than the West at the time, it lacked the crucial ability to build stable institutions. Muslim princes ruled arbitrarily and at a prince's death his state frequently lapsed into civil war. In contrast, Maalouf cites well-known observers of the period like Usamah and Ibn Jubayr who, while noting the barbaric aspects of the crusader's regimes, saw that their subjects had recognized rights and that a king's power had specific limitations. On travelling through Syria, Ibn Jubayr lamented that in Muslim-controlled areas '[Muslims] ... suffer from the injustice of their co-religionists, whereas the *Franj* [foreigners] act with equity'.[3]

This should not obscure the powerful survival of the Crusades in the region as an epic humiliation. Maalouf notes that Mehmet Ali Agca, the Turk who attempted to assassinate the Pope on 13 May 1981, wrote, 'I have decided to kill John Paul II, Supreme Commander of the Crusades.'[4] Despite the bizarre and apparently demented quality of this act, Maalouf concludes that the Muslim East has continued to view the West as an enemy since the Crusades. The temptation to dismiss Maalouf's opinion as raw, simplistic generalization is itself simplistic in the light of frequent confirmation in radical Islamist cant. During Jordan's late-1993 election campaign, for instance, the Islamic Action Front likened 'the new world order' to the crusaders' onslaught.[5] The charter of Hamas, the radical offshoot of the Muslim Brotherhood in the West Bank and Gaza, as discussed further below, repeatedly refers to the Crusades.

The combination of admiration and resentment of the West's impact recorded by Ibn Jubayr persists today. Many aspects of democracy and its accompanying modernization are admired. At the same time, the actions of the Western democracies in the region have blurred and, in some cases, debased democracy as a form of government to be emulated. The post-World War II Western interventions for Israel as well as the entire Cold War epoch saw inherent regional aspirations, however confused and conflicting in the popular mind, subordinated to the strategic requirements of the West. Much current analysis of democratic prospects in the region uses a kind of *tabula rasa* approach in which the impediments to democratic development reside solely in the strictures of Islam on the one hand and the hard grasp of military rule on the other. But the continuity of a deep ambivalence about foreign influences is striking. With the gradual decline and disintegration of the Ottoman Empire after World War I, Albert Hourani notes that the ideological development during the period up to World War II was marked on the one hand by tremendous xenophobia among the masses and, on the other, by enthusiasm among the elites for Western political forms of parliamentary democracy supported by secular-based education.[6] But little had changed substantively. The traditional local family and religious rulers retained the reins of government while ultimate control lay with the European Mandatory powers who had merely replaced the Ottomans. From the popular standpoint, therefore, the connotation of democracy was with continued foreign control over a system whose parliamentary forms became merely a façade over the old unrepresentative way of rule.

In the post-World War II period, Hourani notes, as the old elites began to crack and as socialist philosophy spread, the appeal of parliamentary democracy faded, even among the elites.[7] The very word 'democracy' became associated with European oppression, except in a perverted Marxist sense where the communal divisions, vast inequalities, and military weaknesses of the Middle East states could only be overcome through a single unopposed 'progressive' party. To catch up with the West and defend against its machinations required the adoption of systems employed by totalitarian enemies of the West. Emulation of the West's political system appeared neither desirable nor feasible.

Ultimately, of course, this line of reasoning led to the utopianism and militarism which still dominate the intellectual and governmental life of some of the Middle East states. To this, Marxism made its powerful contribution. From the West, unfortunately, it was not the liberal democratic tradition but the authoritarian, military and fascist strain that was influential after World War II. If the West was to blame for most problems, then surely the models of government based on anti-Westernism offered the greatest appeal. Even through the 1980s, one had to search long and hard among the university and newspaper corridors of Cairo, Algiers, Baghdad, Damascus or even Beirut to find proponents of a democratic multi-party system dependent on a vigorously mixed economy. The Gulf states went their own ways to an extent, with many in pre-revolutionary Iran glued to the mythology that Western intervention had derailed democratic prospects as evolved by Mossadeq. In reality, of course, Mossadeq had led Iran rapidly towards Communist or millitary rule.

The emerging negativism emphasized escape from the foreign influences long seen as the humiliating cause of economic and military backwardness. Yet much of the new model for government was adapted from the military rule of these former 'oppressors' coated with Marxist-Leninist jargon. The rush towards independence from foreign control paradoxically also became involved with rejection of some aspects of indigenous culture. Secular as well as Islamic radicals viewed modernization and change from the West as the enemy, an enemy to be fought with strength achieved through militarism. Instead of co-opting liberal Islamic thinkers in the effort to reorganize polity, the trend (most notably in Iran and Egypt) became repression of the activist clerical elements in favour of tamed and state-controlled religion. Nasser's outlawing of the Moslem Brotherhood and the Shah's draconian measures against the financial and political power structure of the mullahs are exemplars. This issue has returned virtually to dominate current politics today.

THE IRAQI EXAMPLE

Iraq is a useful example of a post-colonial elite's advance to a disaster of suppression and militarism. One of the most authoritative scholars of Iraq concludes that 'in view of Iraq's status of dependence, the decisive causes of its politics lay beyond its frontiers'.[8] Although the reference pertains to the colonial period, Ottoman influence ingrained militarism as did the British Mandate period following the embittering San Remo decisions in 1920 which reversed European promises of independence for the Arabs in return for their wartime support against Turkey.[9] Officers from the Ottoman period remained to help the British run Iraq. While British-installed King Faisal manoeuvred the clans, ethnic groups and tribes of the former Ottoman provinces into the formation of the new state, direct British controls were gradually relaxed in a series of treaties culminating in Iraq's admission to the League of Nations in 1932. But through direct tribal links and parliamentary institutions (beginning as early as 1924) that were largely devices to empower pro-British elders, major elements of British control continued.

Faisal, as leader of the Arab revolt, occupied a unique place in Arab nationalism. By virtue of his origins in Saudi Arabia and role in Damascus as liberator from the Turks, he not only embodied but expressed pan-Arabism. His ultimate focus was not the democratic development of the Iraqi state, but unification of the Arab world. The gradual substitution of Arab for British and French military power was thought to be sufficient to remove the artificial barriers to Arab unity erected by Europe during the Mandate period. Already visible, then, are the strands of utopianism and militarism that ultimately came to dominate politics.

By the end of World War II, utopianism as pan-Arabism coupled with vaguely formulated socialism comprised the overarching principle to unite the mosaic of communal factions which the old order – both Ottoman and mandatory – had governed by co-opting traditional rulers who were then backed by military power. The European dictatorships opposing the democracies appealed to the Arab world to the degree that they were 'anti-Western' and based on following one strong leader. Moreover, the rudimentary parliamentary formations established by the British and French were perceived as tools of foreign control which retained the already entrenched figures of local power. These early formations were not based on true political parties. Real power remained in the hands of the army. And it was military power – again using the Iraqi example – that was seen to be capable of recapturing Arabism's glory. The badly divided Iraq which emerged from Ottoman control became, and has remained, administered by its army, first British-led and ultimately Sunni-led. Initially, Iraq's officer corps consisted of many former Ottomans. To these men, military power was synonymous with government, whether Turkish, British or Iranian.

Furthermore, martial tradition became deeply ingrained and glorified within the educational framework of this relatively powerless nation. Well predating Ba'thism's origins in the 1940s, Iraq's Syrian Director-General of Education from 1923 to 1926, Sati al-Hursi, was a dedicated pan-Arabist who saw military training and the formation of an army by conscription as the avenue to replacing communal divisions by nationhood. As for the raw recruit, 'Military life makes him feel clearly the existence of nation and fatherland. He learns the sacrifice of blood and self in the cause of nation and fatherland.'[10] Continuity of this theme was evident in a famous speech in 1933 by Hursi's successor, Dr Sami Shawkat, to a group of Baghdad students and teachers, later circulated to all schools. Entitled 'The Manufacture of Death', Shawkat's speech extolled the role of the military in restoring past glories such as these of Turkey under Ataturk and of Persia under Pahlevi who mirrored the triumphs of Darius, and who observed, 'If Mussolini did not have tens of thousands of Blackshirts who had excelled in the profession of death, he would not have been able to place the crown of the Roman Emperors upon Victor Emmanuel.'[11] This core emphasis on militarism, one-party rule and pan-Arabism defines Iraq today.

In Syria as in Iraq – and elsewhere in much of the Middle East – it was not the absence of democracy's rudimentary *forms* during the Mandate period that inhibited democratic development, but rather, their misuse. Iraq had a Constituent Assembly as early as 1924, for instance, which ratified an unpopular treaty perpetuating British control. Strong British pressure and a special British relationship with the Assembly's forty tribal members brought ratification in March 1924, and with it, 'a pseudo-democracy for the upper stratum of elderly politicians'.[12] Subsequent treaties somewhat relaxed British controls at the cosmetic level. But with World War II pressures, Baghdad became a focal point of pro-Axis intrigues. British military intervention reinstated those political leaders – previously ousted by military coup – who favoured a continuing British relationship.

OTTOMAN GHOSTS AND LEBANON

The salient factor for democracy's prospects in Lebanon was the continuity of the Ottoman pattern in which a foreign power maintained loose control through selected tribal chiefs, powerful merchants or other leaders. This process inevitably meant playing one group off against another rather than seeking an equitable representative political system. Strong opposition elements had always rejected cooperation with the mandate power. Increasingly, however, politics seemed to centre on that power – its favouritism, the social and economic maladjustment it perpetuated and the supposed natural evolution toward pan-Arabism which it blocked.

Lebanon may be the ultimate and most extreme example of the influence of foreign intervention on state politics. One authority notes, 'Within the Ottoman matrix, Lebanon remained on the periphery, a "haven" to some of the minorities of the Empire, left more or less to its own devices by the Sublime Porte, and protected by the Western powers even when they were in rivalry with one another.'[13] Lebanon's unique relationship with France began during the Crusades. While the small state eventually became known as the Middle East's only democracy (apart from Israel) until its collapse in 1975, in most ways the disadvantages of its Ottoman and European connections outweighed the advantages. Clan chieftains rather than Ottoman-appointed provincial governors wielded real control on a daily basis until communal strife reached sufficient pitch to induce French military intervention (initially in the early 1860s), to protect the beleaguered Christian majority.[14]

Thus, Lebanese rivalries were never settled internally but remained partially the domain of Europe as a result of the special French-Christian and British-Druze connections. This was followed in the post-World War II period by powerful additional outside influences exerted by the USSR, the US, other Arab states, the Palestinian refugees, Iran and Israel. European political structures were introduced into Lebanon as early as the Ottoman period when in 1843, at the behest of Prince Metternich, the military governor, an Austrian deserter turned Muslim, appointed a Maronite district governor to rule in the north and a Druze in the south.[15] By 1926 Lebanon had a French-style parliamentary system and constitution although religion was the basis of citizenship and vote. Divisions between the country's many communities were thus accentuated rather than blurred, freezing the numerous clauses which had been artificially based on a 1932 census. The communities recognized were Maronite, Greek Orthodox, Greek Catholic, Roman Catholic, Armenian Orthodox, Nestorian Christian, Protestant, Sunni, Druze and Shiite. The system denied development of meaningful political party participation that might have enabled the state to survive the severe tests of a new era. These arose in part as the numbers of Shiites in the population far outgrew the static limitations on Shiite political power embodied in the 1932 census. Coupled with growing Arab nationalism, the proximity of Israel, the influx of Palestinian refugees and Cold War pressures an atmosphere of unsustainable social and political stress was created.

Lebanon then, while superficially a functioning democracy, was actually a grouping of ancient clans unable to define a common national interest or to respond to change. Religious and clan leaders focused exclusively on maintaining their power bases. Locked into the communal definition of citizenship, the normal democratic correctives which might gradually have redistributed power remained blocked. In other words, broader voting groups based on common economic interests, for instance, could have crossed and eventually superseded communal lines. Further, there were constant intrigues by foreign powers as Lebanon became a centre for espionage and propaganda warfare, with newspapers and politicians alike often available to the highest bidder. Despite Lebanon's many contributions as an intellectual and trading centre free of the stifling restrictions imposed by most Arab states, the country as a whole was hardly a charismatic model for the democratic system. The case of Lebanon in many ways remains unique. But its example of false democracy heightening communal tensions to the point of self-destruction is a grimly suggestive paradigm for the post-Cold War world.

EGYPT – A SINGULAR KIND OF PLURALISM

While Iraq exemplifies brutal military dictatorship, Lebanon went the other way to unfocused 'democratic' chaos without a centre. Egypt, on the other hand, while representing the strongest continuity of democratic potential, maintains a tantalizing flirtation with forms of pluralism. These fluctuate between genuine progress and setbacks which leave central authority solidly in control. Napoleon's 1798 invasion of Egypt and the brief ensuing occupation resulted in the development of an Arabic printing press which stimulated educated Egyptians to political debate on Islamic as well as Western history. French liberal ideas began to be debated in the context of Arab nationalism and democracy.[16] Napoleon encouraged French scholarly interest in Egypt and a lasting mutual cultural exchange ensued. Muhammad Ali's subsequent independence and defiance of Ottoman rule marked Egypt as having a pro-modernization attitude which was somewhat unique in the region. Egypt's geography itself encouraged a cosmopolitan outlook among the elites, with relative openness to Western ideas. By 1866, Egypt had created a Consultative Assembly of Deputies.

Within 15 years the Assembly had drafted a constitution, called for government ministers to be answerable to the assembly, and demanded the right to vote on the national budget.[17] By the following year, however, the British occupation of Egypt ended the Assembly. Only the 1919 Revolution and partial independence finally opened the way for the formulation of a new liberally based constitution in 1923. Although political parties functioned thereafter until the Officers' Revolution of 1952, Britain continued to exert power through the king and curtailed the basic political freedoms embodied in the constitution. Elections were rigged and newspapers suspended or confiscated. Martial law prevailed frequently and radical groups like the Muslim Brotherhood and the Communists were jailed or persecuted. Once more, as in Lebanon and Iraq, the political pluralism inspired by the foreign power was stunted by the larger strategic and economic needs of that power. Once more, democratic forms of government gradually became regarded as instruments of foreign control as the British presence persisted and the economy stagnated. Inevitably, disillusion overcame the main supporters of liberal democracy like Taha Husayn, Abbas al-Aqqad, Muhammad Husayn Haykal and Tawfiq al-Hakim. The net result was the emerging dominance of nationalists and Islamicists whose view of political pluralism was ambivalent if not negative.[18] Removal of the foreign occupier became the dominant political goal.

In this beleaguered political environment, Nasser's 1952 Officers' Revolution easily eliminated political parties whose vulnerability arose from the inability to achieve full independence after almost thirty years. And in this oversimplified context, Egypt's backwardness, Europe's continued strategic designs, and the new challenge presented by Israel all became justification for further attempts to stifle liberalism. Egypt faced a crisis. The old ways had failed. Central control and military power now seemed the avenues to strength and independence.

But true to Egypt's continuing pattern, democratic ideals and forms were not totally rejected and, in fact, were periodically encouraged. One of the six principles of the 1952 Revolution was the creation of a genuinely democratic system. The new constitution clearly designated the people as the legitimate source of political authority. Several mass one-party organizations – most notably the Arab Socialist Union in 1961 – were created to rally popular support. Frequent elections, while largely a sham, became a regular part of political life, even though control remained with Nasser and his small military clique.

Anwar Sadat, in turn, placed great rhetorical emphasis on creating genuine democracy and made significant efforts to encourage free enterprise. Perhaps in the sense that 'a little democracy is a dangerous thing' his encouragement of political party development coupled with continued strict media and other controls brought mounting dissatisfaction. In 1976, Sadat used the Arab Socialist Union to permit three different political sub-units to function – right, centre, and left – and by 1978 these had evolved into functional political parties. In reasonably orderly elections, Egyptians were given political choice for the first time. Sadat was increasingly pressured by the left, however, and was derided for his pro-West stance, which caused his regime to become steadily more oppressive. Democratic fortunes once more withered. Large numbers of opposition figures were imprisoned and shamelessly rigged elections in 1979 gave Sadat's party an absolute majority. By 1981, he had arrested most of the remaining opposition leaders and journalists.

Sadat's successor, Hosni Mubarak, exercised an initially brave but ultimately losing struggle to revive Egypt's repressed democratic institutions. His early release of political prisoners, restoration of press freedoms and encouragement of a truly independent judiciary immediately changed the country's political climate. By 1984, parliamentary elections allowed political parties to be represented for the first time in the People's Assembly in proportion to the number of votes received nationally. Although five major parties fought the election, the smaller parties complained that the requirement for a party to have more than 8 per cent of the total national vote in order to be represented in the Assembly seriously limited democratic expression. Despite amendments to the electoral law, the elections of 1987 were clouded by opposition parties' accusations of fraud and irregularities; in some districts, the actual population appeared to be smaller than the list of supposedly eligible voters. A member of the conservative Wafd party, Professor Numan Jumah, observed wryly, 'The Wafd has little cause for complaint: the government does nothing to stop the party from organizing, it does not censor Wafd newspapers, and it lets the party run its campaigns freely. The only thing that neither it nor any other opposition party is allowed to do is to win an election.'[19]

Widespread disillusionment prompted three main opposition parties – the Socialist Labour Party, the loosely allied Moslem Brotherhood, and the New Wafd – to boycott the 1990 general election. Earlier public apathy and disillusion were manifest during the elections of 1984 and 1987 when less than 30 per cent of eligible voters in major urban areas actually cast ballots.[20] Given Egypt's deteriorating economic and social condition accompanying this political stalemate, radical reaction seemed inevitable. Cries increased for alternatives to mounting mass poverty, stifling bureaucratic corruption, and unchanging leadership.[21] This reaction

– now well publicized – has transformed Egypt's political environment into violent confrontation between government and radicalized Islamicists dedicated to force as the instrument of change. Not surprisingly, the Mubarak government has responded with the full repressive means at its disposal. Emergency measures decreed following Sadat's assassination give the president virtually unlimited authority. Democratic liberalism – itself an overt target of the Islamicist extremists and possibly a covert target of the Moslem Brotherhood which functions quasi-legally within the party system – has again been submerged. The government has even sought to change voting requirements for the leaders of professional organizations of doctors, dentists, lawyers and engineers in order to displace those backed by religious groups.[22]

This pattern extends in varying forms throughout much of the Middle East as political vitality is increasingly expressed in religious terms whether by radical or moderate groups. In the 1990 elections, the Algerian Islamic Salvation Front (FIS) won over two-thirds of votes in regional assemblies and more than half of municipal council election votes in the spring of 1991. Similarly, in Tunisia, Islamicists running as independents won almost 30 per cent of municipal council votes in 1990; in Jordan, Islamicists and their sympathizers made even more substantial gains until the November 1993 multi-party general elections (Jordan's first since 1956) when the Islamicists lost six of the 22 seats they had previously won (as individuals).[23]

THE BATTERED SUBJECT: ISLAM AND DEMOCRACY

The problem of understanding for Egypt and elsewhere in the Arab world is one of definition and characterization. In Egypt, a significant proportion of those loosely categorized as Islamicists wish to work through the current political party process. This, despite the nagging concern that, once in power, leading organizations like the Moslem Brotherhood might opt for theocratic rule. In contrast, goals of the extremist groups like the Gama'a al Islamiyya, Islamic Jihad, and Ash-Shawkeen openly embrace revolutionary violence. By mid-1993 military courts had sentenced 22 Egyptians to death and charged 32 others with terrorist attacks on police and Christian-owned jewellers, demanding the death penalty for most; all were charged with membership in one of a number of extremist Islamicist groups who allegedly intend to overthrow the government.[24] Over the next year, the Egyptian government's unrelenting pursuit of radical groups appeared to have controlled most of the violence, but at a heavy cost to human rights. The death in police custody during April 1994 of a prominent lawyer, Abd al-Harith Madani, sparked demonstrations by the powerful Lawyers Syndicate which had strongly supported Madani's high-profile defence of alleged Islamicist extremists brought before the military courts.[25]

But nothing distorts Egypt's confrontation more than portraying Islamicists as a monolithic bloc either ideologically or organizationally. Nor is it useful to visualize a confrontation of anti-democratic Islamicists opposing democratically-minded, political pluralists. Enemies of democracy exist on both sides, as do its supporters. Certainly among Egypt's ruling group there are many who pay lip-service to democratic pluralism while refusing to permit the genuine liberalization that would actually transfer power.

So the democratic impulse is beset from both sides, a victim in part of the economic failures and statism characterizing post-World War II Egypt. As elsewhere in the region, the enormous and largely dead-handed bureaucracies that virtually strangle Egypt's polity regard political and economic pluralism as a mortal threat. Sadat's efforts to loosen the hold of state corporations and bring in foreign investment were bitterly resisted on intellectual grounds as counter to embedded orthodoxy about 'independence' and the evils of capitalism. They were resisted by the bureaucracy because of the threat of a vigorous private sector linked to the industrial world economy. This dynamic persists today. As one authority observes, 'It is the culture of the petty bourgeois class from which state bureaucracies are largely drawn (rather than anything inherently Islamic or Arab) which leads to rejection of dialogue with the West.'[26] Thus, democracy's impeders include secular forces and are not confined to the catch-all 'Islamicist' groups.

Islam is as marked by diversity of doctrine and practice as all other major religions. These characteristics are amply displayed in Egypt where the state has long exerted a powerful influence over religious affairs, thus fostering a dichotomy between an establishment clergy and movements opposing government rule. Similar situations exist elsewhere in the Middle East, but the Egyptian example has been notable – at least until recently – for a policy fluctuating between encouragement and repression of what are now popularly called fundamentalist movements. The Muslim Brotherhood, founded in 1928 and thenceforward an integral part of Egypt's ideological spectrum, was initially spared from the dissolution Nasser forced upon other political parties. The Brotherhood had links to the 'free officers', but was permitted to continue to operate openly, mainly because of its public eschewal of ambition to rule or even enter parliament. But when the subsequent request of the Brotherhood to join the cabinet was refused it proposed creation of a Brotherhood Committee to review all laws before their publication.[27] Nasser's refusal was followed by confrontation and a subsequent suppression of the Brotherhood in which some were killed, deported or imprisoned, recalling events in the latter part of the British period.

In Leonard Binder's authoritative study of Islamic liberalism he concludes that, 'Nasser exacerbated the cleavage between the state elite and the religiously oriented members of the lower middle classes.'[28] Moreover, Nasser reverted to Egypt's traditional pattern of '... patronizing al-Azhar academy of Islamic learning ... (which) increasingly has become a part of the state bureaucracy', while a variety of small, separate, largely underground religious organizations developed at the grass-roots level.[29] This raises the continuing interpretive dilemma of establishing cause in the 'state versus Islamicist' struggle. Was not the cleavage or polarization at least equally the fault of the Brotherhood's demand for exclusive political and spiritual dominance over society? Other scholars have observed that while Egypt's nationalists were attempting to unite the country against the British occupation, '*al-Ikhwan* (the Brotherhood) polarized Egyptian society, setting one group against another in the name of religion'.[30] Mubarak's current confrontation with radical Islamicists, albeit in a very different Egypt, resembles Nasser's struggle in which the still quasi-legal Brotherhood disclaimed responsibility for violence and aspired to participation in conventional party politics. The Brotherhood today disowns the shadowy terrorist groups, yet declines categoric criticism or active opposition. This leads to the obvious suspicion that their participation in semi-pluralist politics is merely a short-term device designed as a front for the real programme of destroying secular government.

In an attempt to forestall the descent into confrontation now evident and to incorporate moderate Islamicists into the democratization process, Mubarak appointed supposedly moderate Islamicists to positions of power at various levels of government. Today, however, there are credible accusations that these appointees have used their power to promote the radical agenda. Religious Affairs Minister Mohammed Ali Mahgoub, for instance, has reportedly used the financial and extensive powers of patronage of his office to promote fundamentalism at the expense of Egypt's secular traditions and large Coptic Christian community.[31] Similar indications of the inroads made by infiltrating radical Islamicists posing as moderates have, of course, heavily damaged the prospects for peaceful dialogue.

In a distinct pattern of continuity, related issues arose in the late 1940s, a time of assassinations and bombings in Cairo. When two members of the Brotherhood's secret apparatus killed the respected judge Ahmad al-Khaznidar, there was uncertainty even within the Brotherhood over whether founder Hasan al-Banna's repudiation of the act was genuine, whether he had secretly approved, or whether the apparatus had acted independently of the society's leadership.[32] Prime Minister Mahmud al-Nuqrashi was assassinated by a young Brotherhood member in 1948 and Banna himself was murdered the following year with evident government complicity. His successor, Hasan Isma'il al-Hudaybi, was a respected establishment figure, a senior judge who immediately repudiated the past violence of the organization's secret apparatus and rejected any future role for it, saying, 'There is no secrecy in the service of God. There is no secrecy in the Message and no terrorism in religion.'[33] This produced tension and turmoil in the Brotherhood in which past members of the secret apparatus, many of whom were dead or imprisoned, represented the heroic core, and in which current members believed themselves to represent the heroic vanguard. This tension persists today in Islamicist organizations in Egypt and elsewhere.

Two problems arise in the attempt to identify the real creed and agenda of the Brotherhood. Firstly, from its inception, a variety of religious and political interpretations co-existed within the movement's loose ideological framework. Secondly, while scholars have identified major strands representing these interpretations, the movement has evolved and exhibits consistent fidelity only to general slogans. The same question which was asked in the Brotherhood's early days continues to be asked today. On behalf of which Islam are they acting? While Banna's and other members' writings are signposts, the movement was oriented towards struggle and activism, not definition of a precise doctrine. In a recent interview, a Brotherhood spokesman, Mustapha Mashour, expressed the familiar 'Islam is the solution because the Quran is the word of God ... and all other systems, particularly communism and capitalism, have failed precisely because they are man-made.'[34] Questioned about remedies an Islamic government might apply to Egypt's critical problems of unemployment and poverty he said that clergy attached to ministries would assist officials to apply solutions found in the Quran. Predictably, and entirely within the organization's tradition, Mashour denied Brotherhood links with any of the extremist Islamicist groups responsible for assassinations and bombings. Just as predictably, such protestations met with the kind of scepticism expressed to the interviewer by an unnamed academic, who noted the Brotherhood's failure to oppose terrorism actively, leading to the 'conclusion that the Brotherhood is playing the role of the more politically acceptable face of Islam, while the real game is being played in secret'.[35]

TERRORISM AS HOLY DUTY

If the Brotherhood's role is murky, that of the various terrorist groups inspired by Islam is crudely explicit – violent overthrow of the government to make way for an Islamic state. Often called the Islamic Group (linked to the Gama'a al-Islamiyya and Islamic Jihad) and with many leaders exiled or imprisoned, beyond this basic credo its members have revealed few doctrinal specifics. A notable exception is the manifesto left by Sadat's assassins in October 1981 titled 'The Neglected Duty' (*Al-Faridah al-Ghaibah*) and used by their lawyers as a sanction by Islam for terrorism.[36] The manifesto rejects the concept of working through a political party even though its purpose might be 'destruction of the infidel state ... [to be replaced] ... by an Islamic theocracy', because such a party would have the opposite effect of 'building the pagan State and collaborating with it [including] participating in legislative councils that enact laws without consideration of God's laws'.[37] The underlying theme of the *Faridah* remains the likely common denominator among today's extremist Islamicist groups – that virtually all contemporary rulers of Muslim countries are illegitimate pretenders to Islam who follow laws imposed by the West rather than Islamic law.

The clear association of the notorious Sheikh Omar Abdel Rahman with the assassins and the inability or unwillingness of the Egyptian court to convict him illustrate but one of the many dilemmas inherent in the state-to-religious-group relationship. Can those inspiring violence, but without direct links to specific actions, be allowed to function in either a democratic or quasi-democratic environment? Can Islamic organizations like the Brotherhood, who disown but do not actively oppose the violent fringe groups, retain the right to function? Would Egypt's government be wiser to drop the Brotherhood's technically illegal status and allow it status as a political party, as some have urged? Given the Brotherhood's past policy, it is not clear whether it would even agree to function as one among several parties. Even less clear is whether a sweeping electoral victory by the Brotherhood in cooperation with grass-roots groups of varying degrees of extremism would even produce a cohesive authoritarian government, let alone toleration of secular opposition parties. With absolutely nothing approaching a consensus on interpretation of the *Sharia* to define Islamic rules, the task of displacing Egypt's Western-based laws would invite political and social upheaval.

The more immediate question, of course, is whether secular forces would ever yield such broad electoral freedom to Islamicist groups. Because such an evolution is most unlikely in the near future, continuing *impasse* with oppression and violence is expectable. Such an *impasse* seems destined to delay the discourse between supporters of secular democracy and reformist religious leaders who might find a way out.

For Egyptian intellectuals, there is cold comfort in the view of religious-secular political interaction elsewhere in the region. With the tentative exceptions of Tunisia, Jordan and Morocco, democratization efforts have virtually been aborted. Where Islamicists have come to power, as in the Sudan and Iran, rigid one-party rule exemplifies polity.

ALGERIA – THE SLIDE TO TRAGEDY

Algeria, like Egypt, finds radical Islamicists forming a vital political impetus that has now been captured by the extremists. The cycle of terrorism and responding government repression has brought the country to the edge of civil war. Algeria's democratization process, symbolized by open political discussion following the creation of over 150 new papers and magazines between 1990 and the close of 1991, was abruptly reversed in January 1992. As the first free multi-party national elections approached, the virtual certainty that Islamicist groups (gathered under the Islamic Salvation Front (FIS)) would sweep the polls prompted the government to cancel the elections. Shortly thereafter, the FIS was outlawed. A series of arrests, assassinations of officials, strikes and the imprisoning of thousands of FIS supporters followed. The brief prospect of escape from the circle of violence and deteriorating economic conditions ended in July 1992 with the murder of President Mohammed Boudiaf by one of his bodyguards. The return of the long-exiled Boudiaf had offered the prospect of leadership untainted by the government corruption he had promised to root out. This prospect, coupled with Boudiaf's forthright opposition to the politicization of religion focused blame not only on Islamist radicals, but even more sharply on the senior army officers slated to become the subjects of Boudiaf's corruption probes.

The subsequent widening of the assassination net to cover intellectuals favouring a modern Algeria creates a similar ambiguity. In the opinion of Algerian political scientist Abdel-Kader Djeghloul viewing the tragedy from Paris, the killers could have been Islamicists or 'the politico-financial of the entrenched forces of the old regime. The 'mafia' is the target of liberal-democratic intellectuals as well as radical Islamicists.[38] In mid-1993 Algeria's ruling State Council offered a draft transition plan for review by the principal parties, including two legal Islamicist groups and the leading leftist parties, that would provide for presidential elections between 1996 and 1997.[39] But there are grounds for deep scepticism as to whether the government's economic policies can stabilize the political scene so soon or whether a workable consensus among the political parties is feasible. Without this, an orderly democratic process is impossible. In both Egypt and Algeria, increasing polarization has shrunk the safe political space available for liberal moderates, whether secular or religious. Leading Egyptian intellectuals favouring secularism have been murdered, including the prominent writer, Farag Fodah. At least twenty Algerian intellectuals and journalists known as proponents of a secular society were murdered during the summer of 1993. Thus, intimidation by radical Islamicists, combined with government-imposed security restrictions on all forms of political expression have for now eclipsed all hopes of pluralism.

And what of the familiar charge by Western journalists and academics that governments like those of Egypt and Algeria should allow radical Islamiciists full political sway in competition with other groups and parties within a democratic framework? This approach postulates that once in power, the radical Islamicists would quickly reveal their lack of practical programme and their ineptitude. Pluralist government would naturally follow according to this model. Or, more likely, would the Islamicists' success cause the evolving democratic process to self-destruct? As expressed by Algerian professor of political sociology Lahouari Addi, one choice is to 'permit the democratic process to bring about its own termination, by carrying the Islamicists to power. For a utopia, there is no antidote like reality'.[40] Addi's alternative choice – manifestly beyond reach at this point – is the rapid modernization of the economy in order to neutralize the radical Islamicists' appeal.

So how are the liberal believers in pluralism, both within and outside the folds of the Islamicist movements, to survive, let alone gather strength? As most scholars agree, within the various groups comprising the FIS there is a significant faction dedicated to utilizing the democratic process to achieve an Islamic stage.[41] But this dedication to a process as a means to power in no way assures the ultimate survival of genuine pluralism tolerant of political opposition. Nor does it assure the survival of those genuine believers in pluralism as theocratic absolutism takes hold. Iran and the Sudan exemplify the point. Doubts about the ultimate intentions of FIS have mounted as declarations of devotion to democracy made to Western observers were followed by proclamations to the Algerians that 'democracy is heresy'.[42] When questioned in October 1992 about conflicting statements by several imprisoned FIS leaders on issues like multi-party democracy and women's rights, FIS spokesman Anwar Haddam blandly responded that the comments, 'are within the same framework but said in a different language, because they are addressed to different audiences ... not [in] "double-speak" but a result of the different audiences'.[43]

SUDAN: THE ISLAMICIST-MILITARY COALESCENCE

As noted, the examples of Islamicist-ruled governments now in being compound the doubts generated by FIS ambiguities. In Teheran, the version of 'democracy' practised is simply reminiscent of all the region's old one-party regimes in which the parliamentary process consists of internal debates among party factions. In Sudan, the combined military-radical Islamicist government rests philosophically on Dr Hasan Turabi, a theorist of Islamic revival influential throughout the Middle East and among African Muslims. With impressive credentials in Western education, services as dean of Khartoum University's law faculty and long a leader in Sudan's religious and political life (including leadership of Sudan's Muslim Brotherhood) Turabi skilfully articulates a moderate Islamicist posture. He insists that 'Islam shuns absolute government, absolute authority' and places the blame for Islam's revolutionary excesses on the fact that 'repression has ostracized Islam from democracy and compelled it to become revolutionary'.[44] Turabi heads the National Islamic Front (NIF), a group which had only 25 per cent of the electoral vote in pre-coup voting contests but which now controls most of Sudan's institutions.

Perversely, it is now repression that has ousted democracy from Islam. The NIF replaced almost all university chancellors and vice-chancellors with its own members. The purging of the military that began in April 1990 with the execution of 28 officers (in front of a firing squad one day after arrest and following a two-hour trial) has since removed over 600 officers. Both university students and government employees are forced to take three months of military training combined with political and religious indoctrination with the Popular Defense Forces.[45] Political parties are prohibited. Scores of opposition leaders are jailed, exiled, under house arrest or systematically harassed by the security forces.

Particularly notable here is the relationship between this development and Hasan Turabi's original and continuing rhetorical support for the forms of democracy. Despite the repression and strong resistance within Sudan, Turabi insists that an Islamic state is taking shape and that, 'It will be more true to the liberal tradition than present-day governments in Western Europe.'[46] Against his promises of adherence to the democratic process prior to the 1989 Islamist-supported military coup, this prognosis rings hollow indeed. Thus, Turabi places himself clearly within the utopian/authoritarian tradition of the Communist, Nasserist and Ba'thist movements that have cost Middle Eastern societies so dear since World War II.

OPTIMISM IN JORDAN

Iran and Sudan represent states under Islamicist control which ban pluralism. Egypt and Algeria are approaching civil war under conditions which virtually eliminate earlier progress towards pluralism. But elsewhere in the region, despite latent elements of similar polarization, alternative political methods are being cautiously tested. In 1986, electoral laws in Jordan were amended and political prisoners released. Under the law governing the formation of new political parties, any group with 50 members can form a party, but the Ministry of the Interior has the final say as to whether a party can be licensed or when licences can be revoked. The 90 parties originally proposed were reduced to 60. The resulting objections from liberals were at least partially mollified when Jordan's High Court overruled the ministry to allow licences for the Communists, Ba'thists, and the Popular Front for the Liberation of Palestine (PFLP). Press freedom was also markedly improved, but again with careful strictures controlling press membership, criticism of the king, attacking foreign governments represented in Jordan or making derogatory statements about religion. Most controversial, however, is the requirement for journalists to cite their sources of information. On the other hand, political parties are free to publish their platforms and opinions, a remarkable step forward. Both Hamas, the more radical Palestinian wing of the Muslim Brotherhood, and the Brotherhood itself function within the newly liberalized political framework, with the Brotherhood in the forefront of pro-democracy efforts. Hamas' 1989 Charter expresses a quintessentially paranoid worldview, naming the 'Capitalist West, the Communist East and the Zionist invasion' as continuity from the Crusades and the Tartars to be overcome only under Islam's religious banner. The Charter, which mentions the

Crusades six times, urges tactical cooperation with secular groups like the PLO in the struggle against Israel, but categorically rejects all secular ideology.[47] As elsewhere, therefore, strong doubts have arisen as to whether Hamas' purpose is merely to use the pluralist process as a disposable device en route to theocratic dictatorship. The reduction in seats won by the Islamicists' from 33 to 16 (plus six independent supporters) in parliament reflected the changes to the electoral laws as well as the pedestrian performance of previously appointed Islamicist cabinet members who focused on the minutiae of social behaviour rather than urgent economic issues.

Jordan's form of gradual, paternalistic and carefully calibrated moves towards democratization, though offending liberal purists, may progress because of the unique presence of a monarchy and a military leadership committed to the experiment. While this lasts, the reassurance that each political group can have its say under the slowly shrinking authoritarian umbrella may foster pluralism in greater depth than occurred in Algeria-like models where rapid transition was attempted. Jordan's vulnerabilities, however, are as evident as these particular advantages. More than elsewhere, Jordan's stability depends on the peace process; King Hussein's longevity adds another critical variable.

The thicket of issues affecting democratization prospects is so dense as to obscure some of the fundamentals, like the Palestinian problem, which shape political forces in the region as a whole. These fundamentals appear to be mostly negative for democratic prospects because they create stresses so great that neither the required economic nor the political reforms seem feasible – the economic, because the initial sacrifices requisite for change would risk breakdown of the social order, and the political, because a sudden move from rigid one-party rule to pluralism would mean an Islamicist election sweep. This, in turn, would seemingly unleash even greater antagonism towards Israel and the West at the very time when progress in the peace process is tangible and when almost all of the statist-oriented economies need to increase trade with and investment in the Western economic system.

Among the adverse economic fundamentals Middle East press reports invariably cite are population pressures. While statistics vary, the general impact is unrelentingly uniform. Unemployed youth in Algeria represent some 70 per cent of the 26 million population, Egypt has to feed an additional million people each year, half of Syria's population of 14 million (which grows at 3.8 per cent annually) is under 19 years of age, and so on.[48] While these issues of employment and basic survival predominate, the bitter divisions in the Arab world have been worsened, just at a time when the disintegration of the Soviet superpower increased perceptions of strategic weakness in a Middle East luridly portrayed by the local media as being manipulated by the US and Israel. With the melting away of even Syria's slightest pretensions to being a barrier to Israeli power, and with both Libya and Iraq cut down to size for the moment, there is a sense of diminished pride and confidence in the ability of the Arab states to provide either economic or military security. In the Gulf, while economic security is less of an issue, Desert Storm brought home the total inability of the GCC to defend itself against either Iran or Iraq without Western intervention, despite enormous defence-related investment. None of these factors seem likely to encourage governments to offer opportunities for intensive media probing or rancorous parliamentary debate.

THE POSITIVE MOMENTUM

There are, however, more positive elements at work than may be apparent. Democratic prospects in the region have been long frozen by mass apathy. Today there is evidence, however difficult to document, of heightened appreciation for democracy's benefits. A November 1993 poll in Jordan conducted by the Jerusalem-based Centre for Palestine Research and Studies revealed that among 1855 Palestinians surveyed, 73 per cent wanted the Palestine Governing Council to be elected, versus 15 per cent who preferred a PLO-appointed body. Moreover, 58 per cent wanted a multi-party system and only 19 per cent an Islamic state, a division further supported by a 45 per cent preference for Fatah (the mainstream, moderate Palestinian faction) in contrast to 14 per cent for Hamas and 3 per cent for Islamic Jihad.[49] With its many limitations as a local indicator, let alone as a regional political marker, such a survey must be viewed with caution. Among other reasons, popular desires may not count for much in the short run. But no matter how destructive it may be in the short run or to what extent it is led by Islamicist extremists, the presence of greater grass-roots ferment favours democratic change in the long run.

Many of the moderate secular parties are too enmeshed in the old system to risk the status of their members by supporting real change. Granted the risks presented by Islamicist fervour vulnerable to takeover by extremists, the Islamicist movement represents a basic challenge to the old statist systems. The widely publicized obscurantist and puritanical aspects of the mainstream (as opposed to the extremist) Islamicist thrust tend to overshadow the reality of many Islamicists who would support privatization and political pluralism.

Inevitably, too, a reaction is developing against the extremists' use of terrorism. The death and maiming of innocent bystanders, the murder of popular public figures, and the threats against virtually all who oppose the extreme Islamicist platform have generated disgust. This is not to deny that repressive government acts also have been politically counterproductive. Greater middle class awareness of the ugliness of Islamicist rule in Iran and Sudan has built upon the existing rejection of the Saudi model as applicable, for instance, to Egypt. Nor is the reaction to extremism merely passive. Radical in another way, a new book entitled *The Book and the Koran: A Contemporary Reading* (*Al-Kitab wal-Qur'an: Qira's Musasira*) reportedly circulates widely in the Middle East, though banned in Saudi Arabia, the United Arab Emirates, Qatar and Egypt. The study reinterprets the Quran in a modern context. The 800-page book was written by Dr Muhammad Shahrur, a Syrian engineer whose insistence on reinterpretation has brought attacks from clerics across the spectrum. But the eagerness with which his views are apparently being received may be an indicator of the vitality within and even beyond the liberal Islamicist tradition.[50]

Communications technology may favour the Islamicist or other extremist movements. The Ayatollah Khomeini's taped sermons and tirades were widely noted vehicles for revolution in Iran and beyond. Comparisons are made with the role of Sheikh Abdul Rahman's sermons in Egypt today. However, technology's force as an enemy of obscurantism and thought control is also powerful. A Beirut publisher can produce thousands of copies of Dr Shahrur's book in days. Satellite television receivers (at least until seized) can easily bypass government censorship. The nearly universal ferment for increased cultural and political freedom, so greatly stimulated by the Eastern Bloc's collapse, cannot be confined. Even the quest for a theocracy expressed by the most extreme Islamicists represents a political impetus unlikely to remain within the bounds designated by its creators.

IS IT 'TOUJOURS ÇA CHANGE, TOUJOURS LA MÊME CHOSE'?

In coping with the policy problems surrounding liberalism's struggle in the region, the West should not try to devise a 'policy for Islam' as some have encouraged. To do so would be as dangerously shallow as the Islamic 'policy for Christianity' expressed in the simplistic religious jingoism of the Islamicist radical. Islam, in the broadest sense, is the very culture of the world's Muslims interpreted and practised with great differences. This diversity constitutes a safeguard for the liberal potential in

Islam compatible with democratic pluralism. It also allows narrowly selective interpretations of the Quran to foster aberrations such as those legitimizing the regimes in Iran and Sudan. As noted, many of the strands of today's Islamic revival as practised by extremists were created during revolution against foreign occupation and retain an atmosphere of secrecy and conspiracy that is too often a companion to terrorism. Islam has also played the role of quasi-legitimizer for almost all the region's regimes. So, in several ways, Islamicists have served the secular state willingly or not. Nasser and Sadat used radical Islamicists (as opposed to the tame government-supported Islamicists) against their enemies, and subsequently repressed them. Israel, at one stage, allowed Hamas to function as a counter to the PLO in the West Bank and Gaza. Asad continues to use Iranian-supported Shiite militants in South Lebanon as implements in his complex machinations with Iran, Israel and his own Islamicists and in his effort to control Lebanon itself. Certainly the broad Western-supported coalition liberating Afghanistan from the Soviets leaned heavily on Islamicist leaders. These have been short-lived secular-religious accommodations often widening the underlying divide. Only in Jordan, Morocco and Tunisia, where democratic pluralism is encouraged under firm control, do Islamicists function as part of a politically diverse amalgam. This promising evolution, however, does not answer the question of whether the relatively liberal Islamicists willing to participate in such a process would ultimately survive against radical pressure.

The prospects for the thin layer of liberal secularists and Islamists squeezed between the old single-party tyrannies and those of the radical Islamicists are fragile. Competing at the grass roots against the entrenched power of the state – as principal employer, food subsidizer, master of security – requires genuine political parties offering believable rewards, against radical Islamicists whose siren utopianism gains credibility as the poor receive tangible help from the mosques. In the absence of progress by this thin layer of moderates it is fair to ask whether real change is taking place. Compare the centralized state power in Iran today and the clerics' ideological and economic control coupled with military buildup, on the one hand, with similar power structures in the Nasserist–Ba'thist era. The clerics justify rule by what many Islamicists believe to be a heretical misuse of the Quran. The Nasserists and Ba'thists have borrowed chaotically from Marxism, the Quran, Western democracy and Arab scholars. In both cases, the message was utopian and promised that state economic power would answer social needs, that the West was an exploiter and that progress depended on spreading their system throughout the region. Only because of the long association of a country like Egypt with democratic forms, however halting, and the great diversity of the population does it seem impossible that once again they will fall prey to a utopian tyranny or long tolerate political stagnation. Recall the Wafd politician's sarcasm about government repression preventing opposition parties from winning an election, yet permitting them the freedom to organize and campaign without newspaper censorship. This is a risky formula for those hoping to freeze pluralism. None of the polities of the region, even including Iraq, has remained as static and devoid of the components of a civilian society as it may appear.

NOTES

1. Maalouf, Amin, *The Crusades Through Arab Eyes* (London: Al Saqi Books, 1984), p. 261.
2. Ibid., p. 262.
3. Ibid., p. 263.
4. Ibid., p. 265.
5. *Middle East Insight*, Vol. X, No. 1, Nov.–Dec. 1993, p. 13.
6. Hourani, Albert, *Arabic Thought in the Liberal Age, 1798–1939* (London, 1970), pp. 324–40.
7. Ibid.
8. Batatu, Hanna, *The Old Social Classes and the Revolutionary Movements of Iraq* (Princeton, NJ: Princeton University Press, 1978), p. 45.
9. For a classic review of this period, see George Antonius, *The Arab Awakening*, Chapter XVI, and George Lenczowski, *The Middle East in World Affairs* (Ithaca: Cornell University Press, NY, 1952), pp. 263–75.
10. Hemphill, Paul P. J., 'The Formation of the Iraqi Army, 1921–33', in *The Integration of Modern Iraq*, ed. Abbas Kelidar (New York: St. Martin's Press, 1979), p. 93.
11. Sami Shawkat's collected writings and speeches, *Hadhihi Ahdafuna, Wazarat al Ma'arif* (Baghdad, 1939); as quoted (with slightly differing translation) in Samir al-Khalil (pseudonym for Kanan Makiya), *Republic of Fear* (New York: Pantheon Books, 1989), p. 177, and Hemphill, ibid., p. 102.
12. Lenczowski, George, *The Middle East in World Affairs*, Fourth edn (Ithaca: Cornell University Press, 1980), pp. 268–70. This study provides excellent coverage of political evolution in Middle East states since the Ottoman period.
13. Gordon, David C., *Lebanon, The Fragmented Nation* (London: Croom Helm, 1980), p. 37.
14. Mishaka, Mikhayil, *Murder, Mayhem, Pillage, and Plunder: The History of Lebanon in the 18th and 19th Centuries* (Albany: State University of New

York Press, 1988). See Part I, pp. 9–58, and Part III, pp. 105–59, particularly.

15. Ibid., p. 233–4.
16. Abdel Monem Said Aly, 'Democratization in Egypt', *Arab–American Affairs*, Fall 1987, No. 22, p. 11.
17. Harris, Christina P., *Nationalism and Revolution in Egypt* (The Hague: Mouton, 1954), pp. 44–5.
18. Abdel Monem Said Aly, 'Democratization', op. cit., p. 13.
19. *The Economist*, 6 February 1988.
20. Abdel Monem Said Aly, 'Democratization', op. cit., p. 26.
21. *Al-Wafd*, 8 September 1992, carried 'An Open Letter to President Mubarak', in which distinguished Egyptian establishment member Tahsin Bashir referred to the country's 'unbridled corruption' (as translated in *Middle East Report*, July–August 1993, No. 183, 'Egypt's Islamists and the State', by Ahmed Abdalla, p. 30).
22. *The Financial Times*, 22 April 1993, Survey, p. III.
23. *Los Angeles Times*, 10 November 1993.
24. *The New York Times*, 23 June 1993.
25. *Middle East International*, 24 June 1994, p. 12.
26. Binder, Leonard, *Islamic Liberalism* (Chicago: University of Chicago Press, 1988), p. 337, quoting Abdullah Laroui, *L'idéologie arabe contemporaine* (Paris: François Maspéro, 1967).
27. Husaini, Ishaq Musa, *The Moslem Brethren: The Greatest of Modern Islamic Movements* (Beirut: Khayat's College Book Co., 1956), p. 131.
28. Binder, Leonard, *Islamic Liberalism* (Chicago: University of Chicago Press, 1988), p. 339.
29. Ibid.
30. Al-Sayyid-Marsot, Afaf Lutfi, *Egypt's Liberal Experiment: 1922–1936* (Berkeley: University of California Press, 1977), p. 325.
31. *The New York Times*, 18 August 1993.
32. Mitchell, Richard P., *The Society of the Muslim Brothers* (London: Oxford University Press, 1969), p. 70.
33 Ibid., p. 88, quoted from *Ruz al-Yusuf*, 7 December 1953.
34. *The Financial Times*, 22 April 1993, Egypt Survey, Roger Matthews, p. III.
35. Ibid.
36. Jansen, Johannes J. G., *The Neglected Duty: The Creed of Sadat's Assassins and Islamic Resurgence in the Middle East* (New York: Macmillan, 1986), pp. 159–230 contains a complete translation of the manifesto.
37. Ibid., p. 184.
38. *Christian Science Monitor*, quoted by Howard La Franchi, 2 July 1993.
39. *The Financial Times*, 8 July 1993.
40. Addi, Lahouari, 'Islamicist Utopia and Democracy', *The Annals of the American Academy of Political and Social Science*, November 1992, Vol. 524, p. 129.
41. See Entelis, John P. and Arone, Lisa J., 'Algeria in Turmoil: Islam, Democracy and the State', *Middle East Policy*, Vol. I, 1992, No. 2, pp. 28–35.

42. Zartman, I. William, 'Democracy and Islam: the Cultural Dialectic', *The Annals of the American Academy of Political and Social Science*, November 1992, Vol. 524, p. 189.
43. *The Washington Report on Middle East Affairs*, November 1992, Vol. XI, No. 5, p. 41.
44. Turabi, Hasan, 'Islam, Democracy, the State and the West', summary of a lecture and round-table discussion prepared by Louis J. Cantori and Arthur Lowrie, *Middle East Policy*, Vol. 1, No. 3, 1992, p. 51.
45. Bonner, Raymond, 'Letter From Sudan', *The New Yorker*, 13 July 1992, pp. 80–3.
46. Turabi, 'Islam', op. cit., p. 54.
47. *Journal of Palestine Studies*, Vol. XXII, No. 4, Summer 1993, 'Charter of the Islamic Resistance Movement (Hamas)', pp. 122–34.
48. *The New York Times*, 28 June 1993, for Syria.
49. *Jordan Times*, 23 November 1993.
50. Eickelman, Dale F., 'Islamic Liberalism Strikes Back', *Middle East Studies Association Bulletin*, December 1993, Vol. 27, No. 2, pp. 163–7; *Middle East International*, 23 July 1993, No. 455, p. 15.

Part III Stability or Instability

6 Post-Cold War Security in the GCC Region: Continuity and Change in the 1990s

Brigid Starkey

INTRODUCTION

If there is a fundamental tenet that has characterized post-Cold War security posturing the world over, it is that of uncertainty: incertitude about priorities in an increasingly ill-defined international system structure, by which attempts are made to merge security concerns with economic aspirations, with little regard to the distinctness of these tasks. Regional organizations – the Gulf Cooperation Council (GCC), the European Union (EU), the Association of South-east Asian Nations (ASEAN) – have achieved unprecedented levels of integration for contemporary times, but are still woefully unable to forge unified foreign policies. In the 1990s, tenuous commitments from the world's only contender for superpower status – the United States – have replaced East–West balancing games. Contrary to hopes and some expectations, the international system is not a more peaceful, less dangerous place in the wake of the Cold War. Ethnic bloodletting, much more basic and dangerous than the political-ideological struggles of the Soviet-American standoff, now account for the majority of the system's wars. Aggressive grabs for regional power – on the part of Iraq, Serbia and North Korea – present security dilemmas for all states that continue to actively seek stability. It is this lack of overall system definition that has placed sub-regional protagonists in a state of foreign policy discontinuity with widespread repercussions.

For the six nation-states of the southern Gulf sub-region of the Middle East there has been a most unfortunate continuity across political arenas in the twentieth century, a situation born of regional mistrust and ceaseless competition for hegemony. Most recently, the region has been rocked by a series of shocks with ramifications on both the internal and external

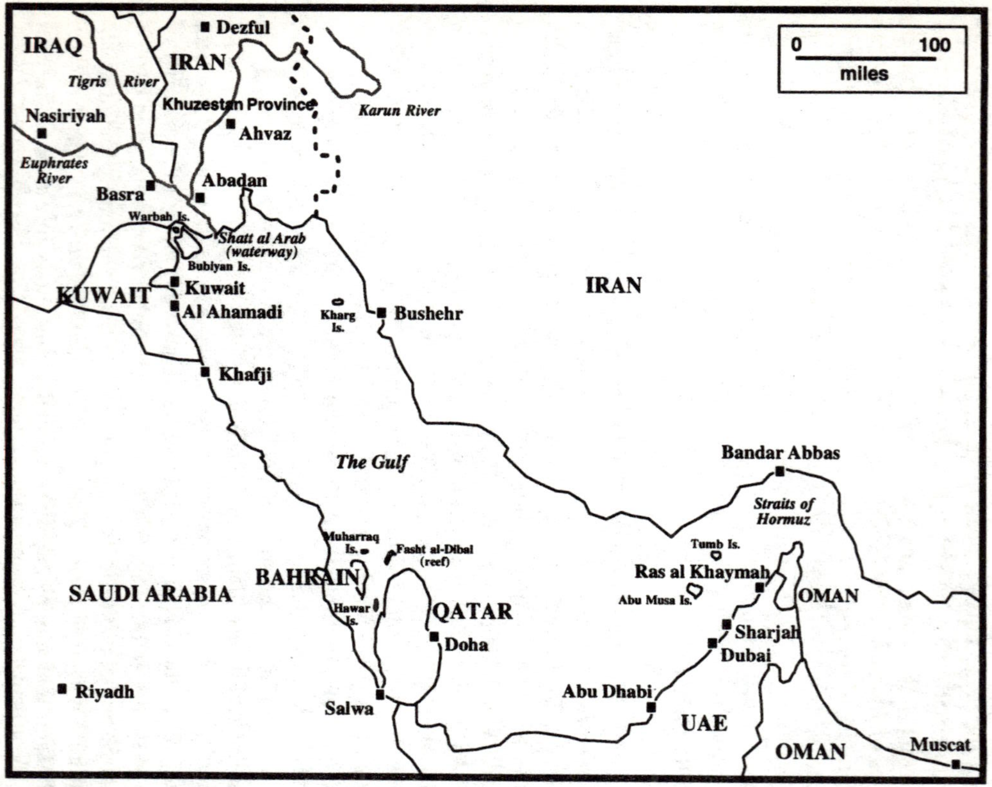

Map 6.1 The Persian Gulf and environs

stability of member states. The Iranian Revolution of 1978–79, the Iran–Iraq War of 1980–88 and the Gulf War of 1990–91 have kept the GCC nations in a continual state of crisis response. The first upheaval prompted the formation of the GCC, while the last exposed its failure to constitute a workable security regime.

As the GCC moves ahead towards the next century, it must overcome the internal and external structural factors which have inhibited it from growing and strengthening as a regional security regime. The member-states of Bahrain, Kuwait, Oman, Qatar, Saudi Arabia and the United Arab Emirates must resolve competitive and contradictory goals in the area of security, as well as their many unsolved territorial disputes.

Dramatic changes in the regional and international political environments provide opportunities for re-orientation and restructuring of GCC security. But first, priority must be placed on the search for multilateral solutions over bilateral and unilateral ones. Threats from the northern Gulf nations of Iran and Iraq must be put into perspective, their importance weighed against that of the internal civil unrest that has already shown a capacity to 'transnationalize' in the region. A coherent and unified security strategy must be developed in place of the still dominant patchwork approach which combines Saudi-style financial diplomacy with a newly guaranteed American security umbrella, a stalled GCC+2 (Syria and Egypt) concept and a lone Omani voice calling for a re-emphasis on Gulf self-reliance and a dialogue with the Islamic Republic of Iran. Regional protagonists must devise approaches aimed at breaking the continuity of a harsh balance-of-power system by taking advantage of the opportunities created by environmental changes.

INTEGRATION AS A RESPONSE TO CRISIS: THE GCC

The Gulf Cooperation Council, an organization born of crisis, functions at its greatest effectiveness during times of regional upheaval, but continues to show a marked inability to expand in scope and cohesion during non-crisis periods. Not surprisingly, economic coordination has proved much easier to achieve than security cooperation.

The articulation of a common economic agenda, at least on a general level, was not difficult and had been underway since the founding of the Gulf Organization for Industrial Consulting (GOIC) in 1976.[1] Common needs due to the hydrocarbon basis of their economies, the universal imperative to diversify beyond that basis and a desire to increase sub-regional trade and collective export potential provided a sound basis for cooperation in the initial stages of the integrative process.[2] The 1981 'Economic Unity Agreement' put the six on a path which is to lead eventually to a common market. While there is no doubt that the economic basis for collaboration has been helpful to the overall process, it is in many ways symbolic. Economic, cultural, religious and political coordination of the larger Arab, Muslim and oil-producing 'worlds' were already central to the purposes of other key organizations, including the Organization of Petroleum Exporting Countries (OPEC),[3] the Organization of Islamic Conference (OIC), and the Arab League. Although the GCC is sub-regional in purpose and scope, membership in these other active organizations produces significant redundancy and institutional overlap in areas other than security. The overriding purpose of the GCC should be to enhance defence cooperation between the six, providing a response to their most pressing common need.

The Iranian Revolution provided an indication of what a tremendous urgency there was for a convincing collective security framework in the southern Gulf. A response was needed to Teheran's suspected efforts to 'export' its revolution to neighbouring countries.[4] This was a threat felt most acutely in the small, vulnerable nations of the Gulf which looked to Saudi Arabia to counter the Islamic credentials of the new regime in Teheran. Suspicions that Iran was behind a series of internal upsets in the other Gulf nations led Saudi Arabia to establish bilateral security agreements with all of the other GCC states, with the exception of a reluctant Kuwait. Meaningful cooperation was achieved between all six in the areas of riot control and the sharing of intelligence information.[5] Still, there was unrealized potential for defence cooperation. The lack of progress was once again highlighted during the Iran–Iraq War.

The initial reaction of the GCC nations to this war was cavalier as it was in the international system at large. It was only in 1982, when Iran began to show an ability to launch offensive attacks, that the southern Gulf nations became sufficiently concerned to once again consider their ability to deter and took steps to establish a unified military force. The result was a GCC Rapid Deployment Force. It was reported by the GCC to be a 10 000-man strong unit, but there is some question as to whether it actually existed, except in theory, prior to the 1990–91 Gulf War.[6] An alliance in any true sense of the term continues to seem unlikely, given the sharp conflicts between the six. There are, reportedly, forty different territorial disputes in the contemporary Gulf region.[7] These include disputes between Bahrain and Qatar, Saudi Arabia and Oman, Saudi Arabia and Qatar and Saudi Arabia and the UAE.[8] In addition, the positions of the six *vis-à-vis* the superpowers and regional powers outside the GCC have repeatedly been at odds. Kuwait maintained a close relationship with the USSR while its neighbours leaned heavily towards the United States; Qatar, Oman, and the UAE have flirted with Teheran in the post-Gulf War period, apparently in an effort to counter Saudi Arabia's power; and Bahrain has already made overtures to the vanquished Iraq.[9]

As the members of other regional organizations have found, trying to formulate a collective security regime in the absence of a collective will does not work. Every international and regional organization must contend with the strength of national sovereignty in efforts to further interstate collaboration, but a collective with as many internal conflicts as the GCC has is facing an even more difficult task. The Council has been a successful forum for coalescence in times of direct external threat. Integration is too strong a term to describe the level of coordination that has been achieved. The member nations' own lack of trust in the organization is well-evidenced by the bilateral agreements which Saudi Arabia has had to forge, individually, with the four smaller states and by similar bilateral efforts now underway between the United States and the six GCC members.[10]

Another crucial shortcoming of this integration scheme is the inadequacy of a defensive alliance – even were it a workable one – to respond to the many internally generated threats faced by the Gulf regimes. While the six struggle to establish a balance between themselves and simultaneously try to deter external aggression transnational and internal challenges loom large.

This 'triple threat' leads to debate about what kind of security strategies best fit the needs of the Gulf states. The importance of enhancing oil production means that any disruption in the flow from neighbouring nations, particularly one or more of the big producers, will have a positive economic effect on the others. Long disruptions, such as the Iran–Iraq War and the Gulf War, have the potential to be especially profitable.[11] Yet, at the same time, they obviously create serious military-security crises for neighbouring states. The result is a Gulf-style variation on the 'guns versus butter' debate. For the smaller Gulf states, in particular, economic and commercial competition can pose a threat equal to or greater than the aspirations of regional aggressors.[12] Competitive goals, unresolved territorial disputes and contradictions between national and regional security strategies have severely inhibited the ability of the GCC to increase its effectiveness during non-crisis periods.

ENVIRONMENTAL FACTORS REDUCING GULF SECURITY

The 1990s have already produced many dramatic shifts in the regional landscape of the Middle East. The collapse of the Communist bloc was a clear catalyst for the unprecedented political movement in this and other regions around the world. The Gulf states felt the repercussions of the resulting uncertainty when Saddam Hussein invaded Kuwait in 1990. This bold aggression, in tandem with the loss of Soviet patronage for the 'hardline' Arab states, opened the way for unexpected foreign policy shifts in Israel, Syria and on the part of the Palestine Liberation Organization. The anti-Israel coalition was broken up, leading to an ongoing regional peace dialogue and a degree of autonomy for the Palestinian people. The United States, having proven its regional commitment during Desert Storm, now plays a solo great power role in the design of the future Middle Eastern order. The Gulf War was a watershed point in the modern political and social history of the Middle East. As such, it increased the visibility of a variety of national and transnational social movements which threaten the stability of the ruling monarchies in the Gulf.

External Factors: The Demise of the Soviet Union

When an international system structure collapses, member states are presented with both new opportunities and new dangers as a result of the ensuing instability. The dissolution of Soviet power did not lead to an immediate or a full cessation of status quo politics in the Middle East as a whole, nor in the Gulf sub-region. It did, however, contribute to some dramatic developments, including Saddam Hussein's perception of a Gulf power vacuum. His subsequent actions tested the post-Cold War commitment of the United States to the Middle East region and to international stability in a new era. The resolve shown by America and its allies, in turn, created an environment conducive to progress in the Israeli–Palestinian and Israeli–Arab peace dialogues. The loosening of the regional anti-Israel coalition was also aided by Soviet leader Gorbachev's last-ditch efforts to win enough international favour to stave off his domestic opponents. His decision to reconcile with Israel in 1990 and the collapse of Soviet patronage for the 'hardline' states, shortly thereafter, left Syria's Assad and Iraq's Hussein, among others, to develop new policies of their own.

In addition to the Iraqi debacle, other developments arose out of the collapse of Soviet power which were to prove ultimately destabilizing to the Gulf sub-region. Yemeni reunification in May 1990 was directly attributable to the loss of South Yemen's Soviet-client status. The larger, more powerful Yemen assumed a pro-Iraqi position during the Gulf War and has tangled dangerously with Saudi Arabia since then on a wide variety of issues including border disputes, oil exploration rights, economic relations and accusations of Saudi meddling in Yemen's internal affairs.[13] Renewed hostilities between forces in the north and south of the country now increase the potential destabilizing effect that a Yemen in chaos could have on the GCC region.

The Palestine Liberation Organization (PLO) is another factor in the Middle East whose own precarious balancing games have been heavily dependent on the macro-balancing act between East and West. Yasser Arafat had taken advantage, however clumsily, of Moscow's unwillingness to let the United States play a hegemonic role in the Middle East. With Israel's international acceptance on the rise in the wake of the collapse of East–West tensions and Gulf patronage on the wane as a result of the PLO's pro-Iraqi Gulf War stance, Arafat finally caved in to American leadership on a peace dialogue.

The demise of the USSR also led to the creation of six newly independent Muslim republics, further widening the eastern flank of the Islamic world, and creating a new battle for regional definition and dominance among Iran, Saudi Arabia and Turkey. The Gulf approach, led by Saudi Arabia, is to continue to practise 'financial diplomacy'. The remainder of a US$1.5 billion Saudi aid package, frozen when the Soviet central government collapsed, is now being disbursed directly to the Central Asian republics.[14] Turkey and Iran have largely departed from their efforts to win influence through cultural persuasion and are instead making economic-based arguments for strong ties to the region. Istanbul emphasizes its position as a gateway to the West in the area of trade and its 'secular, democratic' alternative to indigenous brands of neo-communism and Islamic fundamentalism.[15] Teheran, likewise, has been trying to make the case that it is the most important trading partner for the developing region.

The collapse of the Soviet counterweight in the Middle East has been an interactive factor in most of the dramatic regional developments of the 1990s. But perhaps its ultimate importance has resided in the challenge this has presented to the United States, namely, that of a fork in the road at which greater or lesser involvement in the troubled region are both possible.

External Factors: American Foreign Policy in the Gulf

Washington has long looked to the Gulf region – north and south – as the fulcrum of Middle East stability. Against the backdrop of the post-World War II macro-balancing act between Israel and the Arab world, the 'twin pillars' policy emerged in the 1970s. This Nixon–Kissinger concept placed emphasis on Saudi Arabia and Iran as the harbingers of stability in the region. When the Iranian–American axis was destroyed with the fall of the Shah, and in the midst of the Iran–Iraq War, Washington eventually fell into a policy of 'tilting' towards Iraq in an effort to restore stability. Instead of restoring balance, however, Iraq emerged from the war anxious to utilize its peak military strength against less formidable regional opponents.

The Gulf War of 1990–91 prompted the realization that neither Iraq nor Iran could safely be used to balance the other, prompting a new American policy of 'dual containment'. The resulting high profile American presence provides both opportunity and danger for the Gulf states. Their reluctance to wholeheartedly support containment is evidence of their continuing uncertainty about the 'right' strategic approach.

For the GCC states, the Gulf War provided an awakening as to the limitations of their own deterrent and defensive capabilities. However, it also showed unequivocally that the United States views the region as vital to its own national security.[16] In the aftermath of the war, the US made clear its intention to work with the GCC to further American influence in the Gulf region.[17] However, rather than strengthening the organization, this has prompted the member states to discontinue the introspection begun during the war in favour of cementing bilateral alliance relationships with the United States.

While the unprecedented American commitment to the defence of the Gulf states may lessen their vulnerability *vis-à-vis* Iraq and Iran, it does open them up even further to internal and transnationally generated upheaval. It is not difficult to understand why such comments as Admiral Crowe's praise of Bahrain as 'pound for pound, man for man, the best ally the United States has anywhere in the world', did not receive a lot of media attention in Manama.[18]

In addition to the dangers of the high profile American presence, the dual containment policy is not in any way a recipe for lasting stability in the Gulf. The smaller kingdoms are clearly not willing to dismiss the two northern Gulf powers from their own security equations and have, therefore, been pursuing ties with one or the other at the same time as the United States is attempting to ostracize them.

The United States would clearly like to promote a Middle Eastern security order based on a continuation of the Gulf War coalition. Yet it has further promulgated the misinterpretation of what constitutes a true regional security regime by negotiating bilateral defence agreements with the GCC states rather than a multilateral agreement through the organization. Furthermore, the continued flow of weapons from the United States and other major suppliers to the region guarantees that all of the Gulf states will remain locked in a spiralling arms race, at least for the foreseeable future.

This too contradicts and usurps efforts that have been made to create a stable, collective security arrangement in the region. The wisdom of ignoring the northern Gulf states in that arrangement is an issue on which the GCC states themselves have expressed periodic disquiet and disagreement.

Ramifications of the Gulf War of 1990–91

It was Saddam Hussein's decision to invade neighbouring Kuwait in August 1990 that most impacted the security landscape of the Gulf region and the Middle East as a whole in the post-Cold War era. In some ways, Hussein's move represented more of the same in the endless sub-regional balance-of-power game. However, it also produced some dramatic movement in the political landscape of the Gulf and clarified some unanswered political questions of the post-Cold War era.

For the GCC, the invasion exposed its major shortcoming, namely, that the organizational framework had in no way prepared the Saudis to protect themselves against a major military power such as Iraq.[19] It was built around the security legitimacy the Saudi presence lent to the smaller Gulf monarchies in the face of the Iranian threat. The arsenals of the GCC states are impressive for the size of these nations, but each country suffers from a shortage of manpower. Even after post-Gulf War increases, the total regular armed forces of the GCC countries amount to 216 950 as compared to Iran's 528 000 and Iraq's 382 500.[20] The reliance on high technology equipment as a deterrent proved to be a failed policy during the Gulf War. Yet, this has not slowed the race for acquisition of the 'latest and most lethal conventional weapons' by the states of the region.[21] While it might have been expected that the Gulf War would lead the GCC states to attempt to enhance complementarity and conceive of a long-range integrated plan, any such talk has been overridden by the scramble to purchase more weaponry and cement ties with the West.

Indeed, the 'advice' of the UN Security Council to the troubled Gulf region near the end of the Iran–Iraq War had been to seek a tripolar regional security arrangement among the GCC, Iran and Iraq.[22] The preferred US formula for Gulf security, in keeping with dual containment of the northern powers, was to formalize the Gulf War coalition of Egypt, Syria and the GCC nations. This led to the now-stalled 'Damascus Declaration', based upon the familiar premise that the Lower Gulf nations could purchase security. This time, the payoff was to be the transfer of significant foreign aid to Cairo and Damascus. The 1991 agreement would have created a force of 26 000 to be stationed on the Iraq–Kuwait border.[23] Familiar suspicions of one another's true intentions and a strong negative reaction from Teheran killed the plan before it was ever put into practice, however, providing further evidence that the United States is now expected to serve as the guarantor of GCC security.

The post-Gulf War future of inter-Arab security cooperation is further jeopardized by the cycle of revenge and retribution set off after the defeat of Saddam Hussein. Saudi Arabia did not renew the residence permits of 850 000 Yemenis, whose government supported Iraq during the War. Palestinians and Jordanians were similarly targeted for the pro-Iraqi stances of their regimes and over 300 000 were expelled from Kuwait and other Gulf states.[24] In the aftermath of the war, Saudi Arabia has been much slower to offer support to Islamic and other movements in the Middle East and any such aid now comes with more strings attached.[25]

Despite the clear commitment of the United States to Lower Gulf security, Desert Storm left the GCC nations with an Iraq still under the control of Saddam Hussein and an Islamic Republic of Iran that gained considerably from the face-off between its two worst enemies. The American policy toward Iraq is to wait for Saddam Hussein to be overthrown. In the meantime, his ability to undermine regional stability persists, as evidenced by the October 1994 movement of Iraqi troops back towards the Kuwaiti border. Yet Saudi Arabia and its GCC partners are acutely aware that the demise of Hussein would most probably be linked to success on the part of Kurdish and Shiite movements, neither of which are considered positive alternatives to the status quo situation. In the meantime, despite the restrictions placed on it by successive United Nations resolutions, Saddam Hussein's Iraq is still well-armed, still pumping oil and still maintaining its presence in the Arab League.

Iranian intentions are more obscure than those of Iraq. The GCC states have expressed a willingness to work with Teheran on a regional security arrangement, but this approach is dismissed in both Washington and Cairo as a recipe for future disaster.

For the Gulf monarchs, dual containment is a tremendously high-risk strategy. However, many view the alternative of continuing to alternate between involvement in open conflicts with neighbours to the north as being equally unacceptable. The GCC six can never be sure which country – Iran or Iraq – presents the greater threat.

Internal Factors: National-Transnational Movements

Evidence of social unrest in the Gulf countries has increased since the 1990–91 War. Whereas Islam used to be a cornerstone of cultural solidarity for these nation-states in some of its manifestations, it is now part of the challenge to the legitimacy of their regimes. Yet Islamic movements in the Lower Gulf are less threatening in opposition than are their counterparts in many other parts of the Middle East.[26] State structures in the GCC monarchies are buoyed by the tremendous revenues they control and the economic patronage this leverage buys them with virtually all non-military associations. The impetus to push the demand for Islamicist solutions into civil discontent is, therefore, less strong among populations that are fairly satisfied with the economic performances of their regimes.

As the transnational repercussions of the Iranian revolution continue to reverberate down the Arabian peninsula, however, and there is continued post-Gulf War pressure for greater participation in decision-making structures, the southern Gulf leaders can ill afford to dismiss internal security threats and their possible connections to larger cross-cultural trends.

Gulf elites have responded in the post-1991 period to the sometimes difficult-to-balance calls for Islamization and democratization with incremental concessions and institutional adjustments. What is more threatening than either of these impulses alone is the possibility that they will become further tied to other nascent social movements. The unpredictability of *rentier* economies totally dependent upon oil revenues allows for the possibility of a marriage between relative economic deprivation and Islamization. The class dimension of Middle Eastern and Gulf tensions – the oil-rich 'haves' versus the exploited labourers or 'have-nots' – is another theme which Islamicist movements have seized upon. Large pools of disenfranchised foreign guest-workers, refugees and unemployed youth provide a ready outlet for the revolutionary Islamic idiom.

The demographics of the Lower Gulf region do not bode well for future internal stability. Regional birthrates are among the highest in the world, leading to disproportionately young populations. In Bahrain, half of the population is under the age of 20, contributing to a 25 per cent unemployment rate among males.[27] Foreign guest-workers, brought in *en masse* during the long oil boom have grown to such proportions in these states that their numbers rival those of nationals. The regional average of non-nationals as a percentage of total population in the GCC countries is 47.5 per cent, with a 70 per cent ratio in the United Arab Emirates.[28] It has long been the policy of the Gulf monarchies to deny citizenship to foreign workers and their families, and they became obvious targets of resentment during the Gulf War. Literally millions of non-citizens were forced to flee the peninsula during the early 1990s. Post-war policies of replacing Palestinians, Yemenis and other Arab guest-workers with Asians, thought to be less politically troublesome, has not relieved the potential for tension. Unrest continues to foment among immigrant workers, no matter what their place of origin. Asian immigrant workers waged a violent demonstration in conjunction with an oil refinery strike in Kuwait in August 1993, to protest against what they called 'inadequate living conditions' in that country.[29]

Women's movements are also on the rise and posing a greater threat to social stability in the Gulf in the aftermath of the War. Their connection to calls for democratization are clear, while their ties to Islamicist movements are much less so. Gender politics took to the streets in Saudi Arabia in 1990 and to the polls in Kuwait in 1992. In the infamous 'drive-around demonstration' during the Gulf War, prominent Saudi women protested their inability to legally drive in their country by getting behind the wheels of their family cars and circling through Riyadh.[30] In Kuwait, women's groups have organized debates and other forums to voice their call for the right to vote, to run for elective office and to serve in appointed government posts. Their collective voice was heard by the royal family, which now publicly supports this agenda, pitting themselves against conservative Islamic elements in Kuwaiti society.[31]

Lines of demarcation between internal and external security threats continue to blur in the Gulf, where a combination of oppositional elements have the potential to coalesce and present a real danger to the regimes of the region.

LOOKING TO THE FUTURE: MAJOR CHALLENGES TO LOWER GULF SECURITY

The impact of the Gulf War on the political environment of the region did not provide an escape from the security dilemma which continues to hold all of the Gulf states in its grip. Three major issues must be addressed if any meaningful security dialogue is to be developed. The Gulf States and protagonists from outside the region must jointly consider how this cycle can be broken. The various threats facing all of the states of the region must be articulated and prioritized on a collective agenda. A decision on how to deal with the Islamic Republic of Iran, now in its fifteenth post-revolutionary year, is a particularly high priority. The GCC states must together consider how some degree of cohesion can be achieved to move the Gulf sub-region beyond the archaic balance of power machinations which have so long dominated its security landscape.

Arms and the Regional Security Dilemma

The balance-of-power politics, *realpolitik*, and the notion of credible deterrence continue to define the security panorama of the Middle East. The post-Cold War, post-Gulf War Persian Gulf region finds itself locked in an arms race that is unparalleled in today's international system. In 1994 alone, Iran and Iraq spent a combined US$3.8 billion on arms imports, while the GCC nations spent US$7.35 billion.[32] The spiral effect encouraged by reliance on deterrence calculations of national security is familiar from the Cold War, yet there is a danger in destroying the rough parity which such considerations produce, even in cases where they have not kept the peace. As Cordesman says when describing the security dilemma for the Middle Eastern Gulf states, '[these states] are already so well-armed that even a total embargo on arms would not halt regional conflicts and might well create local imbalances in military capability that would encourage such conflicts'.[33]

The predicament is compounded by the inability of supplier nations to curtail shipments to a region addicted to weapons of all kinds. Despite a clear realization that the Middle Eastern arms race has moved beyond conventional and into the nuclear, chemical and biological realms, the major supplier states – the United States, Western and Eastern European nations, People's Republic of China, North Korea, and selected Latin American suppliers – are unwilling to take collective action to de-escalate the buildups. Since the end of the Cold War, the United States has increased its market share in conventional arms shipments to the region.[34]

Arms control regimes seem to make little difference. Israel persists in its refusal to sign the Nuclear Non-Proliferation Treaty and Iran and Iraq reportedly continue to look for ways in which to develop nuclear capability despite their membership. The 'chemical weapons club' of the Middle East counts Iraq, Iran, Syria, and Libya among its members and biological weapons capability is part of the repertoire of Iraq, Iran and Syria. Egypt and Israel are thought to be included in both the chemical and biological categories as well, although this has not been properly substantiated.[35]

The question is, where will an arms race stop in a region where no amount of deterrence capability seems to be able to eliminate open warfare? The GCC states have embarked on a massive buildup while simultaneously placing themselves under American protection. There is a costly redundancy to this approach. There has been no concerted effort to develop and implement a regional GCC plan which would either take advantage of the new American presence or move to replace it with a more self-reliant regional scheme. Decisions must be made as to whether

Saudi Arabia will complement the American role, develop its own defensive capability, or play the 'swing' role, as it does in OPEC, with its junior Gulf partners. Either the unprecedented, broad commitment by the United States to the GCC nations should be allowed to relieve the pressure posed by bloated, but deeply troubled Iraqi and Iranian military machines, or those nations will have to be included in a regional dialogue.

Iran: Pariah or Player?

The challenge posed by the Islamic Republic of Iran to the southern Gulf region has been compounded over the past fifteen years by the Janus-faced nature of the revolutionary regime's foreign policy. The subject of a GCC containment policy of sorts during its eight-year war with Iraq, Iran is still considered to be a threat in its home region – though, for the moment, the lesser of two evils – in comparison to the regime in Baghdad. Efforts have been made to reduce tensions in the Gulf, but Teheran continues to send mixed signals about its littoral intentions. This leads the Arab peninsular nations to fluctuate between trusting the instinct that Iran must be included in the regional security dialogue and abruptly cutting it out. Two distinct schools of thought have arisen regarding Iran and its position and intentions in the international system of the 1990s. One maintains the image of a terrorist state which should be labelled a pariah and isolated by the international community. US Secretary of State Warren Christopher, for whom the memory of the Carter Administration's hostage crisis debacle has probably not faded, is a principal proponent of this approach. The other asserts that Iran has never been a pariah, particularly not in the economic realm, and that its overtures towards taking a constructive role in the Gulf and Central Asia should be encouraged. Japan and Germany have shown through actions more than words that this is the interpretation which guides their respective relationships with Teheran. Both interpretations receive sustenance from the international actions of the Islamic Republic. The pragmatic Iran signs water agreements with Qatar and establishes free-trade zones in the islands of Kish and Qeshm while the radical Iran sets up installations for Silkworm missiles on islands that are supposed to be jointly administered with the United Arab Emirates, and stands tall in its rejection of the Israeli–Palestinian peace accord.

Teheran's position *vis-à-vis* the principle of national sovereignty continues to be in doubt in the mid-1990s, as does the internal stability of a regime which, to its credit, has survived far longer than most analysts predicted it would. The combination of periodic aggression in the region and continued internal competition for power makes the Islamic Republic a dangerous neighbour for the six GCC states. Yet, the question remains, can Iran be discounted from any Gulf security regime which hopes to be successful?

Accepting that Iran is locked in a domestic tug-of-war between pragmatists and ideologues, realizing that its position on all internal and external political issues is therefore subject to sudden change, an effort must nevertheless be made to identify the dominant foreign policy trend. States that continue to wait for the fall of the Ayatollahs after fifteen years are failing to help shape the security environment of this most important region. Several realities about Iran's own strategic position must be recognized. Foremost among these is the extremely dangerous 'neighbourhood' in which Iran resides. One way to gauge this is through refugee flows into the Republic from the warring and unstable nations which surround it: Afghanistan, Azerbaijan, the Kurdish and Shiite populations of Iraq, and Tajikistan. Secondly, there is Iran's extreme vulnerability to any actions which threaten to cut off its access to the Straits of Hormuz, its economic lifeline.[36] The GCC decision to side with Arab Iraq during its eight-year war with Iran, coupled with the tacit support of Baghdad by the United States and the USSR, were enough to orient the Republic in the direction of an 'independent' and quite belligerent Gulf policy.

Volatility and careless bravado continue to characterize contemporary Iranian foreign policy, but there also seems to be a recognition that rhetoric cannot be substituted for realistic security arrangements. If this was not clear prior to Desert Storm, it is most certainly appreciated now. Realism has been ascendant in Teheran for a number of years, apparent in its return to active participation in regional and international fora (the United Nations, the Economic Cooperation Organization and the Islamic Conference Organization), Iran's cautious, economy-driven approach to the new Muslim republics of Central Asia and its focus on promoting its own credibility and creditworthiness during the 1990–91 Gulf War. With several notable exceptions, particularly in Africa, Teheran has ceased to deal primarily with Islamic movements at the sub-regime level and has re-established active diplomacy with heads-of-state, even in Iraq, Kuwait and Saudi Arabia.[37]

Yet, GCC policy towards Iran continues to be heavily influenced by the American decision to focus on the secondary rather than the primary trend in Iranian international relations. The insecurity of the regime in Teheran, not to mention the tensions between pragmatists and ideologues who continue to vie for dominance, is exacerbated by policies which seek to target Iran rather than include it in the regional security dialogue. Reinforcement of a positive international position in Teheran should be actively pursued by the Gulf nations. This is the direction in which they seemed to be moving in 1991 when the six agreed at a GCC ministerial meeting that even if it did not seem wise to fully include Iran in the dialogue, all future security arrangements should at least be acceptable to Teheran.[38] Public pronouncements such as these could reduce the risk of future 'Abu Musa' type actions, arguably designed to show by force that Iran will not accept a pariah status in its own region.

Saudi Arabia and the GCC: A Failure to Lead?

The al-Saud dynasty emerged from the Gulf War with huge expenses to meet but an enhanced position in the Middle East security system. Forced to test what Twinam calls their 'cadillac-style' military establishment,[39] the Saudis realized quickly that their post-oil boom defence investments were no substitute for an alliance with the West. For their part, other major players including the United States, the European Union, Russia, Israel and the other Arab nations were forced to recognize the key role which the Kingdom plays in Middle Eastern economic and security power-balancing. For the Saudis and all who witnessed their bold hosting of Desert Shield and Desert Storm, the Gulf War was a lesson in political realism. The dollar diplomacy – arms acquisitions unsupported by trained personnel, blank cheques to Arab states and sub-state movements – did not enhance Saudi security. However, the policy response in the following three years has shown characteristic indecisiveness in Riyadh. Some actions have been taken to consolidate the Saudis' new international prestige, including a re-establishment of diplomatic ties with Russia, Mainland China, and Iran and a diplomatic link with Israel. Support of Islamicist and national causes, such as that of the Palestinians, is now funnelled through international and regional organizations. And, perhaps most telling, Saudi Arabia reportedly played a leading role in bringing the GCC into the 'multilateral talks' between the Arab states and Israel, launched in Moscow in January 1992.[40] It has also lent its weight to the notion of suspending the Arab economic boycott of Israel in return for important concessions.[41]

While the Saudis have shown themselves to be committed to furthering GCC security, there is still no clear doctrine on how this will be accomplished. The Kingdom's security relationship with the United States has not been formally cemented, despite a strong desire on the part of the Americans to sign and seal a formal defence pact. A true GCC alliance has been relegated to the back burner in favour of internal discussion as to whether the size of Saudi armed forces should be doubled and whether they should be equipped to fight a large-scale war.[42] The solution which the United States favoured – the GCC+2 formula which shaped the now-stalled Damascus Agreement – was implicitly rejected in Riyadh as unsalable to the Saudi population and to a very attentive audience in Teheran.

For the time being, the old policy of unrelenting arms purchases has gained the upper hand again and bold talk of encouraging the overthrow of Saddam has faded into the recesses of Gulf War rhetoric. Bold extra-regional moves towards peace have been unmatched inside the GCC parameters, where Saudi Arabia has proven unwilling to extricate itself from the many bilateral conflicts which spoil its relationships with its junior regional partners. These unseemly quarrels have escalated into violence on several occasions in the last several years,[43] leading Iran's Foreign Minister Velayati to publicly question why his nation should be left out of a club whose current members hardly seem to be able to get along with each other.[44]

If Saudi Arabia is to help build the GCC into an effective regional organization that can meet the challenges of the new century, it will have to resolve these disputes, erase the lack of trust between members, and substitute a decisive regional agenda for the dollar diplomacy of the past twenty years.

PROSPECTS FOR A RE-ENGINEERING OF GULF SECURITY

Despite its clear shortcomings as a security institution, the GCC has remained in a position to impact the future of not only the Lower Gulf region, but the Middle East as a whole. The respect afforded it by the United States in the regional dialogue provides a guarantee of this.

As the GCC forges its future course, it is worth noting that there are many constants in the security equation with which it must work. The most threatening factor in regional politics continues to be the lack of balance between the southern and northern Gulf nations. The GCC cannot, on its own, withstand an attack from either Iran or Iraq. To continue to engage with these nations in an arms race that is expanding beyond conventional and into biological, chemical and nuclear weaponry is therefore a highly questionable strategy. The Gulf states have tried to offset this troubling scenario by resorting to another familiar aspect of regional politics, namely the acceptance of the role of the external power in redressing regional imbalances. Great Britain, Russia and the United States have all been accused of severe meddling in the politics of the region, and yet the role into which they step during times of crisis has never been successfully eliminated.

It seems highly unlikely that this role, now filled by the United States, will be eliminated in the 1990s. The important changes in the security equation provide a near-guarantee of this. Firstly, the collapse of the USSR has eliminated the Cold War cover for the hegemonic aspirations of indigenous powers. Saddam Hussein proved this with his invasion of Kuwait. Questions about Iran's intentions continue to abound. If the historical record proves a reliable indicator, it will only be a matter of time before Egypt and Syria conceive of ways in which to answer these threats, and in a more direct way than that which the Damascus Declaration would have provided.

The collapse of the anti-Israel coalition is the second environmental change which will also have important repercussions on the developing regional security picture. It, too, changes the context in which offensive and defensive strategies have been conceived over the past 45 years. Indeed, it also opens the way for inter-Arab tensions to come all the way to the surface, with a likely continued overflow into Iran, Turkey, Afghanistan and other contiguous states.

In short, changes such as these result in both danger and opportunity for the Gulf region. If the balance-of-power mechanism remains the security framework of choice in the region, then it is clear that we will continue to see naked aggression, lack of respect for territorial boundaries and insatiable appetites for weaponry. A transformation in the security framework would require a concerted, inclusive, multilateral approach to be allowed to gain precedence over the bilateral security arrangements of the past.[45]

The Gulf Cooperation Council provides an avenue through which this can be accomplished. Up to this point, it has not been allowed to live up to its potential as an institutional channel. This is largely attributable to its own unbalanced nature, with Saudi Arabia greatly outweighing its junior partners in every dimension of power. This makes it unrealistic for Saudi Arabia to rely on the GCC for its own security needs and makes it dangerous for the smaller states to trust in Saudi intentions *vis-à-vis* the organization. If the Council is to provide a true security regime for its members, it will have to broaden to encompass all the nations of the broader Gulf region. This would include Iran and Yemen in the shorter term and Iraq at that point at which it re-emerges as a potentially constructive presence in the region. The difficulty of achieving this task is precisely what would ultimately increase the value of the organization way beyond its current, largely symbolic scope.

To pursue inclusiveness where there has previously been only contention would represent a dramatic re-engineering of Gulf politics. It is a tall order for a troubled region. However, in the wake of substantial progress on the Israeli–Palestinian conflict, it can hardly be considered a mere utopian vision. Saudi Arabia, Iran and the United States must give precedence to long-term over short-term strategy if this redirection is to take place.

NOTES

1. For a detailed account of the history of southern Gulf cooperation and the founding of the GCC, see R. K. Ramazani, *The Gulf Cooperation Council: Record and Analysis* (Charlottesville, VA: University Press of Virginia, 1988).
2. The GCC was formally established on 2 May 1981, approximately ten years after the majority of its members gained their independence from Great Britain.
3. The only two GCC nations that do not belong to OPEC are Bahrain and Oman. Moreover, the northern Gulf powers of Iraq and Iran are leading OPEC members.
4. See James A. Bill, 'Resurgent Islam in the Persian Gulf', *Foreign Affairs*, Volume 63, no. 1, 1984, pp. 108–27, for a description of Iranian 'export' efforts during this period.
5. Ramazani, *The Gulf Cooperation Council*, op. cit., p. 194.
6. Ramazani raised such questions in *The Gulf Cooperation Council*, op. cit., p. 96, and Kenneth Katzman asked similar questions about the same force under its new title – the 'Peninsular Shield' – in 'The Gulf Cooperation Council: Prospects for Collective Security', in M. E. Ahrari and James H. Noyes (eds), *The Persian Gulf after the Cold War* (New York: Praeger, 1993).
7. *Gulf States Newsletter*, Volume 447, 19 October 1992, p. 4.
8. The Hawar Islands are in dispute between Bahrain and Qatar. To the surprise of Bahrain and Saudi Arabia, since the latter was trying to mediate the conflict, Qatar took the dispute to the International Court of Justice in July, 1991. For a description, see Katzman, 'The Gulf Cooperation Council', op. cit., p. 208. In the post-Gulf War period, the dispute has hampered GCC progress in that both nations have periodically refused to attend high-level meetings in which the other was involved. See Mohammed Faour, *The Arab World after Desert Storm* (Washington, DC: United States Institute of Peace, 1993), p. 92. The conflicts between Saudi Arabia and the three smaller Gulf nations are all due to border disputes as well.
9. Katzman, 'The Gulf Cooperation Council', op. cit., pp. 206–10.
10. The United States signed formal defence pacts with Bahrain (1991), Kuwait (1991), Qatar (1991) and the UAE (1993). It has also renewed access

agreements with Oman (1990), and is negotiating with Saudi Arabia. See John Duke Anthony, 'Betwixt War and Peace: the 12th GCC Heads of State Summit', *Middle East Insight*, Volume VIII, no. 6, July–October 1992, p. 58.

11. For a more detailed discussion of this dynamic, see William D. Watson, 'Economic Prospects for the Gulf Cooperation Council', *The Journal of Energy and Development*, Vol. 17, no. 2, 1993, p. 173.
12. Stephen Zunes writes that 'most Bahrainis see their biggest threat not from Iraq or Iran, nor even from internal radical movements, but from competition by Dubai and other regional commercial rivals'. Zunes, 'The US–GCC Relationship: Its Rise and Potential Fall', *Middle East Policy*, Vol. II, no. 1, 1993, p. 110.
13. For more on the troubled relationship between Saudi Arabia and Yemen, see Mark N. Katz, 'Yemeni Unity and Saudi Security', *Middle East Policy*, Vol. 1, no. 1, 1992, p. 117.
14. James H. Noyes, 'Policies of the United States and the Commonwealth of Independent States: A Post-Cold War Perspective', in Ahrari and Noyes (eds), *The Persian Gulf after the Cold War*, op. cit., p. 23.
15. See Allen J. Frank, 'Turkish–Iranian Relations', *US–Iran Review*, Vol. 2, no. 1, January 1994, p. 15.
16. See Zunes, 'The US–GCC Relationship', op. cit., p. 106 for a discussion of US reliance on oil imports from the Gulf.
17. In a March 1991 speech to a joint session of Congress, President Bush stated that in the wake of the Gulf War, the United States would be looking to promote regional security efforts in the Middle East. The GCC, one of the few such frameworks already in existence, quickly became a focal point for the administration. See Robert E. Hunter, 'US Policy toward the Middle East after Iraq's Invasion of Kuwait', in Robert O. Freedman (ed.), *The Middle East after Iraq's Invasion of Kuwait* (Miami: University Press of Florida, 1993), p. 64.
18. See Zunes, 'The US–GCC Relationship', op. cit., p. 105.
19. Abdulaziz Bashir and Stephen Wright, 'Saudi Arabia: Foreign Policy after the Gulf War', *Middle East Policy*, Vol. 1, no. 1, 1992, p. 109.
20. *The Military Balance 1992–93* (London: International Institute for Strategic Studies, 1994).
21. See Anthony Cordesman, *After the Storm: The Changing Military Balance in the Middle East* (Boulder, CO: Westview Press, 1993), p. 381.
22. United Nations Security Council Resolution 598, Article Eight.
23. Katzman, 'The Gulf Cooperation Council', op. cit., p. 203.
24. See Seteney Shami, 'The Social Implications of Population Displacement and Resettlement: An Overview With a Focus on the Arab Middle East', *International Migration Review*, Vol. XXVII, no. 1, 1993, p. 17.
25. At a January 1994 meeting, Saudi Arabia finally agreed to provide support for infrastructure projects in the Gaza Strip and Jericho, but specified that the $100 million in support would go through international agencies. See *Federal Broadcast Information Service*, The Near East and North Africa, 26 January 1994.
26. The Muslim Brotherhood and various offshoots in Egypt and FIS in Algeria, for example, pose much greater risks to ruling elites than do Islamic movements in the Lower Gulf.

27. See F. Gregory Gause III, *Oil Monarchies: Domestic Security Challenges in the Arab Gulf States* (New York: Council on Foreign Relations Press, 1994), p. 150.
28. Ibid., p. 6.
29. *Federal Broadcast Information Service*, The Near East and North Africa, 9 August 1993.
30. For a more detailed description of this incident, see Joseph Wright Twinam, 'The Gulf Cooperation Council Since the Gulf War: The State of the States', *Middle East Policy*, Vol. 1, no. 4, 1992, p. 102.
31. See Mary Ann Tetreault, 'Civil Society in Kuwait: Protected Spaces and Women's Rights', *The Middle East Journal*, Vol. 47, no. 2, Spring 1993, pp. 288–9.
32. Cordesman, *After the Storm*, op. cit., p. 38.
33. Ibid., p. 33.
34. Ibid., p. 43.
35. See Efraim Karsh, Martin S. Navias and Philip Sabin, *Non-Conventional Weapons Proliferation in the Middle East* (Oxford: The Clarendon Press, 1993), p. 2.
36. See Eric Hooglund, 'Iran's Foreign Policy Interests', *US–Iran Review*, Vol. 1, no. 8, November 1993, pp. 8–9.
37. Ibid., p. 9.
38. See *Iran Focus*, Vol. 4, no. 1, January 1991, p. 3.
39. See Twinam, 'The Gulf Cooperation Council', op. cit., p. 128.
40. See *Gulf States Newsletter*, op. cit., p. 3.
41. See F. Gregory Gause III, 'Saudi Arabia: Desert Storm and After', in Freedman (ed.), *The Middle East after Iraq's Invasion of Kuwait*, op. cit., p. 220.
42. Ibid.
43. The most serious border incident involving Saudi Arabia took place in September 1992 when three were left dead after a Saudi–Qatari skirmish at Al-Khafus. Riyadh denied that its forces were involved, blaming the incident on 'bedouins' from the two countries. But the incident prompted Qatar to withdraw its 200 troops from the GCC Peninsular Shield force. See the *Gulf States Newsletter*, op. cit., p. 3.
44. See Nora Boustany, 'Iran Seeks Wider Mideast Role', *Washington Post*, 12 October 1992.
45. Anthony, 'Iran in GCC Dynamics', *Middle East Policy*, 1993, Vol. II, no. 3, pp. 107–20.

7 Change and Continuity in the Middle East Arms Race

Aaron Karp

INTRODUCTION

Progress towards a durable peace in the Middle East has been painfully slow, its path littered with false starts, failed schemes and disappointment. The greatest accomplishments of the peace process are usually understood to be limited almost exclusively to the political sphere in which agreements between Israel and Egypt, the PLO and Jordan stand out as landmarks. Despite steps towards political accommodation, the Middle Eastern armed forces remain the source of greatest international concern and one of the least promising areas for restraint. Nonetheless, it is becoming increasingly clear that the military confrontation – historically the greatest threat to stability, life and property in the region – is not what it once was.

In some respects, military affairs have lost none of their dominance in Middle Eastern security. All the countries of the region maintain large armed forces, most continue to modernize their equipment and some still are expanding the size of their forces. But few if any of the armed forces of the Middle East appear as menacing as they did thirty, twenty or even ten years ago.

Slowly but surely, the race for military superiority in the Middle East has come to an end. The pace of modernization has slowed significantly, and some countries are even allowing their armies to shrink. The trend is clearest in the declining importance of conventional armaments, but it has begun to include restraint in other kinds of weaponry as well. Almost fifty years after the establishment of the State of Israel created an environment of unparalleled tension, the arms race in the Middle East has lost much of its desperation and immediacy.

The decline of the Middle East arms race deserves wider recognition, but it is not in and of itself a reason for celebration. Its foundations lie exclusively in domestic interests and official perceptions. These are not weak forces, but they require considerable reinforcing if they are to form the basis for a long-term settlement of regional disputes. Any informal process of arms control is vulnerable to disruption from previously unimagined events, in the absence of the institutional mechanisms to minimize their effects.

In the Middle East, the process has been reversed temporarily by events such as the 1982 Beka'a Valley War or the 1991 Gulf War. But the effects of such events consistently fade as stronger long-term interests re-establish themselves. Time and again, major arms deals have created the impression that all restraint has been lost, suggesting that the region was plunging ever deeper into a hopeless spiral of arming and counter-arming, a process doomed to lead to war. Upon reflection, though, it has become apparent that hysterical arms buying is a thing of the past. While there have been a few exceptional arms deals, these have done no more than interrupt the overall downward trends in regional military procurement.

Despite the declining danger of regional armaments competition, the roles of regional confidence-building and arms control proposals are no less important than in the past. However, rather than being required to transform regional security politics, Middle Eastern arms control is needed more to re-enforce existing trends. Like other forces affecting regional security, their effects will not be revolutionary but incremental, supporting processes which are already changing the nature of the region. Even so, such measures are essential in order to insulate the gains of recent years, to help insure that factors outside the conventional balance cannot undermine the stability that has emerged so fortuitously.

A Hidden Transformation

The failure to appreciate this unprecedented change in Middle Eastern security is strikingly similar to the greatest blunder of contemporary political science, namely the failure to anticipate the collapse of communism and the end of the Cold War.[1] Five years after the events in the Soviet Union and Eastern Europe, a lively debate has emerged in intellectual circles trying to allocate the blame for that failure.[2] The essential causes of our shortsightedness probably lay within the blinding grip of powerful assumptions and ideologies and the compulsions of political pragmatism and expediency. The practical causes, however, may have been nothing more than lack of imagination and satisfaction with the status quo. While few would admit to liking the Cold War, virtually all responsible observers accepted it; the Cold War was seen as a preferable state of affairs, certainly much better than the worst disasters we could conjecture.[3] The most exciting and influential policies of the Cold War – from *Ostpolitik* and *détente* to arms control and confidence building – aimed not so much at ending superpower competition as at managing it, attenuating its worst aspects while preserving the parts we accepted.

The Middle East is not Europe and its strategic environment is very different from that of the Cold War. Unlike post-1945 Europe, it has seen full-scale warfare between key antagonists, it is marked by widespread unhappiness with the political status quo, territorial divisions remain in dispute and ethnic, religious and ideological rifts have not been allowed to wither. But the status quo is not without its benefits, and it is widely understood that many governments have little interest in changing it. Just as in Europe of the latter Cold War years, Middle Eastern politics tends to inhibit and conceal fundamental change.

The transformation of Middle East security politics has been obscured by many factors, but none greater than the conventional assumption that the region remains the most dangerous place on earth. The numbing repetition of clichés makes it difficult to see the trends moving in the opposite direction.

The decline of the Middle East arms race has been a gentle process, almost invisible behind the rhetoric of political polarization and confrontation. Most regional leaders have an interest in emphasizing only the most provocative acts of their neighbours, not their acts of restraint. In a region in which words often matter far more than deeds, the real trends of geopolitical reality can be easy to miss. To be sure, all countries in the Middle East continue to buy new military equipment, often acquiring advanced weapons and support systems in disturbingly immodest quantities. Yet it has been a long time since the region saw a real arms race.

Change has also been concealed by excessive expectations. By identifying regional peace with the multinational peace process, demands for a comprehensive settlement (including resolution of the Golan Heights problem and establishment of a Palestinian state), overall conventional arms control and nuclear and chemical disarmament, ambitious proposals cast a dark shadow over lesser – but more tangible – achievements. They also confuse the most important lessons of the superpower experience, which demonstrated that there is no inherent link between peace and arms control. The Soviet-American arms control dialogue did not appreciably reduce tensions, and the initial rise of *détente* only permitted the most humble of arms control measures.[4] Stability between the superpowers had other, more fundamental, origins in national self-interest.

Often, we simply have not known what to look for. The passions of confrontation naturally lead responsible observers to hope for radically different politics of mutual respect and accommodation. While no one can criticize such longings, grand aspirations can be emphasized to the exclusion of less dramatic progress. One of the innumerable ironies of

Middle East politics is that all but the most extreme voices clamour for peace, but we do not always know how to recognize them. Peace is not necessarily the opposite of confrontation. Rather it is, above all, the absence of war. While universal amity among nations will always be the long-term goal of international diplomacy, in the short term the avoidance of war is no small accomplishment. There are many serious security problems facing the Middle East today, but the danger of major war is probably less than at any time in modern memory.

One need look only to the former Yugoslavia, the Russian periphery or central Africa to find regions grappling with more immediate threats to human life. The dangers of weapons of mass destruction, long a critical element in the Middle Eastern security equation, are still of some significance in the region today, but they pose considerably more urgent threats in South Asia or the Korean peninsula.

Even so, military dangers remain serious. The mobilization crisis triggered by Iraq's dispatch of troops to the Kuwaiti border in October 1994 illustrated the continuing relevance of conventional forces. Confrontations between Saudi Arabia and Yemen and the Gulf sheikhdoms in the winter of 1994–95 showed that war scares cannot be dismissed as an Iraqi monopoly either. Non-conventional forces, nuclear, biological and chemical weapons and ballistic missiles have become more prominent than ever before. The continual loss of life – whether from Muslim extremism in Algeria, Egypt and Israel, the endless war of succession in Sudan or chaos and terror in Kurdish lands – leaves no doubt that the emerging regional order is not idyllic. But compared to past decades, the Middle East today is more stable than at any time since the collapse of the Ottoman empire.

Ending the Middle East Arms Race?

Despite the progress of the Middle East peace process, major arms deals have continued, leading many observers to the conclusion that the resolution of the Arab–Israeli conflict will not have an appreciable effect on military spending and armaments competition.[5] Some go so far as to question the value of a peace process that allows an arms race to proceed apparently unchecked.[6]

While countries throughout the Middle East continue to buy arms, often in prodigious quantities, their goals and rationales have changed. A few of the smaller Gulf states are expanding their conventional forces. Virtually all the others are concentrating their resources to minimize the effects of inevitable reductions. Rather than expanding their armed forces or investing in new capabilities, they are concentrating on modernization of existing forces. Their arms investments tend to go primarily into new equipment to preserve the utility of forces that reached their maximum size years ago. While this is not the conduct of content and secure states who have no quarrel with their neighbours, neither is it the armament strategy of countries planning to go to war in the foreseeable future.

The events behind this transformation have never been concealed. Many were highly publicized as they occurred. But their strategic significance has been obscured by the nature of the process. Instead of appearing in a single, swift revolution of the sort typically sought in General Assembly resolutions or ambitious regional disarmament proposals, change came slowly and incrementally over a period of decades. Usually it has come not through well-publicized shifts in policy, but in the form of decisions not taken and options not pursued.

Ironically, the roots of this restraint go back to the huge build-ups that followed the 1967 and 1973 wars. Even while the general military build-ups accelerated after these conflicts, the seeds of restraint were germinating. Economic forces played a role, as did diplomatic and military factors. These expansions, whether due to fear or ambition, came at tremendous cost, driving military spending up above 20 per cent of annual GNP throughout the region. But high levels of military spending, although painful, were sustainable as long as military requirements remained extreme.[7]

What allowed high levels of military spending to be reduced was the reduction in perceived threats. More than anything else, it was the gradual acceptance of the status quo that enabled more and more countries in the Middle East to slow their arms procurement. By the mid-1980s the process was virtually complete among Israel and its neighbours. In the mid-1990s, the logic of the status quo has extended to most countries throughout the Middle East.

States in the traditional crucible of Middle Eastern tension – around Israel – no longer fear for their survival. Grand ambitions – achievable only at the direct expense of the security of their neighbours – are gone. While all states of the region still have goals that extend beyond their borders, they understand that these can be achieved only through political initiatives. With this change has come a corresponding change in the roles of armed forces. Instead of being maximized for interstate warfare, they stand ready for small-scale operations and to suppress domestic strife. As in Europe after World War II, general and unrestrained war is increasingly unacceptable.[8] The danger of general war in the Middle East comes not from deliberate choice, but from mistakes and miscalculation. Indeed, the only convincing explanation for Iraq's disastrous war over Kuwait in 1991 is Saddam Hussein's blundering.[9]

The changing priorities and exigency of defence planning can be seen most easily in the reduced pace of military procurement, as well as in the relaxed readiness of the armed forces and greater willingness to divert troops to non-military tasks. Outside forces play no visible role in the process. Foreign arms suppliers have placed virtually no restraints on their Middle Eastern clients, with the partial exception of Iran and the complete exception of Iraq. Rising economic pressure also cannot explain the shift in priorities, which extends beyond simple budget reductions to include widespread reductions in the proportion of GNP going to the military. While many countries in the region have fewer economic resources than they did at the height of the oil boom, none are so poor that they could not rapidly increase defence spending, especially if there were a consensus that national security was in jeopardy.[10] A few countries, moreover, have enjoyed exceptional economic prosperity in the 1990s – Israel is the most obvious example – yet are still allowing military spending to decline.

In the absence of external compulsion, the only forces left to influence the Middle Eastern armaments competition are internal. At the basis of the process is a change in perceptions. While no one pretends that the region is becoming as safe and secure as Western Europe or North America, its leaders show little of the fear and anxiety that characterized their security planning for decades. It is this change in official attitudes and domestic interests that leads so many highly diverse countries to adopt increasingly similar security policies. The process has no relationship to the reduction in Soviet–American tensions as codified in the arms control agreements of the early 1970s. Nor does it reflect any clear reciprocity; one searches chronologies in vain for even a shred of evidence suggesting that one country shows restraint in response to the forbearance of another.[11] Rather the process can be understood exclusively in terms of domestic responses to a generally improving politico-military environment.

The transformation of Middle Eastern security came about unevenly, affecting different areas in different ways. We are accustomed to thinking of the Middle East as a single region in which innumerable linkages make it impossible to separate individual conflicts, in which the Iran–Iraq conflict threatened the entire Persian Gulf, in which Iraq could credibly threaten to escalate its conflict over Kuwait by attacking Israel, in which Saudi efforts to deter Iran and Iraq implicitly threaten Israel and countries as distant as Afghanistan and in which Iran and Libya could directly support terrorism against Israel. This created a unique regional security dilemma, a web in which resolution of individual disputes could be accomplished only through a comprehensive peace resolving all conflicts together.

While there is considerable truth in this perspective, it also unnecessarily complicates the problems of regional diplomacy. In practice, the security environment around Israel has evolved along one path and around the Persian Gulf along another. The linkages between the two cannot be ignored, but neither should they be exaggerated.

The situation around Israel was the first to yield to the logic of mutual acceptance. One by one, Israel's neighbours became reconciled to its existence. The lessons of military defeat were an essential part of this process. By the mid-1980s all sides had abandoned the dream of acquiring strategic superiority and achieving political goals through military conquest. While the armed forces had not lost all relevance, they had

Fig. 7.1 Arms imports in the Middle East, 1981–91 (in constant 1991 US Dollars)

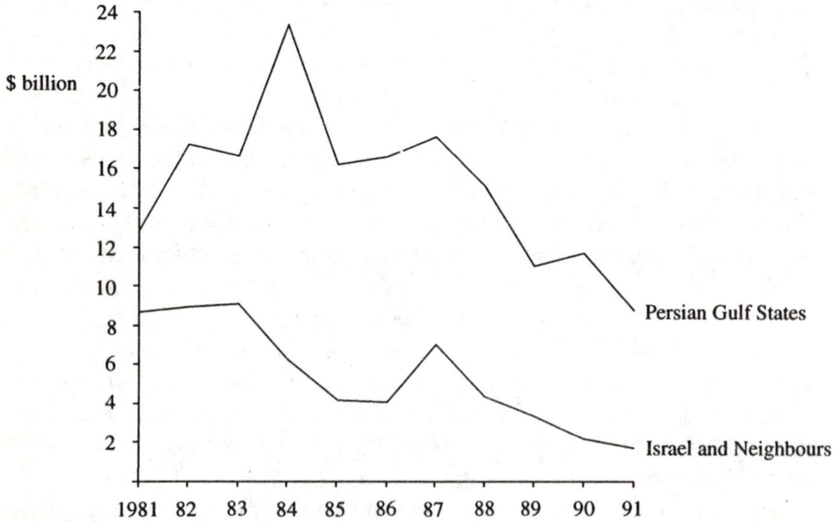

Notes 1. Persian Gulf countries included here are Kuwait, Iran, Iraq Oman, Qatar, Saudi Arabia, and the UAE.

2. Egypt, Israel, Jordan, Lebanon and Syria.

Source: *World Military Expenditures and Arms Transfers 1991–1992* (US Arms Control and Disarmament Agency, 1994).

ceased to be a serious instrument of geopolitical change.[12] This is manifested in the procurement choices and deployment patterns which became increasingly defensive. While the neighbouring military establishments were not exactly allowed to wither away, they ceased to grow and, in some cases, actually shrank.

This transformation first affected Jordan, which swiftly came to accept – *de facto* if not in formal policy – the loss of the West Bank in the 1967 War. Small and internally divided, Jordan could not hope to challenge Israeli power militarily. After the 1970 crises with the PLO and Syria, moreover, Jordan came to rely on indirect security guarantees from Jerusalem. By the late 1970s the Jordanian military began a steep decline. King Hussein signed his last major arms deals in 1982 (for Mirage F-1 fighters and American ground radar). After these deals, Jordan ceased to modernize its army seriously.[13] While major arms deals were discussed and sometimes even negotiated, none were finalized. The sole exception was a deal to buy Mirage-2000 fighter planes in 1988, which was cancelled the following year.

Fig. 7.2 Arms imports by Israel and neighbouring states, 1981–91 (in constant 1991 US Dollars)

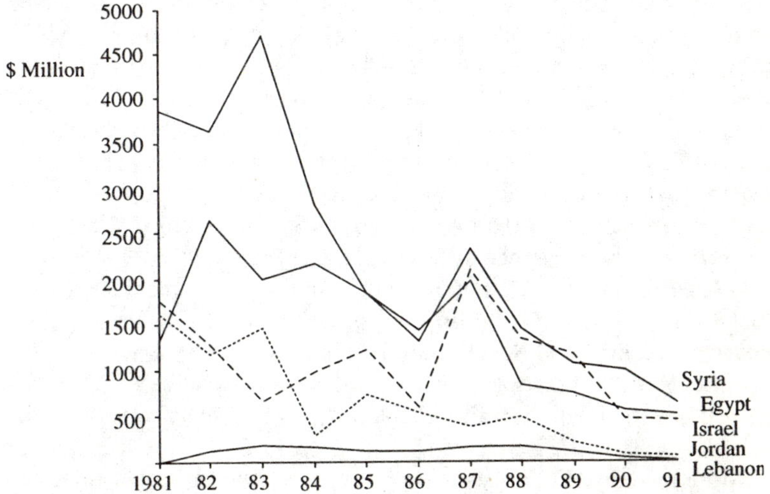

Source: *World Military Expenditures and Arms Transfers 1991–1992* (US Arms Control and Disarmament Agency, 1994).

New equipment has been acquired, but almost exclusively by happenstance. The most impressive example came when Saddam Hussein gave Jordan several hundred armoured vehicles his forces had captured from Iran. Lucky breaks, however, could do no more than slow a broader pattern of contraction. In the late 1980s, Jordan began to expedite the decline of its forces, cannibalizing weaponry for spare parts and selling excess stocks to raise capital.[14] The very idea of excess arms was an extraordinary innovation in the Middle East.

A smaller recent transaction is especially illuminating. In November 1994 seven Jordanian F-5E fighters previously declared in excess of requirements and decommissioned were sold to Singapore in a deal worth $21 million. Only a cursory effort was made to replace these aircraft and later abandoned, although the sale will help to finance the modernization of Jordan's remaining F-5 fleet.[15] Other, more marketable equipment such as helicopters and transport aircraft has been sold off as well. Behind these sales lies a new security strategy. Like many other nations that do not face a major military threat, Jordan has dropped the strategy of relying on large standing forces in favour of maintaining a small but highly-qualified cadre. Although this cadre cannot defend the nation, it will serve as a basis for long-term training and expansion should regional threats re-emerge.

Egypt's decision to step back from strategic parity with Israel was more tacit. Instead of a clear decision or change in strategic policy, a series of events gradually led in that direction, events with a clear cumulative direction. The path that emerged was not entirely intentional, but Egyptian leaders did not vigorously try to pursue others. The first step came when Anwar Sadat severed the nation's arms relationship with Moscow in 1973, even though he had no alternative supplier. This decision can be described only as a massive change in priorities; Sadat calculated that his country did not need the assurance of Soviet military aid sufficiently to justify the loss in autonomy.[16] After signing the Camp David accords five years later, Sadat found a new supplier in the United States. But American aid was never as generous as Soviet assistance had been. The strict formula for American military assistance ensured that Israel always received considerably more ($1.8 to $1.3 billion annually), while Israel also has greater wealth and domestic resources.

More recently, Egypt has been one of the greatest beneficiaries of the end of the Cold War, receiving hundreds of 1960s-vintage M-60 tanks, armoured personnel carriers and other equipment decommissioned by United States forces in Europe. This 'cascade' served primarily to permit Egypt to finally get rid of 1950s-vintage Soviet hardware. More serious modernization includes the assembly of roughly 500 M-1 tanks and the purchase of some 160 F-16 fighters which will form the real nucleus of Egypt's future military capability.

Despite the limits imposed by American aid policy, Egypt has displayed little interest in striking out on its own, having abandoned most efforts at domestic arms production and made few major agreements with European suppliers or the Soviet successor states. The nation's extreme economic difficulties make it impossible for it to sign major new agreements except under tremendous pressure, while peace with Israel removes any motives for such investment.

Syria's transformation came about not through changes in policy goals so much as from the lessons of war, the pressures of economics and technology, and strategic choice. In 1982, Syria found itself more isolated than ever after its disastrous Beka'a Valley war with Israel. Fighting alone – except for some co-ordination with Palestinian factions – it suffered the most one-sided defeat in the history of Middle Eastern conflict up to that point.[17] Among the most prominent casualties were Syrian military self-esteem and trust in its Soviet-designed military hardware. While Moscow and its Eastern European allies were delighted to sell replacement equipment, and Syria bought readily, there was no possibility of matching Israel's technical wizardry. The arms shipments that followed – including over 1400 T-72 tanks, 2400 other armoured vehicles, 200 combat aircraft and air defence missiles including the massive SA-5 – only confirmed Syria's quantitative superiority, something that was never in doubt.

The futility of building further numerical superiority became evident to Damascus by 1986. Syrian officials ceased speaking of pursuit of 'strategic parity' with Israel and allowed defence purchases to decline rapidly.[18] Smaller purchases of Soviet-style equipment continue to this day. Since 1988, a total of 70 MiG-29s have been ordered to replace the obsolete MiG-23s.[19] At this rate, the MiG-29 force may grow to 120–150 by the end of the decade. But this should be compared to an Israeli force of F-16s and F-15s that soon will amount to 350 aircraft. Smaller orders are adding more modern SU-24 bombers and SA-10 air-defence systems to the Syrian inventories. In each case, the main effect is not to build overall capabilities but to preserve elite units from total obsolescence.

Syria's investments in new Russian and East European armaments make it the leading arms customer for several ex-Warsaw Pact producers.[20] Although its suppliers undoubtedly would sell even greater quantities of even more advanced hardware if Damascus asked, Syrian officials have not shown much interest. The money is there; in the early 1990s, defence spending amounted to an average of just 10 per cent of GNP, far below the 20 per cent levels the nation tolerated ten years earlier.[21] As long as it is forced to depend on its traditional suppliers, however, Syria has no hope of matching Israel's qualitative superiority. Having participated at the margins of Iraq's overwhelming defeat in 1991, Syrian leaders can be under no illusions regarding their nation's conventional capabilities.[22]

From recognition of these realities has come a revolution in Syrian security policy. A political dialogue with Israel was one result. Assad has convinced many observers that he has made a strategic choice for peace, even if it must be on terms that satisfy his domestic requirements.[23] New policies de-emphasizing combat readiness and training are another consequence.[24] Another, less reassuring, result is greater commitment to a long-term shift in armaments strategy. Syria places less emphasis on the ability to win wars through conventional forces. Instead it relies more on weapons of mass destruction designed not to win military victory in time of war, but to influence an adversary's policies in peacetime.

The data in Figure 7.2 show these trends graphically. After peaking in the mid-1980s, arms imports by Israel and its immediate adversaries slowed greatly. Despite aggressive promotional efforts by China, Russia, Western firms and regional manufacturers, sellers have found few takers among the core states of the Arab–Israeli conflict. Israel continues to modernize, as discussed below, as do Egypt and Syria. Their acquisitions appear to be motivated almost exclusively by long-term domestic procurement plans. They also take advantage of occasional bargain offers, especially for second-hand equipment. When viewed individually these arms deals can look alarming. But when viewed in sequence and in comparison to previous eras, the trends are far less disturbing.[25] Regional arms buying remains dangerous – these are instruments of death and destruction, after all – but it takes increasing imagination to see them as a potential *cause* of war.

When evaluating recent Arab–Israeli arms trade trends, it is helpful to speculate on hypothetical alternatives. How great would the regional arms trade be if the Arab–Israeli conflict did not exist at all? While it undoubtedly would be less, it probably would not be considerably so. Given the size of the armed forces present in the region and their special importance in non-democratic regimes, a significant arms trade would exist under almost any political circumstances, even the most peaceful.[26] For the same reason, the failure of the Middle East arms trade to slow even more than it has need not mean that old arms races continue. The more likely explanation is that in the Middle East, as elsewhere in the world, armies retain a symbolic and domestic political value regardless of the likelihood of actual fighting.

The Persian Gulf Disruption

While trends in the immediate vicinity of Israel are clear, there is greater ambiguity among more distant Middle Eastern states. Over the years, hardline states elsewhere have engaged in their own build-ups. Sometimes their military policies have been justified largely in terms of their own local disputes; at other times, Israel has been used to justify these developments. Among these protagonists as well, the logic of the status quo has gained greater weight. Like Syria, they may seek specific adjustments to make the regional geographic order more palatable, but these objectives are essentially political in character.

For many years, the most troublesome dangers appeared to come from Libya, where Muammar Qaddafi evinced vigorous support for revolutionary causes around the world and justified his massive military build-up in order to challenge Israel. As long as its oil income and Soviet patronage permitted, Libya was able to acquire remarkably advanced conventional forces. It was the first export client for numerous advanced Soviet weapon systems, such as the SU-24 strike-bomber and MiG-25 interceptor.

The decline in oil prices in the early 1980s made such purchases increasingly painful, but Libya continued to buy when possible. Often suppliers said no. China and Pakistan refused to share nuclear warheads, Brazil and the Soviet Union turned down requests for long-range ballistic missiles. Tired of Qaddafi's political and military excesses, Moscow became less sympathetic. After the embarrassing defeat of his forces in Chad in 1987, even Qaddafi lost interest in military adventure. Economically weakened and politically isolated, Libya ceased much of its previous support for terrorism and allowed its military establishment to atrophy.

Tripoli has not ordered any major conventional weapons since 1989.[27] Like Syria, Libya continues to invest in alternative technologies instead, especially chemical weapons and ballistic missiles.[28] These may allow Tripoli to remain a serious factor in regional strategic stability equations, in other words, to continue to be taken seriously. Libya is keeping its options open, but, without a conventional army at the core of its capabilities, its goals cannot extend beyond influence on the margins.

Today, the greatest risks of Middle East destabilization come not from the traditional confrontation states but from the Persian Gulf. The Iranian revolution and the rise of Iraqi military power created threats that have the potential to leap-frog over the more settled confrontation states in order to engage Israel directly. So long as the two Gulf superpowers fought each other, the dangers could be managed. The key was to insure that neither side defeated the other decisively.[29] This priority led Israel to send military help (mostly weapons components) to Teheran and later compelled Washington to align itself strongly behind Baghdad.[30] The war was a major success for outside diplomacy. While the war itself could not be stopped and was punctuated by serious events like the USS *Stark* and USS *Vincennes* incidents, the fighting was contained successfully through eight years of aggressive and flexible diplomacy.

With the end of the Iran-Iraq war in August 1988, the dangers to outsiders grew again. The Iranian danger to regional stability has been widely debated. Support for the highly disruptive Hizbollah forces in Lebanon and an inexcusable delight in vicious rhetoric have created a fearsome image. The substance behind the language is more obscure. The purchase of two or three advanced Kilo-class submarines from Russia and several squadrons of the latest MiG-29s initially appeared to justify grave concerns. Even if they did not make Iran into a superpower overnight, they suggested to some that Teheran might have long-term ambitions.[31]

While Iran's goal for the coming decades is unknown, it has become evident that the nation is in no position to continue to sign major arms deals. Only a decision to alter national priorities dramatically could make it possible for Iran to re-emerge as a major military power.[32] Iran still has a long way to go before its forces approach the strength of those it inherited from the Shah in 1979. Even in defeat, Iraq retains considerable superiority over its old enemy. Geography and its own growing strength help ensure that Saudi Arabia can also defend itself against an Iranian attack.[33] While Iran's ballistic missile capabilities have grown substantially, its nuclear capability remains nascent, expressing distant intentions that must be taken seriously but have little effect on contemporary strategic planning.[34]

Iraq remains the strongest land power in the Gulf region, but Saddam's threats increasingly rely more on his personal unpredictability than his military resources. The allied destruction of Iraqi weapons and facilities in Desert Storm, and the subsequent United Nations disassembly of much of its remaining infrastructure, left Iraq far weaker than before. With the most numerous armed forces in the Middle East, Iraq can still be worrisome. However, deprived of supplies, spare parts and foreign technical assistance, Saddam's military poses no serious danger to its neighbours, provided they have enough warning to mobilize in response. The near-certainty of American intervention reduces the Iraqi danger even further.

Iraq will almost certainly grow weaker during the next decade compared to its neighbours. The armaments binge among moderate Gulf regimes that followed the 1991 war will begin to show results by the end of the century, allowing the countries of the Gulf Cooperation Council to deploy unprecedented capabilities. While these nations' lack of personnel and constitutional instability undermine their potential somewhat, the Gulf military balance seems more reliable than ever. Even Iran can acquire new military hardware with greater ease than Iraq. United Nations inspections under Security Council resolution 715 will make it difficult – though not impossible – for Iraq to resume development of non-conventional armaments, which remain its most likely hope for military influence.

The scale of GCC arms contracts during 1991–93 aroused concerns that a new arms race was being created. Every GCC government signed contracts for state-of-the-art aircraft and armoured vehicles. Several also purchased exotic equipment like advanced military communications gear and highly sophisticated air-defence and anti-submarine systems. For foreign suppliers, this unique windfall cushioned sagging industries from painful domestic cuts. Saddam Hussein, through his personal excess, accelerated his neighbours' military development by a decade or more. By the year 2000, Saudi Arabia, Kuwait and the Gulf sheikhdoms will have some of the best-quality forces in the world.

All that is missing is quantity. No country can afford an indefinite military build-up, not even Arab oil sheikhdoms. The arms race that some feared would emerge from the trauma of the 1991 Gulf War proved to be a two-year spending spree.[35] Instead of continuing uncontrollably, it ended almost as suddenly as it began. In effect, a normal five- or ten-year modernization cycle was compressed into two years by the fear of Iraqi or Iranian revanchism. As this procurement cycle was completed in 1993, its total dimensions became evident. Rather than expanding their armed forces, the GCC countries have created segmented military establishments, divided between a well-armed and -trained nucleus and less impressive reserve and militia units. New equipment is going almost exclusively into modernization of existing units, not the creation of new ones.

Saudi Arabia and the other GCC countries have not gained the ability to attack Israel or more distant adversaries. Rather, their acquisitions will enable them to defend themselves somewhat more effectively against foreign aggression, hopefully slowing an attack long enough for an international response to assemble. The gradual relaxation of tensions after Saddam's defeat is perhaps the strongest evidence that governments throughout the region are bent on nothing so much as preservation of the status quo. It is revealing that after completing a series of arms purchases that logically should have raised their self-confidence to an all-time high, Saudi leaders chose not to confront Israel, but to initiate steps intended to lead to political accommodation.[36] In the new atmosphere of accepting the military status quo, it is through steps like this that states show the real degree of their security.

Another sign is Israel's new confidence. The end of the Gulf War did not occasion a military investment programme comparable to those that followed the wars of 1967, 1973 and 1982. Despite the fact that its economy is healthier than it has been for over a decade, growing by over 5 per cent a year in the mid-1990s, defence spending is being cut.[37] Instead of an arms build-up to face new dangers, Israel's leaders across its political spectrum seek primarily to trim defence where possible, while preserving existing military capabilities. Several army and air force units are being reduced, allowing greater investment in the modernization of old equipment. A few critical projects continue to move forward, such as the Merkhava tank, Eilat-class corvettes, and the Arrow missile interceptor. Otherwise domestic defence industries are being closed or streamlined.[38]

Like others in the region, Israel has deliberately avoided being drawn into a new arms competition. Its leaders remain deeply suspicious of countries like Iraq – even after Saddam's defeat – but show no interest in expanding their armed forces.[39] The clearest example came after President Bush announced the sale of 72 F-15X fighters and several hundred missiles to Saudi Arabia in September 1992. The deal, worth $9 billion, was criticized for destabilizing the regional balance.[40] Yet the country potentially most threatened hardly batted an eyelid. Instead of demanding a huge package of comparable weaponry as compensation, Israel allowed its previous procurement planning to stand unmodified. Instead of seeking new arms it used the proposed deal primarily to justify a long-sought American commitment to share intelligence, something of far greater military importance than additional hardware. In January 1994, Israel purchased 20 additional F-15Es, but this had no direct connection with events in Saudi Arabia; the deal fulfilled a requirement established several years before to replace aging F-4 Phantoms. It was a classic example of force modernization, not expansion.

Reinforcing Regional Peace

The greatest problem with the declining intensity of conventional armaments in the Middle East is that the process is not based on any concept of self-restraint, let alone charity towards neighbours. Rather, it is based exclusively on narrow self-interest and on perceptions of declining threats and ambitions, coupled with economic pressures. For a few countries like Iran and Iraq, the hesitancy of foreign suppliers is also a serious barrier to greater procurement. Despite the strength of recent trends, there is every reason to suspect that if the economics were less pressing and the availability of foreign arms were greater, some of the countries examined above would be expanding their armed forces once again. With the gentle erosion of threat perceptions and adjustment of national priorities, the trend could reverse altogether.

Without a comprehensive peace – especially an Israeli–Syrian settlement or an amicable resolution of the Palestinian issue – no regional arms slow-down can be sufficient for long-term confidence. Thus, efforts to promote regional amity and arms control remain as important as before. The range of Middle Eastern arms control and confidence-building proposals is very broad.[41] Good ideas have accumulated in a way typical of regions in which such proposals have been advanced for years without success.

Unfortunately, the many schemes under consideration offer little justification for optimism. The impact of formal peace politics has been especially disappointing. The Camp David Accords, as has been widely noted, did nothing to slow Israeli defence preparations and allowed Egypt to upgrade its capabilities, something which had been impossible since the end of Soviet aid in 1973. The 1994 Israeli–Jordanian agreements came at the end, not the beginning, of a long process of informal de-escalation. Both sets of agreements are of singular importance, if not because of their role in ending old arms races, then because of the future arms races they may prevent.

Syria continues to distance itself from similar agreements, pending the return of the Golan Heights. The Madrid process, which it was hoped would advance military transparency and offer a basis for regional arms control, foundered on this issue. If anything, the minimal arms talks organized under the Madrid process's Arms Control and Security Working Group (ACRS) have been counterproductive. Syria's refusal to participate, along with the non-participation of Iran, Iraq and Lebanon, undermined the credibility of these talks and highlighted the extent of regional differences. Having spurned the ACRS forum, the governments of these countries will not be able to join it without sacrificing their domestic credibility and international dignity. Unless these governments are replaced with more accommodating ones, or another, unforeseen revolution alters the regional security equation, it will not be possible to reinvigorate the current dialogue. If and when a regional agreement becomes feasible, a completely different forum will be necessary.

The outlook for confidence-building measures has been damaged further by the excessive politicization of Confidence and Security-Building Measures (CSBM). The need to score political points domestically and among each other encourages Arab governments to present proposals emphasizing demands for Israeli nuclear transparency and disarmament.[42] Israel's nuclear forces must be brought into a comprehensive system for long-term security, they claim. In the near term, though, insisting on this as the primary goal of regional arms control eliminates possibilities for cooperation on conventional forces, which would do more to enhance Middle East security today. There is more to be gained by building on the processes which are already restraining conventional forces, rather than by trying in the first step to encompass the region's most contentious armaments.

A variety of confidence-building and arms limitation proposals have been advanced in initiatives such as those proposed by Presidents Bush and Mitterrand in 1991, but all must wait for political breakthroughs, especially with Syria, and changes in political priorities in other Arab countries. Meanwhile, it may be easier to organize a new forum among arms suppliers to co-ordinate and reduce transfers. The previous effort, the Perm-5 (or P-5) Dialogue initiated in 1991 by the five permanent members of the UN Security Council, agreed on nothing more than a list of banal generalities before it collapsed in 1992. While it should be possible to start similar discussions again, competitive pressures make it unlikely that suppliers' restraint will achieve much without direct support from the recipient countries.[43] In the final analysis, it appears that arms trade control will be inhibited not by good intentions, but only by the same political forces that make other forms of regional arms control so difficult to achieve.

Throughout the foreseeable future, Middle Eastern arms restraint will rely more on domestic factors and informal understandings than on formal international agreements. This undoubtedly is an enormous improvement over the uninhibited competition of the past. But it is a weak basis for long-term stability. In lieu of formal agreements, the greatest danger of renewed arms races will come from forces outside the conventional balance. It is these factors that will be of greatest importance to regional security.

A New Regional Arms Race?

The competition in conventional weaponry may have abated, but few countries in the Middle East have shown a comparable willingness to reduce their non-conventional weapons programmes and some have clearly shifted priorities in that direction. Has a competition in the acquisition of the weapons of mass destruction and ballistic missiles risen to replace the stymied quest for conventional superiority? If so, does this rising competition threaten to undermine the stability that has emerged in the conventional area?

The threat of nuclear weapons, chemical and biological weapons and ballistic missiles has been part of the Middle Eastern security framework since the late 1950s. Starting with Israel's decision to acquire nuclear weapons after the massive Soviet–Egyptian arms deal of 1956, weapons of mass destruction were originally seen in the Middle East as a substitute for weakness in conventional weapons.[44] Similarly, during the long war with Iran, Iraq developed chemical weapons in an attempt to circumvent a battlefield stalemate. Syria's chemical weapons programme and its efforts to acquire long-range ballistic missiles both accelerated in 1986, the year in which Damascus apparently abandoned efforts to achieve parity with Israel in conventional forces.[45]

At the moment, competition in unconventional weapons is suppressed by the patchwork system of treaties and export control regimes, such as the 1968 Nuclear Non-Proliferation Treaty and the Nuclear Suppliers Group, the 1972 Biological Weapons Convention, the 1993 Conventional Weapons Convention and the Australia Group, and more informal mechanisms like the Missile Technology Control Regime and the still-emerging follow-on to Cocom to deal with dual-use technologies. All have become stronger since the discovery in 1991 of Iraq's covert progress, having increased membership, tightened restrictions, and improved enforcement. But all face threats from evasive states and profit-minded exporters.

Of these regimes, the nuclear regime is the strongest and yet the most fragile. Impressive barriers have been erected to halt the further spread of nuclear weapons, but if only one more Middle East country acquires a single bomb, the credibility of the entire effort will be lost and the region's security gravely weakened. Arab countries have been increasingly vocal about their discontent with Israel's nuclear status, but few are seriously interested in acquiring nuclear weapons of their own. Although Egypt leads Arab protests in the United Nations against Israeli nuclear capabilities, it long ago lost interest in acquiring a nuclear option of its own. Syria has never assembled the technical resources. Others, like Saudi Arabia, toyed with the possibility but were never seriously interested. The few that remain interested, like Iran and Libya, have had little luck, although Russian assistance and illegal exports of fissionable materials could change that.

The situation regarding chemical and biological weapons is much less stable. While they are difficult to use and their effects are difficult to predict, they have become the strategic weapon of choice for hard-pressed Middle Eastern governments. To be sure, several Middle Eastern governments have signed the Chemical Weapons Convention, agreeing to its intrusive inspection requirements, but none of them are contiguous with Israel. Where regional interest in chemical and biological weapons survives, it is cultivated mainly to keep pressure on Israel's nuclear programme. Although Iraq's large stockpile has been destroyed by UNSCOM, other countries, including Iran, Libya and Syria, are widely believed to maintain comparable stocks of chemical agents. Recent revelations suggest that some of these countries continue to develop their chemical warfare potential.[46]

The ballistic missile situation is probably the most delicate of the three. Virtually very country in the region now has a missile force. Middle Eastern interest in ballistic missiles goes back to the late 1950s when Nasser brought a German rocket team to Egypt. Israel's response culminated in its own French-designed missiles deployed just before the 1973 war. Meanwhile, the Soviet Union began to sell SCUD-Bs to virtually all its clients in the region. The number of Soviet SCUDs transferred to the Middle East has not been made public, but undoubtedly is large. Iraq is known to have received over 900, and the total number still in the inventories of other Arab states could be over 2000.[47]

For defence planners in Europe and the United States, the danger of Middle Eastern missiles is increasingly pressing. Long-range missiles directly challenge the outside world's automatic reaction to any regional war, to contain it and prevent it from spreading. Since Saddam Hussein's dramatic use of modified SCUDs in 1991, NATO and the European Union have undertaken major studies of theatre ballistic missile defences (TBMD). The United States has reoriented its plans to deal primarily with this kind of threat,and plans to invest roughly US$20 billion over the next 12 years to deploy TBMD systems, largely – but not exclusively – with the Middle Eastern threat in mind.[48] Israel and Western Europe seem likely to follow with systems of their own.

In the past, most of the ballistic missiles in the region came from the Soviet Union, and to a lesser extent from America, China and France. Since the late 1980s, the list of possible suppliers has narrowed dramatically, leaving North Korea as the pre-eminent supplier. The future of Middle Eastern missile proliferation largely depends on whether North Korea will change its export policy and accept the new international culture opposing missile exports. If it does not, there is a serious danger that North Korean missiles like the 1000 km-range NoDong-1 could reach its clients in the region, as could more powerful rockets which are still under development.[49]

Despite the very real successes of the various non-proliferation treaties and export control agreements, greater competition for weapons of mass destruction and long-range missiles remains a strong possibility. It is far less certain that such competition could undermine the region's conventional stability. Non-conventional forces are developed for very different reasons and serve distinct goals. They have greater implications for the region's enduring political conflicts than for its diminishing military confrontation. These weapons may have been sought as a substitute for conventional power or a last resort in case of its failure. But there are clearly limits to their potential as substitutes. Today, the two kinds of weapon serve different ends. Just as in Europe and between the superpowers, the various kinds of armaments have become progressively more specialized over the years.

The importance of the weapons of mass destruction in the Middle East increased as the importance of conventional weapons waned, but the relationship between the two has since lost is flexibility. The day when one could substitute for the other appears to have passed. The logic that has been apparent since the birth of the nuclear era, which was first understood in terms of the superpower relationship and in Europe, now seems increasingly appreciated in the Middle East as well. Only under the most peculiar circumstances can WMD be used to conquer territory. They are poorly suited to defeat a standing army in the field. This is true even of chemical weapons, which are most effective when used on unprotected civilians. Weapons of mass destruction are overwhelmingly political instruments. In Europe and among the superpowers this was understood to mean deterrence of a potential attacker in times of peace and inhibiting escalation in times of war. The same rule applies in the Middle East, albeit with important differences. As Saddam Hussein's attacks on Israel in 1991 demonstrated, in the Middle East the list of political missions can also include the deliberate escalation of a conflict.

While conventional forces can shrink in response to changing domestic priorities and the logic of the status quo, unconventional forces develop through a more independent process. There is a strong consensus that the only way to bring reductions in their spread will be through verifiable arms control agreements, probably beginning with confidence-building measures and progressing toward negotiated caps and reduction.[50] Others argue that the only hope for control is through global measures to reduce the salience of these weapons.[51]

Where we used to see the Middle East arms race as a single phenomenon requiring overarching solutions, we now face a widening split between the outlooks for conventional and for unconventional weapons. Solving the Middle Eastern nuclear quandary will be far more difficult than the resolution of its conventional arms race. The unfortunate side of this schism is that progress towards conventional stability may create little if any momentum for control over the weapons of mass destruction. The fortunate side is that the possible escalation of the nuclear, chemical and biological weapons situation or missile confrontation will probably not weaken the underlying conventional stability.

The New Long-Term Threat

A greater danger of destabilization comes from the threat of terrorism and the violent acts of religious extremists. Its rising importance poses a direct threat to safety, but except in the most extreme circumstances, this is not a threat which can be countered by military means. The exceptions, however, are of such importance as to require serious and searching consideration. While terrorist violence in and of itself cannot justify the procurement of highly advanced major weapon systems, the danger that terrorists might acquire weapons of mass destruction cannot be dismissed, nor can the potential for destabilization. Should religious extremists take power in the Arab world as they have in Iran, moreover, the possible renewed conventional escalation would be very difficult to control.

The rising importance of terrorism and religious extremist-related violence reflects not their growing deadliness but a change in their political nature. Any terrorist organization, no matter how sincerely motivated, can operate only to the degree of its outside support. By themselves, such organizations are capable of a minimum level of violence, sometimes sufficient to cause serious political problems, but to act with more certain effect against the authority of a state they require external support. In the past, this came primarily from foreign state sponsors. The most serious terrorist groups of the 1970s and the 1980s – the Red Army Faction, the IRA, the PLO and Hizbollah – relied on foreign state support; their deadliness waxed and waned with the favour of their sponsors.[52] Through its reliance on foreign support, terrorism became, in effect, an instrument of covert policy, a way for countries like East Germany, Libya or revolutionary Iran to assert themselves indirectly.

As long as terrorism was directly related to state policy, the dangers could be addressed by going to the states which sponsored it. Whether or not Washington could track down the bombers of the La Belle Disco in Berlin in 1986, an air strike could be mounted against Libya. Similarly, the international community could react to the Lockerbie bombing without knowing the identity of the bombers by applying United Nations sanctions to Libya. Regardless of whether the West could reach terrorist factions based on Damascus, it could deal directly with the Syrian authorities.

When France apprehended the terrorist leader Carlos in August 1994, it was reportedly with the direct assistance of Sudanese (and probably Syrian) officials.

The capture of Carlos was widely acknowledged as a climactic event left over from another era. The end of the Cold War brought an end to terrorism-sponsoring by the states of Eastern Europe and convinced most others like Libya to abandon the business. Today's most demanding security dangers come not from states or their proxy cells. Islamicist parties like the Islamic Salvation Front (FIS) in Algeria, the Muslim Brotherhood in Egypt or Hamas in Israel do not rely on the support of the state sponsors. While they gladly accept cash and arms from Iran, Iraq or other patrons, their most important support comes from well-organized individual supporters.[53] Having evolved beyond state sponsorship, terrorism has lost its key vulnerability, making the most important instruments of antiterrorism almost irrelevant. Today's terrorists are all but immune to formal diplomacy.[54]

The toll from such groups does not compare to the destruction caused by orthodox state-against-state warfare. But the slow and unpredictable haemorrhaging of human life can be no less deadly over time, and the erosion of public confidence is no less palpable. The made-for-television gruesomeness creates a special burden by convincing people that their government cannot defend their lives, stripping the state of a key element of its legitimacy.

The Palestinian *Intifada* stands out as a model of dangers these new threats pose. The seemingly random chaos and ungovernability was instrumental in convincing Israel to relinquish control of Gaza and allow the PLO to establish formal rule in part of the West Bank. The possibility of new Iranian-style revolutions elsewhere in the Middle East torments any security planner. There is growing reason to suspect that Muslim extremists may take power in Algeria. Whether or not they can take control of Cairo, their violence could determine the credibility of Egypt's central government.

The danger of ungovernability must not be underestimated, but it is not the same as facing hostile armies directly across one's borders. It is not a problem that justifies major military build-ups, if only because extremists – in and of themselves – do not pose a conventional military threat. For extremists to undermine the basic elements of regional stability, they must either take control of governments and national armies or acquire weapons of mass destruction.

The latter scenario is the source of widespread fear. One need look no further than the lists of best-selling paperback novels, in which the theme of nuclear-armed terrorists long ago became common enough to bore anyone not addicted to cheap thrillers.[55] Since the collapse of the Soviet Union, the international community and the governments of the former Soviet states have taken several steps to prevent nuclear weapons from falling into the hands of sub-state protagonists. Since the Russian plutonium smuggling scares of July–August 1994, action to control fissile materials has also become more aggressive. Yet the possibility that nuclear weapons may be given or sold to a sub-national group remains serious.

Other weapons could be harder to control. The possibility that terrorists will threaten to use biological agents is especially realistic and troubling. Even so, this is a danger that must be responded to not with full-scale warfare, but with discrete uses of force, however real the threat. Renewed large-scale military confrontation could still result. While the threat of a Muslim Brotherhood bomb, for example, would not justify a massive Israeli arms build-up, it could provoke uncontrollable tensions that would impel government leaders on all sides into a new arms race.

Aside from the risk that they could detonate a nuclear bomb over a major city, the greatest danger that extremists pose is the possibility of igniting a July 1914-style crisis. By threatening to use weapons of mass destruction they could compel governments to react with extreme measures. The Middle East is accustomed to Israeli strikes against terrorist PLO factions and the Hizbollah in Lebanon, usually in response to relatively limited attacks on Israelis. But Lebanon is weak and powerless, virtually a regional punch-bag, unable to respond in any effective manner.

If confronted by nuclear or biological threats from terrorists based in another, much stronger, state like Egypt or Iran, Israel undoubtedly would feel compelled to threaten more forceful action. In this scenario, however, the host state – one which is much stronger than Lebanon – might feel equally compelled to react. However intended, the use or threat of force against extremists based in a neighbouring state could provoke a cycle of arming and counterarming, re-starting the arms race and possibly culminating in outright warfare.

CONCLUSION

While the Middle East arms race may not be completely and permanently over, one of the most powerful engines of regional instability is not the threat it once was. With the increasing acceptance of the region's geopolitical status quo and changing domestic priorities, the Middle Eastern race for superiority in conventional weaponry has diminished greatly. In and of itself, this is not a sufficient basis for regional peace, but it should encourage those who believe that regional security can be strengthened.

It may be premature to speak of the end of the Middle East arms race, but a new watershed in regional security affairs undoubtedly has been reached. The transformation remains informal and incomplete; it lacks the reinforcement of international commitments and treaties, and it still does not fully embrace nuclear, chemical, and other weapons technologies. Despite its shortcomings and limitations, the process has proven to be surprisingly durable. Gradual and inconspicuous rather than sudden and dramatic, it has acquired a momentum and strength of its own with clear and beneficial consequences for regional stability. While the decline of the Middle East arms race may still not be easy to see, its effects are increasingly obvious.

As the danger of interstate war recedes and military preparations cease to be of overwhelming importance in relations between states, the Middle East becomes increasingly like other regions of the world. While a comprehensive peace of the kind described in innumerable speeches before the United Nations may not be close at hand, important aspects of it are being established through a piecemeal, incremental process. Above all, fewer countries of the region pose a direct danger to the security of their neighbours. While this may not be the peace the world has long sought, it is one with which the world can live.

As a result of this transformation, the outlook for Middle Eastern confidence-building and arms control is much better than ever before. Although the conventional confrontation has been reduced informally, formal agreements still have a vital role to play, enforcing and institutionalizing the stability so felicitously achieved. The key to successful negotiations will be the trimming of expectations, the shift from long-term goals of comprehensive settlement and general regional disarmament. Greater progress will come by focusing on closer objectives, stressing more modest but still vital mechanisms controlling conventional forces.

As in other regions, the most serious threats to international stability come not from the excesses of demonic leaders and rogue states, but from the collapse of power in otherwise normal countries. Efforts by sub-state protagonists to take power or carve out sovereignties of their own are as destabilizing in the long term as official government revanchism. In a world increasingly divided between strong states and ineffectual ones, groups acting beyond the authority of any government are emerging as the dominant source of havoc.

Terrorism and religious extremism do not render military forces irrelevant, but they do change the way in which those forces must operate. Instead of orthodox large-scale operations by army brigades or air force squadrons, the new threat calls for small-scale operations by special forces. In the Middle East as elsewhere, armies which are Napoleonic in scope are increasingly irrelevant, preserved more out of respect for ageing memories and the symbolism than for any day-to-day functional ability. In the Middle East as elsewhere, the armies of the future will tend to be small, highly-trained forces designed to deal with specific contingencies. Such forces pose a minimal threat to neighbouring states, while they have a greater ability to deal with the thorny challenges of terrorism and violent acts perpetrated by religious extremist groups. The immediate goal of the international community should be to encourage this trend through arms control initiatives, diplomacy and aid.

NOTES

1. The only serious analyst to anticipate the end of the Cold War was Andrei Amalrik, who wrote in 1969, although his reasoning had little connection with actual events. Amalrik, *Will the Soviet Union Survive Until 1984?* (New York: Harper and Row, 1970). See a literature survey by Timur Kuran, 'Liberalization and democratization in the Soviet Union and Eastern Europe', *World Politics*, v. 44, n. 1 (October 1991) pp. 10–11.
2. This debate was anticipated in Paul Johnson's *Modern Times: The World From the Twenties to the Nineties*, rev. edn (New York: HarperCollins, 1991), pp. 696–704, 750–68. Also see the symposium on 'The strange death of Soviet Communism', in *The National Interest*, no. 33 (Spring 1993).
3. John Lewis Gaddis, 'International relations theory and the end of the Cold War', *International Security*, v. 17, n. 3 (Winter 1992/93), pp. 5–57.
4. Colin S. Gray, *House of Cards: Why Arms Control Must Fail* (Ithaca: Cornell University Press, 1992).
5. Julian Ozanne and Roger Matthews, 'Ploughed back into swords', *The Financial Times*, 9 September 1994, p. 13.
6. Michael Eisenstadt, *Arming for Peace? Syria's Elusive Quest for Strategic Parity*, Policy Paper no. 31 (Washington, DC: Institute for Middle East Policy, 1992); Gerald M. Steinberg, 'Middle East Arms Control and Regional Security', *Survival*, v. 36, n. 1 (Spring 1994) pp. 129–30.
7. It has been argued that even in the Middle East, high military spending is not economically sustainable over time. For example, see Yahya M. Sadowski, *Scuds or Butter? The Political Economy of Arms Control in the Middle East* (Washington, DC: Brookings Institution, 1993). In practice,

however, economic pressure rarely reduces military spending before the political causes of a conflict have been minimized first.

8. John Mueller, *Retreat from Doomsday: The Obsolescence of Major War* (New York: Basic Books, 1989). Whether Mueller's hypothesis applies to regions other than Europe and North America is the subject of lively debate. See Akhtar Majeed, 'Has the war system really become obsolete?' *Bulletin of Peace Proposals*, v. 21, n. 3 (December 1991), pp. 321–8; and Mueller, 'A response to Akhtar Majeed', ibid., v. 23, n. 1 (March 1992) pp. 103–7.
9. Lawrence Freedman and Efraim Karsh, *The Gulf Conflict, 1990–1991: Diplomacy and War in the New World Order* (Princeton: Princeton University Press, 1993), pp. 19–41.
10. On the great flexibility of defence spending, see Saadet Deger and Somnath Sen, *Military Expenditure: The Political Economy of International Security* (Oxford: Oxford University Press, 1990), pp. 3–8.
11. In this respect the decline of Middle Eastern arms competition bears little connection to the processes outlined in Bennet Ramberg (ed.), *Arms Control Without Negotiation* (Boulder, Co: Lynne Rienner, 1993).
12. Glen Frankel, *Beyond the Promised Land: Jews and Arabs on the Hard Road to a New Israel* (New York: Simon and Schuster, 1994).
13. In the early 1980s, Western observers began to express concern that Jordan was becoming too weak to defend itself against Palestinian or Syrian intervention. Anthony H. Cordesman, *Jordanian Arms and the Middle East Balance* (Washington, DC: Middle East Institute, 1993).
14. Philip Finnegan, 'Jordan cuts armed forces; plans to sell off aircraft', *Defense News*, 25 November 1991, p. 1.
15. 'Jordanian F-5s to Singapore', *Military and Arms Transfers News*, v. 94, n. 14 (2 December 1994), p. 5.
16. Alvin Z. Rubinstein, *Red Star on the Nile: The Soviet-Egyptian Influence Relationship since the June War* (Princeton: Princeton University Press, 1977), esp. ch. 6, 'The end of illusion'.
17. John Laffin, *The War of Desperation: Lebanon 1982–85* (London: Osprey, 1985), pp. 119–21.
18. Efraim Karsh, 'The rise and fall of Syria's quest for strategic parity', *RUSI and Brassey's Defence Yearbook 1991* (London: Brassey's, 1991) pp. 197–215.
19. *Military Balance 1994–1995* (London: International Institute for Strategic Studies, 1994), pp. 123, 140.
20. Craig Mellow, 'Saber-rattling helps Russia ring up arms sales', *International Herald Tribune*, 19 December 1994, p. 9.
21. *World Military Expenditures and Arms Transfers,* 1991–92 (Washington, DC: US Arms Control and Disarmament Agency, 1994).
22. Geoffrey Kemp, 'Impact of the Gulf War on attitudes toward advanced weaponry', presentation at a conference sponsored by the Institute for Foreign Policy Analysis and the United Nations Institute for Disarmament Research, Geneva, 14–15 February 1994.
23. Roger Matthews, 'A crisis of leadership', *The Financial Times*, 21 December 1994, p. 13; 'Syria in "secret" talks with Israel', *The Financial Times*, 23 December 1994, p. 4; 'Father figure', *The Economist*, 7 January 1995, pp. 33–4.

24. James Bruce, 'Syria's inner circle's reshuffle', *Jane's Defence Weekly*, 17 September 1994, p. 27; and Bruce, 'Assad sanitizes agencies to prepare for peace deal', ibid, 26 November 1994, p. 13.
25. A similar point is made by Saleh Al-Mani, 'Conventional weapons and arms transfers in the Middle East', in Chantal de Jonge Oudraat (ed.), *Conference of Research Institutes in the Middle East* (Geneva: United Nations Institute for Disarmament Research, 1994) pp. 58–9.
26. Keith Krause, 'Middle East arms recipients in the post-Cold War world', *Annals of the American Academy of Political and Social Science*, v. 535 (September 1994) pp. 73–90.
27. According to Sipri, the last Libyan order for major weapons systems was a 1988 contract with Moscow for 15 SU-24 bombers. *Sipri Yearbook 1991* (Oxford: Oxford University Press, 1991) p. 262. According to the IISS, though, the order was apparently cancelled after only six of the aircraft had been received. *The Military Balance 1994–1995* (London: International Institute for Strategic Studies, 1994), p. 145.
28. W. Andrew Terrill, 'Libya and the quest for chemical weapons', *Conflict Quarterly*, v. 14, n. 1 (Winter 1994), pp. 47–61.
29. Stephen C. Pelletière, *The Iran–Iraq War: Chaos in a Vacuum* (Westport: Praeger, 1992); Dilip Hiro, *The Longest War: The Iran–Iraq Military Conflict* (London: Paladin, 1990), ch. 3.
30. European support for Iraq was unambiguous from the start of the war. See Kenneth R. Timmerman, *The Death Lobby: How the West Armed Iraq* (London: Fourth Estate, 1992). The strength of American support for Saddam is more obscure. An extreme position is developed by Alan Friedman, *Spider's Web: Bush, Saddam, Thatcher and the Decade of Deceit* (London: Faber and Faber, 1993).
31. Testimony by R. James Woolsey, Director of Central Intelligence, before the US Senate Committee on Governmental Affairs, 24 February 1993.
32. James W. Moore, 'An assessment of the Iranian military rearmament program', *Comparative Strategy*, v. 13, no. 3 (Fall 1994) pp. 371–89; Elaine Sciolino, 'Iran's difficulties lead some in U.S. to doubt threat', *New York Times*, 5 July 1994, p. A1.
33. Shahram Chubin, *Iran's National Security Policy* (Washington, DC: Carnegie Endowment for International Peace, 1994), pp. 29–38.
34. Iranian efforts to find a country willing to aid in the completion of its two Bushehr reactors have caused alarm. For example, Chris Hedges, 'Iran may be able to build an atomic bomb in 5 years, U.S. and Israeli officials fear', *New York Times*, 5 January 1995, p. A10. The reactor's light-water design, however, does not offer a practical basis for nuclear weapons production. See the repudiation of the previously cited article in Clyde Haberman, 'U.S. and Israel see Iranians "many years" from A-bomb', *New York Times*, 10 January 1995, p. A3.
35. An explicit statement of post-Desert Storm concern is Chris Smith, 'From bust to boom', *Peace and Security*, Spring 1991, pp. 10–11.
36. Youssef M. Ibrahim, 'Muslims argue the theology of peace with Israel', *New York Times*, 31 January 1995, p. A9.
37. 'Emerging-market indicators', *The Economist*, 28 January 1995, p. 102.

38. Israel Military Industries (IMI), for example, cut employment from 21 000 in the mid-1980s to 3000 in 1995. Eric Silver, 'Israel aims to cut 5000 defence jobs', *The Financial Times*, 6 January 1995, p. 3.
39. The Director-General of Israel's Ministry of Defence, David Ivry, interviewed in *Jane's Defence Weekly*, 9 April 1994, p. 32.
40. Natalie J. Goldring, Testimony before the US House Subcommittee on Arms Control, International Security and Science and the Subcommittee on Europe and the Middle East of the House's Foreign Affairs Committee, Washington, DC, 23 September 1992.
41. Useful introductions to this extensive literature are Avi Becker (ed.), *Arms Control Without Glasnost: Building Confidence in the Middle East* (Jerusalem: Israel Council on Foreign Relations, 1993) and Alan Platt (ed.), *Arms Control and Confidence Building in the Middle East* (Washington, DC: US Institute of Peace, 1992).
42. Mounir Zahran, 'Strengthening the Nuclear Non-Proliferation Regime', *UNIDIR Newsletter*, no. 26/27 (June–September 1994), pp. 16–18; 'Nuclear peace', *The Economist*, 28 January 1995, p. 40.
43. David Mussington, *Understanding Contemporary International Arms Transfers*, Adelphi Paper 291 (London: IISS and Brassey's, September 1994).
44. Avner Cohen, 'Most favored nation', *Bulletin of the Atomic Scientists*, v. 51, n. 1 (January/February 1995), p. 45.
45. Joseph S. Bermudez, Jr, 'Syria's acquisition of North Korean "Scuds"', *Jane's Intelligence Review*, June 1991, p. 250.
46. Philip Shenon, 'Libya expels Thais in chemical weapons dispute', *New York Times*, 10 November 1993, p. A14; Daniel Pipes, 'Trust Assad? Not yet', *New York Times*, 18 January 1994, p. A22.
47. Aaron Karp, 'Ballistic missile proliferation in the Middle East', *Contemporary Security Policy*, Winter 1994/95.
48. *1994 Report to the Congress on Ballistic Missile Defense* (Washington: US Ballistic Missile Defense Organization, July 1994).
49. The latter are described in David Wright and Timur Kadyshev, 'The North Korean missile program: how advanced is it?' *Arms Control Today*, v. 24, n. 3 (April 1994), pp. 9–12.
50. Efraim Karsh and Yezid Sayigh, 'A cooperative approach to Arab–Israeli security', *Survival*, v. 36, n. 1 (Spring 1994), pp. 114–25.
51. Eliza D. Harris, 'Towards a comprehensive strategy for halting chemical and biological weapons proliferation', *Arms Control*, v. 12, n. 2 (September 1991); Geoffrey Kemp, 'The Middle East arms race: can it be controlled?' *Middle East Journal*, v. 45, n. 3 (Summer 1991).
52. Max G. Manwarring (ed.), *Uncomfortable Wars: Toward a New Paradigm of Low Intensity Conflict* (Boulder, CO; Westview, 1991), pp. 20–4; Edward E. Rice, *Wars of the Third Kind* (Berkeley: University of California Press, 1988), especially ch. 4.
53. Claire Spencer, 'Algeria in crisis', *Survival*, v. 36, n. 2 (Summer 1994), pp. 149–63.
54. J. F. Holden-Rhodes and Peter A. Lupsha, 'Horsemen of the apocalypse: gray area phenomena and the new world disorder', *Low Intensity Conflict and Law Enforcement*, v. 2, n. 2 (Autumn 1993) pp. 212–26.
55. Tom Clancey, 'Five Minutes Past Midnight', *National Interest*, Winter 1991/92, pp. 3–12.

8 Weapons Acquisition and Arms Racing in the Middle East

Raymond Picquet

It has become commonplace to view the Middle East as a region of unbridled arms races – a dangerous dynamic relieved only occasionally by conflicts of arms and often naïve and ill-fated attempts at 'arms control'. Unfortunately, the image of an armaments-swollen region is even more disturbing in the light of the recent surge in regional efforts to acquire nuclear, biological (BW) and chemical (CW) 'weapons of mass destruction' (WMD).[1] In general, because of the strategic importance of the Middle East, the presence of critical oil resources and the continuing political instability of the region's major states, the possession of such weapons is widely assumed both to threaten global interests and to make possible potential Armageddons.[2] In this chapter, the focus is on the current and future status of arms acquisitions in the region, particularly with respect to WMD. The emphasis is on the nature of the weapons acquisition process, particularly with respect to its potential for impacts on the international system.

In this chapter, arms acquisitions are analyzed on two levels. In the first section, in a survey of the WMD programme status of each proliferation state,[3] the focus is on weapons acquisition decisions. The emphasis is on the political, cultural, organizational and leadership factors associated with the acquisition decisions of specific proliferation regimes. In the second section, the focus is on the competition for arms between states and on specific 'arms races' in the region. A third section analyzes regional trends in the acquisition of WMD.

Arms racing implies that states are constantly striving to outpace their rivals in the pursuit of military capability, and, in so doing, that they seek to obtain a decisive advantage. On a conceptual level 'arms racing' suggests an ambiguous nature; is it a close-run competition over an extended period of time or a sporadic or extraordinary contest for short-term advantage? From the system perspective, does it resemble the tortoise or the hare?[4] A thesis produced by this analysis is that WMD-proliferation arms races in the Middle

East involve both extraordinary efforts and ongoing competitions. Indeed, it is the presence of both characteristics which makes the regional phenomenon so costly and so potentially dangerous. Unfortunately, arms racing appears to be an enduring aspect of international relations in the Middle East. In addition, arms racing also portends the possibilities of potentially destabilizing developments resulting from technological 'breakthroughs' or technology transfers, or, worse, from a surprise use of such weapons in war.

A major source of the changes associated with the end of the Cold War was the Soviet Union's loss of superpower status. Two key developments have resulted from this change. Firstly, the United States is generally much more influential in the region; secondly, in the wake of the Gulf War, certain key US allies (i.e. Israel, Egypt and Saudi Arabia), are rearming with financial and technical help from the United States and with access to sophisticated Western technologies. A third regional development has been the continuing inclination of former Soviet-client, radical-secular, and Islamic-revivalist states to develop indigenously produced WMD. The thesis of this analysis is that regional WMD developments have resulted largely from the driving ambitions of states' leaderships for regional influence, status and prestige and only subordinately as responses to calculations of strategic threat. In other words strategic weapons acquisitions, particularly of WMD, appear to be driven primarily by leadership orientations and intrastate politics, some of which have a regional dimension, rather than as linear responses to either strategic-regional or global agendas. The two exceptions to this generalization are the results of arms races associated with major regional conflicts: the Arab–Israeli dispute and the Iranian quest for regional hegemony.

From a decision-making perspective, armament decisions are typically multi-dimensional. They tend to involve more than strategic issues to include a range of political interests; they transcend domestic, foreign and defence policy realms, both as a function of the complexity of the political issues and objectives and due to cost considerations.

On a conceptual level, strategic armament acquisitions are based on: (1) the leadership's 'rational' calculations of the balance of power associated with the international political system and with respect to other interests at stake in the international political environment, and (2) the definition of available political and military means required to obtain foreign policy objectives. Such calculations are generally premised on definitions of national security interests, operational means–ends analyses, such as 'grand strategies', and formal or informal 'force doctrines'. In practice, decision-making involving important political issues in the real world is seldom a totally 'rational' process; certain important components, such as definitions of national security or bureaucratic interests, are, by definition, subject to value judgements and non-rational political haggling. The implication of this concept of decision-making is to suggest that neat and logical decision-tree flow charts do not represent political reality – in the Middle East or anywhere else.

In the real world, acquisitions of WMD undoubtedly result from *both* the internal political motivations of state leaderships and motives associated with conceptions of strategic interests. Authoritarian regimes often use weapons programmes in order to employ political and military cohorts and to co-opt rivals with the lure of lucrative positions involving power, money and prestige. In some countries, weapons programmes, including WMD, are used to integrate both strategic ambitions and domestic interests in high priority, government-sponsored public projects for the benefit of major political support groups, such as the scientific and military professional groups of the new middle class. For the regime, the need to establish links with such groups is largely a function of the weak legitimacy characteristic of authoritarian regimes.[5]

As in other areas of political life, defence policy decisions in authoritarian regimes are subject to the idiosyncrasies of the leadership elite. In such environments, personalistic or radical decision-making modes are not subject to democratic electoral mechanisms or routinized institutional checks and balances. In many cases, such regimes are checked mainly by economic constraints and the perceived propensity of the military to intervene in political life. In regimes with strong traditions of military-influenced politics or outright intervention, ruling elites will often attempt to reach a political accommodation with rival institutions and groups.

Authoritarian regimes are characterized primarily by the dominance of an individual or a small ruling elite. In such systems, decisions are functions of arbitrary authority and force of personality on the political process. Indeed, most of the major regimes of the region are characterized by strong leaders of either the charismatic-radical or bureaucratic-authoritarian types, and these individuals are not generally accountable to institutions or social forces outside their own elite groups. The implication for defence decision-making is that such leaderships typically command great latitude for defining the political agenda and establishing their own defence strategies and military force postures. In such a political context, high-status, high-prestige weapons programmes in the Middle East have often resulted mainly from the personal disposition, political commitments and leadership style of the individual ruler. Thus, the leaders of several major states were almost certainly directly responsible for the sponsorship of WMD programmes; Egypt's Gamal Abdel Nasser with a CW programme, Iraq's Saddam

Hussein with the full spectrum of non-conventional weapons, Libya's Muammar Qaddafi with CW, Syria's Hafez Assad with CW, Israel's David Ben Gurion and Moshe Dayan with Israel's nuclear weapons programme.

On the international and regional level, the theme of 'continuity' implies the status quo, an ongoing competition for both conventional and some non-conventional arms, from initial phases of technology acquisition, development and deployment to potential use on the battlefield. In theory, the process is conceived here as an intense dynamic between rival states, which tend to act and respond to the 'racing behaviour' of their counterparts in a political atmosphere of increasing and prolonged political tension and exorbitant defence expenditures – a ceaseless dynamic of recycled confrontation and war. In the Middle East, continuity implies that states will continue to acquire more and higher quality weaponry and that they will continue to make incremental progress towards the acquisition of non-conventional weapons.

Within the framework of an existing arms racing 'system', change implies one or more of the following conditions: (1) a significant increase in the scale of the acquisition programme or in the sophistication/effectiveness of the weapon sought, (2) an intensification or acceleration of the acquisition effort, or (3) a substantial abatement of the acquisition phenomenon, presumably as a consequence of a defence policy change by one or more of the major states of the region. Obviously, these possibilities assume that something akin to arms racing is a normal phenomenon in the region. This proposition is consistent with statistical trends that mirror the increasing defence expenditure in the region over the last three decades.[6]

Throughout modern history, a major objective of states has been to ensure security by acquiring new and more destructive weaponry. As weapons have become inexorably more sophisticated, states have been increasingly inclined towards the independent production of such weapons and continuing access to related infrastructure. In the twentieth century, the struggle for technological superiority has grown more intense as states continue to seek decisive advantages with new and increasingly destructive 'wonder weapons' – as such technological marvels were sometimes called. Thus, the battleship, submarine, machine-gun, armoured tank and aeroplane each had its heyday as the ultimate or decisive weapon.[7]

This process of weaponry development eventually resulted in a new and more ominous category of 'weapons of mass destruction'. This term generally refers to the genre of highly destructive weapons which destroy an entire area, rather than with respect to specific targets, such as personnel or buildings. During World War I the first modern 'mass weapon', chemical weaponry, underwent frantic technical development and battlefield use, and resulted in thousands of casualties during that conflict; each side struggled to develop deadly new gases and superior protective equipment. In the post-World War II era, by far the most destructive and sought-after weapon was the nuclear bomb, due to the enormous magnitude of its destructive potential.

However, the relative utility and glamour of a given weapons system is to some extent driven by current fashion. In the aftermath of a global war in which CW was not used, and in the context of a new emphasis on nuclear deterrence, all non-nuclear weapons were overshadowed by the symbolic mushroom cloud.

Since the mid-1960s, interest in CW has been rekindled by both the use of such weapons in the Middle East and the apparent lack of effective sanctions against their military use. Indeed, several Middle Eastern states are currently believed to be actively pursuing WMD through relevant technology transfers and research and development programmes. In addition, several states in the region are experimenting with BW, a potentially far more powerful device that could be exceedingly difficult to control or protect against.

NON-CONVENTIONAL WEAPONS IN THE MIDDLE EAST

The Middle East includes at least six countries which are in possession of, or interested in obtaining, non-conventional weapons or WMD. In general, Third World states have attempted to acquire WMD and related technology as a function of largely European-based commercial sources. Although some of this effort is for legitimate business purposes, much of it has consisted of state-sponsored clandestine efforts to circumvent international norms against proliferation-oriented technology transfers. In general, the presumed goal of such transfers is to facilitate the acquisition of the technical infrastructure required for the development of an indigenous weapons production capability.

Table 8.1 evaluates the status of nuclear, biological, chemical and ballistic missile programmes in the Middle East.[8] The data indicate that the region is currently replete with non-conventional weapons. In addition, the following observations are suggested. (1) Approximately seven Middle Eastern states have acquired non-conventional weapons, a relatively large number by any measure for a single area; (2) several of the countries on the list hold adversarial relationships and could conceivably pose threats involving non-conventional weapons; (3) several of the countries of the region have recently been upgraded to a 'probable' status (i.e. reliable but unconfirmed reports of proliferation activity have emanated from one or more sources) or such states have been subsequently assessed by official sources as possessors of a non-conventional weapons development

Table 8.1 Proliferation programme status in the Middle East

	Nuclear	*Biological*	*Chemical*	*Ballistic missile*
Algeria	R&D			
Egypt			R&D, Stkpl	R&D, Stkpl, P
Iran	R&D	R&D	R&D, P, Stkpl	R&D
Iraq**	R&D	R&D	R&D, P, Stkpl	R&D, P
Israel	R&D P, Stkpl	R&D	R&D, P, Stkpl	R&D, P, Stkpl
Libya	R&D*	R&D*	R&D, P, Stkpl	R&D, P, Stkpl
Morocco				
Syria			R&D, P, Stkpl	R&D, P, Stkpl
Saudi Arabia			R&D ?	R&D, P, Stkpl

KEY:
R&D – Research and Development
P – Production
Stkpl – Stockpile

* The status of such programmes is not clear, but is not thought to be more than R&D.

** Assessment refers to pre-Gulf War status. The number of existing clandestine programmes is uncertain.

Sources

1. *Proliferation of Weapons of Mass Destruction: Assessing the Risks* (Office of Technology Assessment: US Congress, Washington, DC, 1993).
2. Gordon M. Burc and Charles F. Floweree, *International Handbook on Chemical Weapons Proliferation* (Westport, CT: Greenwood Press, 1991).
3. Leonard Spector and Jacqueline R. Smith, *Nuclear Ambitions: The Spread of Nuclear Weapons* (Boulder, CO: Westview, 1990).
4. Leonard Spector, 'Nuclear Proliferation', Efraim Karsh, Martin Navais and Philip Sabin (eds), *Non-Conventional Weapons in the Middle East* (Oxford: Oxford University Press, 1993), pp. 151–3.

programme. Examples of this apparent movement are Iran (NBC and ballistic missiles), Syria (CW and missiles) and Libya (NBC and ballistic missiles). In more general terms the table suggests a dynamic upwards shift in the number of mass weapon acquisition programmes.

CASES OF ARMS ACQUISITION IN THE MIDDLE EAST

The following section describes NBC/missile programmes in terms of the known intentions and capabilities of key countries. In each case the proliferation-relevant activities of each state are tentatively assessed with respect to the full range of known WMD programmes. In addition, a brief analysis of the weapons-relevant decision-making process suggests the major motive forces behind the acquisition decisions. State capabilities are analyzed in terms of both 'programme status' and infrastructure potential.

Iraq

The current status of the Iraqi NBC/missile programmes is the subject of the current intense scrutiny of UN inspectors acting under the authority of Security Council Resolution 687.[9] In general, it can be assumed that most, if not all, of Iraq's WMD capabilities have either been destroyed or are currently being dismantled under the aegis of the inspectorate. In particular, the Iraqi CW programme appears to have been completely destroyed. However, according to UN reports, the Iraqis have consistently resisted the efforts of UN inspection teams, particularly with respect to allowing genuine and full access to suspected nuclear weapons facilities.[10]

The key issue regarding Iraq is probably more a question of when, not whether, it will resume its weapons development activities. In this context, the important issues are whether the Iraqi leadership is currently hiding nuclear and BW materials and what the timeframe is for what is assumed to be the inevitable resumption of nuclear and BW weapons development. Suffice it to say that the Iraqi case is compelling evidence of the importance of using political intentions as a key index to future development. Perhaps the most significant implication of the Iraqi case is the need for continuing vigilance in the assessment of future proliferation threats, particularly in the context of impending arms control agreements concerning WMD.

If Iraqi capabilities in the aftermath of the Gulf War are, indeed, on the rebound, it is not clear that the motivation of the regime has been substantially altered by either the war or the inspection regimes that were imposed on it by the Coalition allies. A brief analysis of this motivational structure is suggested here. In general, Iraqi proliferation decisions result from a combination of factors, including a leadership committed to increasing state power through military means, an ambitious and expansionist grand strategy associated with that leadership, and a legitimizing strategic culture oriented towards anti-Western, radical political values and military solutions to political issues. Indeed, the Iraqi regime under Saddam Hussein suggests a 'proliferation regime' type. The defining aspects of such a regime are reflected in the political ideology and the political culture of the elite in several ways. Firstly, there is the development of a radical, militarist and strategic culture that puts a heavy emphasis on the nation-state's status and prestige. Secondly, the importance is stressed of technology and technical development and the relationship between technology and national power; thirdly, the political leadership defines national interests and national security in terms of a 'grand strategy', which serves to integrate the relationships between political ends and military means, in particular with respect to defining general force doctrines. Fourth, states which seek to acquire mass weaponry require an economic base that can furnish the resources for an expensive, multiphased programme, from research, development and training, to field deployment. This observation is assumed to be valid for chemical and biological weapons as well as for nuclear weapons, in spite of the well-worn, but largely inaccurate, refrain about the 'poor man's nuclear weapon'.

Post-war Iraq satisfies all four criteria. The Ba'thist political elite in Iraq is a fanatically radical, fervently nationalistic and highly authoritarian group that places great weight on its standing in the region. In addition, as secular modernists, Ba'thist elites place a major emphasis on the role of technology in modern economic development and as an index of modern political power and national prestige. Furthermore, since 1973 Iraq has spent enormous sums of oil wealth on both a conventional and a non-conventional arms build-up.

As the ruler of Iraq, Saddam Hussein is the ultimate source and arbiter of all defence decisions. Hussein articulates a strategic ideology or a 'grand strategy', which both establishes political goals and integrates them into a set of political, military and economic means. In addition, Hussein has invariably committed the economic resources necessary to acquire, develop and sustain major military development programmes, including the exceedingly costly WMD programmes. In the context of the outcome of the Gulf War and Iraq's relentless effort to rebuild its weapons inventories, Hussein can be expected to continue to be heavily committed politically to Iraq's resumption of its prewar status as a rising star in the Gulf and, indeed, in the Middle East.

Egypt

Egypt appears to have an active interest in chemical weapons (CW) and probably has an active CW programme. However, it does not appear to have a current interest in the development of either nuclear or biological weapons (BW).

Egypt is reported to have a CW programme capable of mustard and nerve gas production.[11] Egyptian CW dates back at least to the early 1960s. During the Yemen civil war, circa 1964–67, Egypt is known to have used mustard gas on Royalist forces.[12] Subsequently Egypt's programme maintained a very low profile – and has been officially denied by Egyptian authorities. According to Egyptian President Hosni Mubarak, however, Egypt has no current interest in such weapons: 'We are against chemical weapons. Of course, we do not build such a factory. We do not like the idea at all. We want to make peace not war.'[13] Nevertheless, enough evidence of an active programme exists to suggest that Egyptian denials are probably disingenuous at best.

Although Egypt is assumed here to possess the necessary infrastructure for the development of nuclear and biological weapons, it is unlikely that more than exploratory efforts have been conducted in this direction.[14] On the other hand, Egypt has exhibited a long-term interest in the development of ballistic missiles, primarily as a function of its acquisition of FROG and SCUD missile technology from the Soviet Union and as a consequence of the dynamics of its intense arms race with Israel, at least until the late 1970s. Egypt currently has two active surface-to-surface missile regiments with twelve FROG-7 systems and a regiment of approximately ten SCUD-B launchers.

Egyptian denials notwithstanding, there are abundant grounds for concluding that Egypt is trying very hard to develop both an effective chemical weapons capability and the means to deliver such weapons. Prominent among the indicators of an Egyptian interest in these weapons is the considerable number of Egyptian individuals recently under investigation for illegally exporting weapons materials.[15] In addition to the development of advanced SCUD missiles, by the mid-1980s, Egypt was involved in at least three other missile projects, the Sakr-80, an advanced artillery rocket designed to replace the FROG-7A, the RS-120 programme, a long-range missile programme initially designed to reach 120 km, and the Condor II/Vector Programme, a 1000 km-range missile in conjunction with Argentina.[16] The Saqr 80 can hurl a 200-kg warhead 80 kilometres. This rocket is 6.5 m long and 210 mm in diameter. According to one source, this system could be easily configured for chemical weapons.

In addition to the delivery systems configured for the use of non-conventional weapons there are conventional weapons or delivery systems that have multi-purpose functions. These include many types of artillery and attack and bomber aircraft that could effectively deliver a wide array of weapons, including most non-conventional types. In this review of weapons developments in the region emphasis is placed on sophisticated aircraft and other systems that are neither readily available on the world market nor from those which have become available as a result of the demise of the Soviet Union. In general, descriptions of aircraft of Soviet origin are included in the Syrian sub-section of this chapter – except where specific countries have acquired or developed unique domestic versions of a particular imported aircraft.

According to one report, there are rumours that Egypt intends to develop 'advanced chemical and biological warheads for its missile systems and modern binary bombs and [Egypt] may be reviving its nuclear weapons research effort'.[17] If true, such developments could have important implications for the balance of power in the region and subsequent efforts for arms control.

Egypt's acquisition and subsequent use of CW during the Nasser regime is seen here as a consequence of a leadership and a strategic culture that viewed Egypt as a state legitimately acting out the role of a great power – albeit regionally defined. In this perspective, Egypt's foreign policy and concomitant defence policy involved the grand political 'ends' and the political and military 'schemes' of a state in search of status and prestige. Thus, Nasser concocted the military intervention in Yemen, an imperialistic adventure, and resorted to the technological 'fix' with CW when conventional doctrine didn't achieve the desired military success. CW was acquired and/or used by a new nation swollen with pride and pretensions, and it was used by a military desperately searching for a way in which to defeat unprotected guerrillas. The point is that there was no clear foreign-threat-oriented rationale for the acquisition of CW. Indeed, some experts have suggested that CW was acquired by default (i.e. as a consequence of weapons materials left by the British army in the wake of World War II) – in which case the issue is not the initial acquisition, *per se*, but one of making use of existing material, and ultimately using it as weapons some years later. In this context, weapons acquisition was more akin to 'warehousing', possibly a result of the military's not uncommon desire to possess a technical 'ace up the sleeve', if and when it were needed.

Egypt's quest for power and status in the 1950s should be seen in the context of its emerging nationalism and the mass support generated by Nasser's leadership and the series of wars with Israel in 1948, 1956, 1967 and 1973. These conflicts were the causes and consequences of a struggle between the Arab states and Israel for military parity as well as political dominance of the region. For Egypt, arms acquisitions have been largely defined by the relationships (or the lack thereof) with the superpowers. Under Nasser, Egypt parlayed its ostensible and official neutrality in the Cold War into a mechanism of political influence and economic trade and access to weapons from the Soviet Union. Under both Sadat and Mubarak, Egypt has continually relied on superpower support for military assistance and access to arms.

For several reasons, the Egyptian political elite tends to view Egypt as the natural leader of the Middle East, both because of its ancient Pharaonic legacy and prestige and due to the growing weight of its relatively large population in calculations of national power. The Egyptian leadership has also tended to assume that the Arab World owes a debt of respect to Egypt as the cradle of early anti-colonial nationalism and out of deference to the legacy of the international non-aligned movement and to 'Nasserism'. In foreign policy, the prerequisite for leading the Arab world has involved confronting the Israeli challenge to Arab interests according to Arab values of honour, courage and dignity. In this context, Egyptian political interests appear to have demanded a 'grand strategy' – based on an assessment of Israeli military power and technological prowess – that can be most effectively accommodated with the acquisition of non-conventional weapons. Such weapons are conceived by important elements of the strategic culture as requirements for the redemption of national honour lost in the succession of humiliating defeats suffered by a technologically inferior army and for the prestige associated with possessing an undeniably potent offensive weapon and a formidable deterrent.

The implication of this conception of Egyptian 'motivations' is to suggest that the acquisition of a mass weapon is to a large extent a function of the political and psychological agenda of the 'strategic culture' as well as a strategic response to particular aspects of the international system. In other words, the motive to acquire such weapons is as much to achieve psychological parity with an adversary that already has them, and the concomitant international prestige of acquiring them, as it is a response to the political or military threat of such a weapon.[18] In specific terms, Egypt views the acquisition of WMD as a legitimate response to the Israeli nuclear threat. It is therefore inclined to acquire chemical weapons both as a direct political response to that challenge and as a potential military response (i.e. a 'retaliation in category'). Thus, Egypt relates to the acquisition of chemical weapons on several levels: (1) it seeks to acquire such arms because of the threat posed by the Israeli weapon; (2) it wants chemical weapons because it believes that a 'great' state should possess weapons of the non-conventional type – commensurate with its political status; and (3) it wants the mass weapon-type simply because *Israel* possesses such weapons. It should be obvious from the motivations listed that those of prestige and the desire to increase offensive military power tend to 'interpenetrate'. Consequently, it is not always easy (or possible) to determine precisely which sets of factors (or what mixture) are relevant to a particular decision-making context. In the 1990s, Egypt continues to seek the status and prestige that attend the dream of decisive military power – in spite of its new and tentative relationships with former adversaries.

Iran

After responding to the initial Iraqi use of CW against its own forces with a rudimentary CW programme, Iran embarked on a full-blown weapons development programme. It now appears to include all types of non-conventional weapons. Indeed, since the summer of 1987, Iran has built a substantial indigenous infrastructure for the production of CW, and it has made major strides in the direction of developing nuclear and biological weapons. In addition, Iran has been very aggressive in obtaining necessary infrastructure and equipment on the world market, even when such efforts are carefully scrutinized by foreign intelligence bureaus and are frequently subjected to public censure as proliferation-oriented transgressions of international law.

Iran is suspected by the US Government of developing of non-conventional weapons with respect to all of the major categories, i.e. nuclear, biological, chemical and ballistic missile.[19] However, although Iran does indeed possess a nuclear weapons programme, it is not generally assessed as constituting a serious near-term threat, and it will probably not materialize for the balance of the decade. On the other hand, apparent Iranian involvement with such pariah states as North Korea, presumably to acquire weapons development materials censured elsewhere on the world market, should be viewed as cautionary.

With respect to CW, Iran is known to have an active development programme and to be capable of producing both mustard and nerve gas.[20] In addition, the Iranians have been suspected of developing BW offensive weapons since the mid-1980s.[21] However, it is unlikely that the Iranians have developed a suitable delivery system for such a weapon. In general, it is probable that such a possible BW effort is largely an R&D effort at this time.

Iranian missile development has proceeded apace with its WMD programme, which was, at least initially, another manifestation of threat-response behaviour to the vulnerabilities made obvious in the Iran–Iraq war. The Iranian missile development programme is reportedly dedicated to short-range ballistic missiles (SRBMs) in the 150-to-300-mile range and to bombardment rockets designed to provide massive firepower as 'area' weapons. In this context, the Iranians have developed the IRAN-130, the

R-17E, a version of the SCUD B, and the Chinese-manufactured Oghab, a 40-kilometre-range rocket.[22]

According to one authoritative source, Iran has a growing capability in the development and manufacture of ballistic missiles. At the present time it is producing reverse-engineered SCUD-type missiles and solid-propellant short-range missiles.[23] Perhaps the most intriguing and ominous fact is Iran's well-known interest in Chinese missile and nuclear technology. A key question is: why would Iran need a missile of the IRBM type? None of its Persian Gulf rivals nor other states which present an obvious threat require that much range.[24] Reportedly, Iran currently has the infrastructure required to assemble and produce foreign-designed ballistic missiles, for example the Chinese '8610', and the North Korean SCUD-B and SCUD-C. More ominously, Iran is currently in the process of designing and producing, with Chinese assistance, ballistic missiles with range of 700+ and 1000+ km, for example, the Tondar-68.[25]

Iran almost certainly acquired CW (and an interest in biological and nuclear weapons) as a direct response to the Iran–Iraq War. This suggests that the initial motive probably had relatively little political content, except to the extent that CW was viewed as a deterrent by the decision-makers. However, Iran's more recent behaviour with respect to non-conventional weapons does indeed suggest a very definite political and military motivation with respect to current weapons acquisition efforts. In brief, Iran is reportedly attempting to acquire all types of NBC/missile weaponry. Part of this effort is no doubt an attempt to redress the substantial weapons losses incurred during the war, but it also appears to be the enterprise of an aggressive, neo-hegemonial power bent on acquiring the means of achieving revolutionary ambitions (i.e. establishing a greater Islamic order throughout areas proximate to the Persian Gulf).[26] Indeed, according to Shahram Chubin, Iran probably seeks to acquire nuclear weapons for the following reasons: (1) to become the dominant power in the Persian Gulf and, thereby, to intimidate its neighbours, (2) to inhibit a US presence in the Gulf and deny the United States access to the Gulf, (3) to assert leadership in the Muslim world and to activate an eastern front against Israel.[27] In this context the assessment of Anthony H. Cordesman emphasizes Iran's *potential* threat. 'The problem is the future. The threat posed by Iran's weapons of mass destruction could be far more important if Iran acquired more effective chemical weapons, highly lethal biological agents, or even one or two nuclear devices.'[28]

The implication of this analysis is to suggest that Iran may well be difficult to deal with in future regional issues involving conflicting definitions of security in the Gulf or along its borders or with respect to regional arms control efforts. Revolutionary Iran is not necessarily motivated by conventional strategic threat phenomena. In other words, a rational calculation of national interests and threat elimination would presumably accommodate a substantial reduction of arms *quid pro quo*. Unfortunately, however, it is by no means clear that Iran's current leadership thinks in these terms. Rather it is a distinct possibility that it conceives of modern armaments as the practical means to create a new hegemony in the Gulf or even an Islamic political order of Iranian design.

However, if Iran is viewed as a threatening power in the Gulf and near its own borders, it is nevertheless a state that perceives itself as the potential victim of great-power manipulation and threat. Indeed, there is no doubt that Iran has a massive fear of the Western powers, particularly with respect to the United States with its unique potential for intervention and its close links with the monarchy of Shah Pahlavi. In addition, the United States' close alliance with Iran's regional rivals in Saudi Arabia and Egypt means that it is the effective guarantor of a status quo that Iran finds inimical to its interests and aspirations for status and leadership in the Gulf. In addition to perceptions of threat based on national interests defined by a revolutionary elite, Iranian hostility towards the Western powers is partly a function of a historical domination by Britain and Russia and a revolutionary experience that has not yet passed its peak.

Syria

Syria is generally believed to possess both active and highly secret CW and ballistic missile programmes. Although some reports of the Syrian CW programme date back to the 1970s, substantial evidence began to emerge in the early 1980s of a significant CW effort.[29] As in the case of other Arab states, speculations about the origins of technology and technical knowledge have often pointed to the Soviet Union and Egypt, often with scant or unconvincing evidence.[30] However, it is highly unlikely that Syria's weapons programmes were developed without considerable assistance from competent sources. Certainly the level and sophistication of its CW programme suggests a massive influx of money and technical assistance. In addition, recent reports have suggested that Syria may have assisted Iran in its CW programme.[31]

According to credible reports, the Syrian CW programme has concentrated on the production of nerve agents, e.g. sarin, a non-persistent agent, for use in surface-to-surface missiles (SSMs) and artillery.[32] According to some reports, Syria has integrated CW assets with a strategic doctrine emphasizing threats to Israeli cities in a deterrent role. More recently, Syria's development of tube and artillery rounds filled with blister agents suggests a tactical use in the terrain-denial role against advancing troops.

A recent report asserts that Syria produces several hundred tons of chemical agents a year at two sites near the cities of Damascus and Homs.[33] In general, Syria has exploited dual-use technology procured in Germany and France to develop its CW production capability. In addition, Syria has successfully obtained precursors from Western Europe and India.[34] The report claims that Syrian chemical warheads were developed with the assistance of Western European and North Korean engineers and technicians.[35] Surface-to-surface missiles have been used in two of the last four wars fought in the Middle East. In October 1973, both Syria and Egypt launched SSMs against military targets – to no avail; neither inflicted substantial damage. During the Iran–Iraq war missiles were used against cities by both sides.

The use of FROG-7 rockets by Syria against targets in northern Israel during the October War prompted a massive retaliatory strike by that country against the general staff and air force headquarters in Damascus as well as economic targets throughout the country.[36] Syria's inability to repel these attacks may have precipitated the decision to acquire SCUD-B missiles in 1974 and North Korean SCUD-C missiles in 1991, the backbone of Syria's strategic forces.[37] The current inventory of SCUD missiles numbers about 250 B and C-type missiles. The use of these missiles during the Gulf War indicated a circular error probable (CEP) of 500–1000 metres, which is not sufficiently accurate to be effective using conventional high-explosive munitions against pinpointed targets, but would presumably be useful against area targets or with chemical warheads. The SCUD-C has a range of 500 kilometres.[38]

Syria is also acquiring the more advanced Soviet/Russian SS21 'Scarab' and the Chinese M-9 missile.[39] In addition, according to one report, Iran, North Korea and China are assisting in the construction of underground factories near Aleppo and Hama. Reportedly, Syria has acquired German precision machinery for this project. Production of the SCUD-C at these sites is expected to start in one year, production of the M-9 is anticipated within two to three years. The Chinese M-9 offers additional range, estimated at 600 kilometres, is more accurate than the SS 21, and is less vulnerable due to its greater mobility and shorter reaction time.

It is worth noting that Syria possesses several types of strike aircraft capable of delivering conventional and non-conventional munitions. They are the Su-24, MiG-23 BN and Su-20/22. However, only the Su-24 has sufficient range and the low-level penetration capability necessary to present a substantial threat to Israeli air defences.[40]

On a more ominous note, Syria reportedly tried to obtain the SS-23 medium-range ballistic missile from the Soviet Union, a request denied by the erstwhile superpower. Nevertheless, the request, if reports are accurate, serves to suggest the inclination of the Syrians to push for technology that could easily threaten both Israel and Iraq.

Syria's CW programme and its effort to develop long-range delivery systems were, at least initially, designed to counter Israeli capabilities and to achieve a strategic parity with that state. This ambition was intended to compel negotiations for a satisfactory Middle East peace settlement. In addition, Syria was also interested in various non-conventional weapons as a 'legitimate' accoutrement of an emerging regional power. The latter context included Assad's well-known aspirations to establish the framework for a 'Greater Syria'. This ambitious strategy carried the pretensions of a reshaping of the map, including the political incorporation of much of Lebanon. In addition, Hafez Assad's ability to solicit technical assistance from the Soviets and from various other states, including Iran, for the acquisition of an enormous war machine in the late 1970s and 1980s was, of course, the linchpin of his policy.

In the case of Syria, weapons proliferation appears to have been a function of the aforementioned factors of political leadership, culture and an ingenious grand strategy. Indeed, Assad's ambitious and shrewd leadership has conceived a grand strategy that successfully parlayed Syria's strategic location into a political asset in its dealings with the Arab world and flattered a Ba'thist culture that is inclined to support virtually any level of political commitment necessary to enhance regional political stature in the Arab World and produce concomitant military parity with Israel. On the other hand, Syria appears to have decided to acquire WMD in the context of strong perceptions of strategic threats emanating from Israel and emphasized by the continuing string of humiliating defeats in Arab wars with that country as well as the increasingly obvious superiority of Israeli armaments.

Libya

Libya is believed to have an active interest in nuclear, biological and chemical weapons. Libya's attitude to such non-conventional weapons is reflected in the militaristic posturing of its leadership and the radical nature of its foreign policy.

Libya's well-known efforts to obtain nuclear weapons date from the early days of the regime when Muammar Qaddafi's lieutenant, Major Jalloud, was sent to Beijing to beseech Chou En-lai for the purchase of an 'Arab' bomb, a request that was politely rebuffed.[41] Since that event, Libya has reportedly pursued every possible avenue leading to the acquisition of nuclear weapons, including aggressively networking with European and South American nuclear aspirants.

Libya probably did not develop a substantial non-conventional programme involving indigenous production objectives until the mid-1980s. However, in the foreseeable future Qaddafi is likely to continue his struggles to obtain the military power and political prestige associated with those states which possess nuclear weapons. Libya's programme was largely the result of Qaddafi's personal desire to acquire these weapons, probably as a function of a concomitant grand strategy designed to thrust Libya into the role of leadership of the Arab world as head of the Arab nationalist 'revolution' and, on the state level, as the champion of the Palestinian cause in the Arab–Israeli conflict. In this concept of Qaddafi's motivational set, non-conventional weapons furnish the prestige of the required political status, and a means of obtaining the prestige that is less politically risky than that posed by his inimitable military-political adventures throughout the area. Indeed, for Qaddafi, non-conventional weapons constituted the political membership card he desperately sought, probably for reasons of personal esteem, as well as the status issues of nationalist political movements and 'modernizing' (i.e. mobilization and neo-mercantilist type) regimes of the Arab world. In this context, non-conventional weapons constituted the price of admission to the elite community of Arab states that seemed to matter in the high-stakes game of international power and influence. Indeed, viewed from this perspective, non-conventional weapons were an entirely rational choice. Without such weapons, Qaddafi was just another rich oil sheik who could buy himself an army outfitted with foreign arms and advisers; with non-conventional arms he was the leader who could demand status for himself, his revolution, Libya and the Arabs – and not be ignored.

Unfortunately for Qaddafi's quest for status, his policies of a massive armaments build-up and his predilection for backing anti-Western radical groups has left Libya politically isolated – in the Middle East. This alienation has seriously hindered Libya's ability to develop WMD.

For the foreseeable future nuclear weapons are likely to remain beyond Libya's near-term technical grasp. Its indigenous capabilities are too rudimentary to permit the production of weapons-grade nuclear materials and the embargo that the major nuclear suppliers have placed on nuclear transfers to Libya is likely to prevent it from making further advances for some time.[42]

In the 1980s Libya made a major effort to obtain an indigenous CW production facility, and it probably succeeded in constructing the major elements of an infrastructure capable of manufacturing CW at a facility near Rabta, about 40 miles south of Tripoli – before the confrontation with the United States over the very issue of CW production. This effort relied primarily on corporate business networks in Europe and in particular, in Germany. Indeed, Libya's international networking approach to the acquisition of an indigenous-based WMD capability is assumed here to constitute a potential model for future proliferation in the Third World.[43]

Although Libya is reported to have begun its CW programme in the mid-1970s, efforts were intensified in 1983-84 as a reaction to Iraq's use of CW in the Iran–Iraq war.[44] Although some reports have suggested that Libya obtained CW from Egypt after the October War in 1973, it is not certain what the actual source of Libyan CW was. Nevertheless, by the late 1970s Libya may have possessed a small stock of mustard and nerve gas.[45] Although reports of Libyan CW development are sparse and speculative, there is a reasonable consensus that the Rabta facility was (or is) a CW production plant and that Libya was therefore capable of producing copious amounts of this agent, probably exceeding the capabilities of any other country in the Middle East or the Third World.[46]

The current status of the Rabta site is unclear; reports of a fire there in early March of 1990 were probably designed by Libyan authorities to suggest an accidental and face-saving end to the CW programme – on that site. On the other hand, numerous reports have emerged to suggest that CW activities are being conducted at other locations.[47]

Libya is assessed by authoritative sources to possess an undeclared offensive biological warfare programme; however, there is no credible evidence of such activity in the public domain.[48] Although some reports suggest that Libya's 'second plant' at Sebha includes a BW research and development function, such assertions have not included a material basis on which to justify such claims. On the other hand, Libya's attempts to cover its CBW efforts with pharmaceutical rationales are not convincing in the least.

Libyan delivery systems follow the familiar Soviet client-state pattern of SCUD missile technology – plus a capability that is dependent on whatever indigenous engineering is available or that can be garnered from the Third World market for missile development. Delivery systems which could be used to employ non-conventional weapons include jet attack aircraft and missiles. The Libyan air force includes approximately ten Su-24s, long-range swing-wing strike fighters roughly equivalent to the General Dynamics F-111. The variant of this aircraft delivered to Libya is probably the 'D' version, which includes a sophisticated radar warning receiver, an improved electronic warfare suite, an improved terrain avoidance radar, satellite communications and an aerial refuelling probe.[48] The Su-24 can carry nearly 25 000 pounds of payload and has an operational radius of 1300 kilometres with 6600 pounds of fuel.[49]

Libya has SCUD-B and FROG missiles that could be used to deliver non-conventional weapons. Indeed, it has sufficient quantities of the former type to have transferred some to Iran during the Iran–Iraq War. For the last ten years, Libya has supported missile development programmes with a number of states. A recent ACDA report suggests that it may now possess the SS-21 and a longer-range missile developed with German assistance.[50] According to some reports, the Libyans may have been involved in ballistic missile development with the West German firm Otrag about 60 miles from Sebha, developing a missile with a 500-to-700 mile range.[51] Other reports have indicated R&D on a missile named 'Al-Fatih', which reportedly has a range of at least 490 kilometres. In addition, Libya has been reported to be interested in the Chinese M-9 missile, with a 600-kilometre range, the CSS-2, and Brazilian long-range systems (i.e. 1000 kilometres).[52] According to some reports, Libya has established a missile range or facility at Al-Qarait and Tauwiwa as well as production sites, but there are no details available.[53]

Qaddafi's Libya exemplifies the case of an armaments programme that is a manifestation of the leadership's ego and ambition. This factor both defines and transcends other elements of state decision-making, such as the more general shaping influences of culture and history and the orientations of the strategic elite. In Qaddafi's Libya that orientation is largely a reflection of his political personality. In this context, Libya's propensity for the acquisition of WMD is largely a function of the political character and the subjective orientations of its political leadership and its ambitious foreign policies. Libya is conceived here to be relatively less influenced by either perceptions of national interests, such as regional or global balances of power, concomitant threat phenomena or other interactive manifestations of the international system.

Israel

Israel's decision to acquire non-conventional weapons was made in the early 1950s by no less a personage than David Ben-Gurion and a coterie of like-minded proponents. This decision was based on Israel's well-known perception of political isolation – of being surrounded by hostile states. In this view mass weapons, particularly nuclear weapons, were necessary to deter attacks by Israel's numerous enemies or to retaliate in the event that such a deterrent failed. This concept of Israel's mass weapons acquisition motivations is basically a strategic-rationalist interpretation. Added to the deterrent component of the formula is a strong penchant by the Israeli strategic elite to strive for political independence with respect to vital necessities, a value that was reinforced by Charles de Gaulle's refusal to resupply Israel after the June 1967 War. The Israelis have never been convinced that the United States will always and invariably support them in a crisis. In addition, they often appear to be quite suspicious of and occasionally quite unhappy with American efforts to intervene politically in the current stage of the conflict, which is presumably a preliminary bartering process leading up to serious negotiations with Syria.

An important aspect of Israel's motivation to acquire arms is a world-view that has evolved conceiving of Israel as a 'destined' and historically derived regional power, a role thrust on it by a series of wars and the challenge of the relentless enmity of Arab states. Israel's desire for WMD was not 'rationalized' for strategic reasons (i.e. a response to regional threats); it was a function of destiny and the accoutrements of such a destiny, namely, formidable and decisive military power. Non-conventional weapons were, after all, sanctioned by the Biblical story of David and his unconventional sling.

Another component of the acquisition decision was the emergence of a very substantial defence industry, the largest single economic enterprise in the country, with an abundance of material interests at stake. Although such criteria as the bureaucratic-economic interests of the defence establishment may not have played a role with respect to Ben-Gurion's initial weapons acquisition schemes, they almost certainly had an impact in facilitating the momentum of the decision once it was made and once the interests began to develop in the wake of a full-blown research and development effort at Dimona and elsewhere. Such decisions are difficult to reverse, as interests become linked to their successful outcome. Indeed, it is quite possible that CW was developed as a piggybacked, collateral effort of prior work on nuclear weapons at the Dimona site. In any case, what probably started as a linear response to a perception of threat has become a complex mix of motivations – the skeins of which are difficult for the analyst to unravel.

Israel is generally thought to possess the capability to develop nuclear, biological and chemical weapons, and, indeed, it is assumed to have existing inventories at its disposal. In Israel's case, the issue of capability is more a question of capacity (i.e. 'how many?' rather than 'can it be done?'). Indeed, the case of Israel mandates a unique consideration of 'proliferation' *fait accompli* in the region since its technical capabilities have far outpaced those of its rivals.

According to a respected authority, the Israeli nuclear programme has actively sought an offensive capability since the mid-1950s. Although official US sources did not acknowledge the Israeli nuclear capability until 1974, a nascent capability at least was widely assumed by most Arab states well before that. The current assessment of respected authorities is that Israel is either on the verge of developing or already has a thermonuclear weapon, a destructive potential several magnitudes beyond that of its Arab rivals.[54] A recent assessment of the Israeli nuclear programme by Leonard Spector asserts, rather pessimistically, that 'it is highly probable that Israel will maintain its nuclear monopoly for much, if not all, of the 1990s; the nuclear map is changing dramatically'.

The Israelis have probably had an offensive CW capability for some time, although the exact date of acquisition is not certain.[55] However, the development of such a weapons system has undoubtedly been substantially hastened by the use of CW by Iraq in the Iran–Iraq War and by the subsequent proliferation of CW in other countries of the Middle East. In any case it seems likely that the Israelis began to view CW as a deterrent as the perception of Arab-state CW threats began to emerge in the 1980s.[56]

With respect to biological weapons, Israel is suspected of having conducted some research on offensive BW agents.[57] However, it probably does not have an active offensive BW weapon at the current time. In general, the consensus among most experts is that Israel's technical sophistication in related fields, such as medical research and microbiology, puts it within the category of the technologically advanced states capable of producing such weapons at will. Israel could almost certainly produce such a weapon within a brief period.

Israeli delivery systems appropriate for non-conventional weapons configurations are operational, sophisticated, and effective.[58] Both Israel's ambitious missile development programme and the quality of Israeli Air Force technology indicates an ability to develop the warheads, munitions or other technologies required for sophisticated and effective nuclear, biological or chemical weapons systems. Israel's aerospace research programme has included the creation of the broad-based infrastructure necessary for quality weapons development. Israel's inventories include Lance missiles obtained from the United States and Jericho 1 and 2 missiles developed domestically. The 1500-km-range Jericho 2 gives Israel the ability to strike targets virtually throughout the Levant. Israel is also developing the Arrow anti-missile missile, which is currently undergoing field tests. It will eventually replace the Patriot missile supplied by the United States during the Gulf War.[59]

Algeria

Algeria is suspected of embarking on a nuclear weapons research programme. This suspicion is based on the acquisition of a highly specialized research reactor that is thought to be much smaller than is normally required for efficient economic power production. In addition, at its site about 150 kilometres south of Algiers, it is protected by a military compound and a nearby SA-5 surface-to-air missile system. Although experts differ on the relative utility of this plant for weapons development (estimates suggest that it would take about three years to produce enough material for one weapon), it is nevertheless an intriguing facility. Some experts believe that the relatively large cooling towers represent a much larger scope of operations than suggested by the purported 15 megawatt capacity.[60] Another report indicates that Algeria purchased uranium oxide from Argentina and may have transferred some of it to Iran. Some experts are also concerned with the Libyan 'connection'; Algeria is believed to have developed 'troubling ties' with Libya, which could have resulted in that state's gaining access to Argentine nuclear knowledge through Algeria.[61]

According to one source, Algeria has conducted research in chemical and biological weapons and 'seems to have stepped up its chemical weapons research significantly since 1988'.[62] On the other hand, Algeria has not displayed any interest in ballistic missile development and does not currently have such weapons.

Algeria's political system is in the midst of an instability engendered by a host of factors. Foremost among them are an economy that has not developed and a political system that cannot deliver on promises for a better life. A second factor is the crisis of legitimacy engendered by a succession of military regimes that have intervened as a result of the economic and political failures of the short-lived civilian government. A third factor is the emergence of a fundamentalist Islamic group that has threatened political unrest and had the audacity to actually win a democratic election – an opportunity quickly withdrawn by the military, which used the occasion to intervene once again.

Given this obvious political turbulence, it is quite clear that none of the above-mentioned motive forces are firmly established. Neither ideology and organization nor strategic culture nor leadership are firmly institutionalized – nor is there any assurance of more than a temporary stability for longer than the next change of leadership in the next coup.

In brief, the political movement that began with the struggle for independence from France by the Front de Libération Nationale led initially by Ahmed Ben Bella has not lived up to the promise of economic progress that accompanied the Revolution. When Ben Bella's minister of defence, Houari Boumédienne, effected a coup in 1965, a precedent was set for military intervention in Algeria that has continued to plague its political leadership. Boumédienne suspended the constitution and ruled with the authority of a Revolutionary Command Council. A major thrust of Boumédienne's regime was central planning of the economy under an ideology of Arab Socialism. Eventually, political issues were resolved as a function of intra-military conflict, and on the basis of military force criteria (i.e. who possessed the forces for implicit coercion).

Unfortunately, Algeria's chronic crises of authority and economic vitality date back to this period. By the time of his death in December of 1978, Boumédienne had reduced Algeria's economy to that of a socialist basket case; worker incentives were eliminated, housing shortages were widespread and unemployment was massive. The succeeding regime under Col. Chadli Benjedid, a pragmatist, attempted unsuccessfully to move back in the direction of a capitalist system. However, Benjedid had none of Boumédienne's qualities for political manoeuvring and charismatic leadership. Algeria's economy continued to founder in an ill-conceived quasi-socialism. By 1985, Algeria's economy was becoming desperate; only 5 per cent of the population owned 45 per cent of the land; unemployment was roughly at 20 per cent; 95 per cent of national income came from gas and oil. By 1982, a substantial portion of the population was ready to try an alternative political agenda in an Islamic revivalist movement.

Simultaneously with the demise of the economy, the government took several steps in the direction of the liberalization of women's rights. This had the effect of further alienating the conservative elements of the population. During 1987 and 1988, the army was forced to suppress rioting connected with residual fundamentalist outrage and against economic austerity measures. In addition, the effect of the liberalization of the electorate was to provide a forum for the fundamentalists. However, when the Islamic Salvation Front Party (FIS) dominated the first free municipal elections on 12 June 1990, it set the stage for a political confrontation. Subsequently, when the FIS won the elections in December 1991, the army staged a coup in order to prevent any chance of a fundamentalist takeover.

The subsequent regime was headed by Mohammed Boudaif, who had been in exile, but the new government's policy was shaped by Defence Minister Khaled Nezzar and Chief of Staff Abdelmalek Guenaizia and others. But on 29 June 1992, Boudaif was himself assassinated by an unknown party. He was succeeded by Ali Kafi, and Belaid Abdesalam was chosen as prime minister to replace Ghozali, who had resigned on 8 July 1992, due to the faltering economy and continuing political instability.[63]

It should be clear from this brief survey of Algeria's political life that it has been fully 'militarized'. Indeed, Algeria constitutes in a sense a military interregnum regime, which is both self-serving and decadent and probably paranoid about the direction and impetus of a revolution of colonial independence that has long since died. In this case, the military can be expected to dominate the political panorama for the near future and to determine the agenda of all defence decisions.[64] Thus, it is hardly surprising that the military rulers have decided to flirt with the major status symbol in the regional political club, namely, the acquisition of a nuclear weapon, however inchoate or far removed from the logic of an arms race or other strategic rationales to justify it.[65]

Algeria's quest for strategic weapons is basically determined by domestic factors, or at the very least is heavily influenced by them. In brief, no credible scenarios of threat or other international environmental factors appear to be compelling with respect to the initiative to 'go nuclear'. Neither Libya, an aspiring nuclear power, nor Morocco, can pose a real nuclear threat in the near term. Rather, it is more likely that Algeria is seeking such weapons as a function of domestic political issues, such as its prestige appeal to the strategic elite. Indeed, it is quite possible that Algeria's strategic elite is basically motivated by 'self-esteem' issues and seeks to enjoy the status associated with the nuclear 'club'.[66]

REGIONAL ARMS RACING

Regional arms racing is mostly a competition between the major regional powers for qualitative changes to their military capabilities. Thus, an analysis of regional arms racing is largely confined to a discussion of the *relationship* between these particular powers. On the state level, competitive arms acquisition processes have so far been related to decision-making. However, on the international scene 'arms racing' refers to a type of strategic interaction, an emphasis on the 'international political environment'. That environment implies the relative balance of power between states; it constitutes the framework for foreign policy and national security-oriented decisions and often defines or influences the domestic policy agenda. The implication is that certain characteristics of that environment will have important impacts on decisions to acquire weapons. In the Middle East, several environmental factors have had important impacts on such decisions and the patterns of relationships they generated.[67]

In this concept, arms 'races' are focused on obtaining the physical accoutrements of political/military power according to perceptions of strategic threats. Indeed, according to Samuel P. Huntington, the race usually concerns a single weapons type.[68] In general, the regional arms race for WMD has been stimulated by several factors:

- The apparent military utility of non-conventional weapons in various countries in the region has been highlighted by effective use of such weapons in several local conflicts; examples are Iraq's use of CW in the Iran–Iraq War, Egypt's earlier use of CW in the Yemen conflict, Libya's use of CW in Chad in 1987, Syria's development of CW in an ongoing arms race with Israel, and Israel's development of non-conventional arms that spans three decades and all major categories of strategic weaponry.
- The development of non-conventional weapons by other Third World states, such as Iran, India and Pakistan, and allegations of WMD use by the Soviet Union in Afghanistan.
- The increasing costs of conventional weapons have generated a need for a cheap force-multiplier, a technological fix for the relatively disadvantaged state that cannot afford the costs of vast supplies of conventional arms.
- The availability of key weapons systems and sub-systems and infrastructure has expanded to European, Latin American and Asian suppliers and sources of technical expertise.[69]

According to Samuel P. Huntington, arms competitions are either quantitative or qualitative (or both), and such interactions typically occur among weapons that are functionally related, either in terms of 'similarity', e.g. jet fighters versus rival jet fighters they would engage in combat, or of 'complementarity' that concerns weapons designed for combat with each other but that are different types of weapons (i.e. fighters versus bombers). In addition, some states are motivated to seek 'absolute' weapons that 'would render superfluous further military effort, regardless of what other states might do'.[70]

In general, regional proliferator states have sought to obtain both 'decisive' or 'absolute' power in the case of nuclear weapons acquisition and a combination of 'absolute and relative' power in the case of chemical and biological weapons, because these weapons types share a definitive capability for mass destruction. In addition, their presumed functional complementarity is of roughly equal importance on a psychological level; all of these weapons types are capable of offering some level of deterrence against virtually any type of weapons capability, if not on precisely equal physical terms (i.e. with respect to destructive magnitude), at least with a degree of psychological parity or functional equivalence. On the other hand, states that seek indigenous production capabilities must possess either a broad technical infrastructure or engage in very large-scale R & D programmes and related training efforts. In addition, weapons technology must eventually be coupled with an effective delivery system, which typically requires a major engineering effort in its own right.

Several assumptions about the nature and conditions of regional strategic interaction frame the analysis of arms racing. Firstly, the size and shape of regional political geography tends to structure interaction within certain interlocking sub-regions, which are historically important in terms of the distribution of power, culture and international relations. In the Middle East, the relatively large number of middle-sized and roughly equal states (i.e. Egypt, Iraq, Libya, Syria, Algeria, Saudi Arabia, Morocco, Turkey) and the absence of a single consistently dominant regional state are key facts of life and facts which encourage the tendencies of these states to compete for leadership roles. Secondly, certain regional institutions have formed the basis for a common regional-national and/or ethnic political identity, such as the prevalence of Islam and the importance of traditional Arab lifestyles and values. Third, foreign influence, particularly with respect to political and military intervention, has had an important impact on indigenous elites in terms of their willingness to assimilate foreign culture and concomitant definitions of perceived threats to national autonomy and dignity. Fourth, the perception of political autonomy of the state, particularly *vis-à-vis* the superpowers or former colonial powers, is one of the most important political values in the region, one that skilful leaders carefully cultivate and none will safely ignore. Finally, modern technology, in particular sophisticated Western weapons technology, is a highly prestigious entity in its own right, regardless of the ironic inclination by some regional elites to summarily reject certain other facets of materialist Western culture.

As for arms acquisitions, several new elements or characteristics of the current political environment tend to structure the interaction. The first is the end of the Cold War as a result of the collapse of the Soviet state. The immediate effect of that collapse was to deprive the client states of the former Soviet Union of the reassurance that their political mentor would be able or willing (particularly after Gorbachev's ouster) to support their military armaments acquisition programmes. As a result of this development, Syria, Libya, Iraq and Algeria were compelled to search elsewhere for weapons types formerly obtained from the Soviet Union, with due allowances for the Russian government's recent tendency to view arms transfers as a means of sustaining the weapons establishment in that country and for obtaining hard currency. On the other hand, the Soviet Union's well-known propensity to avoid helping aspirant nuclear proliferator countries suggests that there was probably relatively little net change in status or access to Soviet nuclear, chemical or biological programmes as a result of the political changes in that country.

Another impact of the demise of the Soviet Union was to place the United States in the position, whether by default or not, of foremost arms supplier to the region. This development meant that the United States was often in the discomfiting position of trying to cap arms sales in one area, while simultaneously leading the fray in other areas of arms marketing, particularly with respect to supplying sophisticated conventional weapons to US allies.[71] With respect to WMD, the US policy against proliferation was consistently on the record in favour of arms control measures, even if the nation did not always or consistently back measures against treaty noncompliance.[72]

REGIONAL STRUCTURES

In general, WMD proliferation driven by strategic factors in the region has been related to two dominant structural foci; it is either related to the Arab–Israeli dispute or is largely a function of sub-regional rivalries between Arab states. Revolutionary Iran currently constitutes the key element of the second focus.

The series of conflicts between the Arabs and the Israelis, Israel's seemingly paramount military power, and Israel's 'opaque' possession of nuclear weaponry have all had an important impact on the proliferation phenomenon in the region.[73] Indeed, in spite of whatever combination of motivations are in fact responsible for Arab-state proliferation decisions, the dispute with Israel ranks high on the list of 'official' rationales. Undoubtedly, this reflects both genuine political calculations of the perceived Israeli threat to national interests and associated sentiments. However, it is also indicative of disingenuous Arab state posturing against an unpopular enemy with other interests in mind, such as the internecine rivalries between Arab states.

Unfortunately, the traditional dynamic of conflict between the Arabs and Israel is not likely to change substantively in the near future, primarily because international rivalries are not generally resolved as linear consequences of issue-oriented negotiations. Israel and the Arab states will continue to behave as sovereign rival states with distinct sets of competing national interests. On the other hand, it is by no means clear that the traditional patterns of enmity will indefinitely subvert the prospects of more normal relationships between Israel and the Arab states. At the current time it appears that the anti-Israeli ethic is too deep-seated in the strategic cultures of the major regional powers for there to be short-term changes. Indeed, crowd-pleasing posturing against Israel has been a fundamental source of political legitimacy in Arab capitals and Jerusalem since the early 1950s. In addition, that rationale is justified by the simple and not unreasonable argument that Israel is the most formidable military power in the region. Alternatively, the Israeli elite also suffers from hard-core, anti-Arab sentiments that will not be readily quashed by regional negotiations for 'arms control' purposes. In addition, it is difficult to exaggerate the symbolic and psychological impact of Israel's identification with the sophisticated technologies of the Western powers.

On the speculative level, one could hope that those with a pragmatic orientation and young people untouched by first-hand tragedies of war may one day lead the region out of the political black hole. Indeed, Israel's economic prowess and technical sophistication could conceivably be viewed by some of the newly emerging pragmatic political elites, particularly those of the new middle classes, many of which are emerging within non-traditional, military-led regimes, as a potential source of technical assistance – in the framework of a yet-to-be-realized new regional order.

Perhaps more ominously, Israel has not hidden the fact that it has a nuclear capability. Rather, it occasionally issues 'opaque' official statements about not being the first to use such a weapon, which are presumably intended to avoid either humiliating the Arab states by publicly highlighting their inferiority or embarrassing Israel when the truth of their existence eventually becomes public knowledge and irrefutable. This issue, of Israel's techno-superiority, is a major driver of Arab passions precisely because it is beyond the cultural grasp at this moment in history of either the traditionalist, authoritarian or radical mobilizing Arab states to develop an Israeli level of technical sophistication.

If Israel and interested Arab parties fail to reach a lasting agreement on the Palestinian and related issues, the cycle of strategic arms competition will almost certainly continue into the future, with due allowances for the relative inability of the former Soviet client states to purchase arms in the current economic environment. Nevertheless, frustrated Arab proliferator states can be expected to try, and their domestic agendas will force them to do nothing less.

The primary arms race with Israel in the recent past has mainly involved Syria. In the case of Syria, however, the immediate prospects for resuming its intense arms race of the 1980s are minimal, if not impossible. Indeed, in terms of WMD it is not clear what a Syrian acquisition effort could accomplish, because from an economic perspective, such a capability is not within an easy or even a mid-term grasp. On the other hand, Syria is known to have a substantial capability with respect to both chemical weapons and missile delivery systems.

On the international side, Syria's efforts to upgrade its capabilities will need to wait for the development of a new mentor. Syria's efforts to maintain a modicum of stability (i.e. to keep the Israelis and the Iranians at bay) as well as to facilitate its political stature and influence in Lebanon have earned it some respect from the conservative Arab states. In the past, relations with Saudi Arabia have been troubled by Assad's radical secularism and his tendency to court the Soviet Union. Syria has been credited by conservative Arab states with helping to stave off Saddam Hussein's aggressive designs for the region. However, the Saudis are more likely to view Syria with respect for its wily and prudent leadership, rather than for its potential as a strategic ally.

At this point, most of Saudi Arabia's defence efforts appear to have been absorbed by an enormous defence build-up that has important implications for the whole Gulf sub-region. Indeed, Saudi 'rearmament' in the wake of the Gulf War has probably helped to stimulate the size and tempo of the massive current Iranian arms build-up. The Saudi build-up included a massive conventional arms acquisition programme, including the 'big five' American weapons systems: the M1 Abrams main battle tank, the M2 Bradley infantry fighting vehicle, the UH-60 Black Hawk helicopter, the AH-64 Apache attack helicopter and the Patriot air defence missile. In addition, the Saudis are implementing plans to augment the size of their F-15 inventory with another 72 of the expensive fighter planes. In addition, they are upgrading the sophistication of their already formidable air defence command and control systems.

The scale of the Saudi build-up is extraordinary. Since the Gulf War, the Saudis are estimated to have imported arms worth US $30 billion, with the United States, Britain and France as the major suppliers. In the 1990s, Saudi Arabia has emerged as the developing world's leading arms importer. Unfortunately, both the magnitude of the build-up and the types of weaponry involved tend to precipitate both the strategic and non-strategic factors which could serve to justify subsequent WMD acquisition efforts in both Iran and Iraq.[74]

Perhaps the most problematical aspect of the Saudi build-up is not its magnitude, but the types of technology the Saudis seek to acquire. In brief, the Saudis want the high technology items that were effective against Iraq in the Gulf War: (1) 'C3I' – command, control, communications and intelligence items, (2) defence suppression technology, and (3) precision guidance technology.[75] The disturbing aspect of this build-up is that it suggests the possibility of driving regional rivals in the direction of more and more sophisticated arms and indeed to technological 'fixes', such as those supplied by WMD.

Iran is involved in a massive arms build-up, which is undoubtedly partly a response to the massive and high-tech Saudi acquisition efforts. However, it is not clear whether its acquisition of WMD is designed to ward off real or perceived enemies or is rather a consequence of Iranian domestic politics and ambitions for regional hegemony. Unquestionably, Iran has certain legitimate security needs that are largely the result of the military and economic devastation resulting from its war with Iraq.

Even if there is a perception of threat from the Saudis, the scope of the Iranian build-up is clearly ambitious. Evidence of the massive scale is indicated in numerous recent international arms trades. In 1989, the Iranians signed a US $5 billion arms agreement with the Soviet Union that was subsequently reconstituted with the separate states of the Commonwealth of Independent States. The intention was to rebuild the air force by importing fighters and bombers.[76]

A more difficult question is, in addition to the wound-licking after the war with Iraq, what strategic factors are driving Iran's acquisition efforts? What are the regional factors that compel Iran to spend badly needed economic resources on a military build-up? Three possible reasons are: (1) the Iranian perception of Iraq as a continuing threat, a resurgent Iraq, presumably bent on revenge for the previous war (1980–87) and guided by a radical-militarist regime which was probably toughened by a recent defeat by the Western powers; (2) a developing arms race with Saudi Arabia, which is to some extent also a function of post-war rearmaments; (3) an Iranian grand strategy that conceives Iran taking its proper hegemonial role in the Gulf and assuming leadership over the Islamic world. Unfortunately, each of these strategic drives or calculations has its own merit. Iran is, indeed, responding to the potential of a resurgent threat from Baghdad, an active arms build-up on its southern flank and renascent ambitions for regional hegemony that have been largely frustrated since the mid-1980s.

REGIONAL TRENDS

Several regional trends are indicated by recent developments. Firstly, most of the capable states in positions of substantial economic strength and political ambition for a regional or sub-regional role are embarking (or have already embarked) on acquisition programmes for WMD. Secondly, countries that have economic and technological capacity and/or strong economic and political ties to the West and, in particular, to the United States, are either deferring commitments to such programmes or are involved in certain corollary programmes, such as potentially associated delivery systems and concomitant personnel training. Thirdly, several of the proliferator countries are developing acquisition-relevant ties with Third World suppliers, such as China, Brazil, North Korea, India and others, which will be difficult to influence substantially through either international efforts, such as arms control, or unilateral foreign policy. Fourthly, the multinational corporation has become an increasingly important player in the international arms trade, and it is particularly difficult to track and to hold accountable – given the dual-use nature of the technologies transferred and the clandestine nature of such programmes.

As the preceding analysis makes clear, the major states of the region will continue to acquire more and more advanced weaponry, and this tendency will occasionally assume the traditional pattern of strategic competitions associated with racing behaviour. This conclusion is neither counter-intuitive nor surprising. However, one related trend is particularly ominous: *the concerted new effort to establish indigenous and autonomous WMD programmes*. Ironically, this effort is probably to some extent a result of Western non-proliferation policies. In the quest for autonomy, proliferation states will probably continue to attempt to limit their future dependence on the technically sophisticated West. Instead, states aiming at proliferation will rely on dedicated international business consortia and rogue scientists from the former socialist bloc countries and other 'scientists of fortune'. In addition, economic incentives, such as economies of scale and off-market profits (i.e. bribery), should facilitate the necessary technical expertise from Western corporate sources. The problem with this trend is that it is difficult to influence, and, by definition, once the status of autonomy is reached, it will be virtually impossible to control subsequent developments.

On the narrowest, technical level, most of the states of the region can be expected to have taken due note of the technological lessons of the Gulf War. In that conflict, the demands for highly effective weapons, such as the Precision Location Strike Systems, Global Positioning Satellites (GPS), laser-guided 'smart' bombs, cruise missiles, and anti-missile missiles are already the object of intense scrutiny in the arms bazaars of the region. This interest is, of course, motivated by both security interests and non-strategic security concerns, such as prestige and status and the bureaucratic-organizational agendas of regional elites.

In summary, besides striving to acquire the advanced anti-armour and guidance technologies highlighted in the Gulf War, most of the regional proliferator states can be expected to continue their efforts to obtain WMD. In addition, the Gulf War may well have contributed additional resolve to the predilection to reject all arms control agreements that leave those states without an ostensible or arguable parity with Israel.

NOTES

1. On the general characteristics of such weapons, see US Congress, Office of Technology Assessment, *Proliferation of Weapons of Mass Destruction: Assessing the Risks*, OTA-ISC-559 (Washington, DC: US Government Printing Office, August 1993), Chapter 1, 'Introduction and Summary', pp. 1–32. The term 'weapon of mass destruction' refers to nuclear, biological, and chemical weapons. In this chapter, it implies a weapons 'system' including both the destructive 'agent' of a nuclear, biological, or chemical device and the concomitant technological and human infrastructure required for its effective use. The term 'non-conventional weapons' is used herein to describe such weapons types and their complementary ballistic missile delivery systems.

   Nuclear weapons destroy primarily by explosive shock wave and nuclear radiation. Nuclear weapons are by far the most destructive. Biological weapons consist of live, pathogenic organisms used as infectious agents. Chemical weapons are highly toxic organic chemicals used as poisons. The key difference is that biological agents are capable of reproducing, and are, thereby, capable of magnifying the threat exponentially. CW are derived from organic chemicals, but they are not live organisms or 'biological'.

   In general, although in theory both biological and chemical weapons are highly destructive, their effectiveness on the battlefield is limited by the efficient use of dedicated physical defences and by certain ameliorating and ambiguous environmental factors, such as wind direction, temperature and humidity. On the other hand, such weapons can have important negative impacts on civilian and troop morale and psychology, and their potential effects could play an important role as a deterrent.

2. For a recent discussion of the concept of the 'arms race', see Michael Sheehan, *The Arms Race*, (New York: 1989), pp. 9–11. This chapter borrows from a discussion of the history of the concept in Patrick M. Morgan, 'Arms Races and Strategic Surprise', a paper presented at the International Studies Association – West, Convention, March 1980. According to Morgan the concept implies 'an unusual level of effort, and does not continue indefinitely' (p. 3). In addition, the arms race embodies a heightened level of hostility and suspicion, a greater concern in each party about the other's incremental improvements in military power, a greater willingness to sustain military burdens, systematic attempts to predict the course of prospective wars, and a psychological context for perception and interpretation of rival behaviour that affects the decision-making involved (p. 4).

   Samuel P. Huntington's earlier definition of the concept suggested that it was 'a progressive, competitive peacetime increase in armaments by two states or coalitions of states resulting from conflicting purposes or mutual fears. An arms race is thus a form of interaction between two states or coalitions.' (*Public Policy*, 1958, pp. 385–96.) Huntington also suggests that the competition typically involves one weapon type or one form of a single weapon type (pp. 374–6). See the comments on Huntington's conception and its shortcomings in Patrick M. Morgan, *Theories and Approaches to International Politics: What Are We to Think*, Second Edition (New Brunswick, NJ: 1977), pp. 275–7.
3. 'Proliferation' refers to the spread of such weapons to states which have not previously possessed them, and which, for the most part, have not previously had the technical capability to possess them. In practice, however, the term has come to imply non-Western states which are not generally viewed as politically stable or which have recently tended towards foreign policies perceived as threatening Western interests.
4. Ibid., *Theories and Approaches*, pp. 275–7.
5. On the relationship between weak legitimacy in third world authoritarian regimes and arms acquisitions, see M. E. Ahrari, 'Arms Race in the Persian Gulf: The Post-Cold War Dynamics', in M. E. Ahrari and James H. Noyes, *The Persian Gulf after the Cold War* (Westport, CT: Praeger, 1993), p. 172.
6. On the upward spiral of Middle Eastern arms purchases in the 1980s, see Richard F. Grimmett, *Conventional Arms Transfers to the Third World, 1983–1990*, Congressional Research Service, 2 August 1991, p.CRS 20. See also M. E. Ahrari, 'Arms Race in the Persian Gulf: The Post-Cold War Dynamics', in M. E. Ahrari and James H. Noyes (eds), *The Persian Gulf after the Cold War*, op. cit., pp. 172–96, esp. pp. 181–5. See also the description of technical trends in Anthony H. Cordesman, *After the Storm: The Changing Military Balance in the Middle East* (Boulder and London: Westview Press, 1993), pp. 51–82.
7. For a historical treatment of this process, see J. F. C. Fuller, *Armament and History* (New York: Charles Scribner's Sons, 1945), pp. 1–23.
8. A more comprehensive analysis of the decision-making processes associated with mass weapons is covered in the author's doctoral dissertation: *The*

Acquisition of Chemical Weapons in the Middle East (Claremont, CA: Claremont Graduate School,1994) Part I.

9. This resolution stipulated the terms for the cessation of hostilities with Iraq that terminated the Gulf War in August 1991. Iraq had agreed to destroy all weapons of mass destruction, and it acceded to ongoing UN on-site inspections that verified the destruction and monitored Iraq's progress towards compliance with the terms of the agreement.
10. For a discussion of the problems confronting Iraqi-based UN inspection teams operating under Security Council Resolution 687, by no means irrelevant to future arms control efforts on behalf of treaty 'verification' objectives, see R. Jeffrey Smith, 'Secretive Iraq Parries UN Arms Inspectors', *The Washington Post*, 4 November 1994, pp. A1,30; Rolf Ekeus, 'Iraq: the Future of Arms Control', *Security Dialogue*, Vol. 25 (1994) no. 1, pp. 7–16; Nikita Smidovich, 'The Russian and Other Perspectives', in Benoit Morel and Kyle Olson (eds), *Shadows and Substance: The Chemical Weapons Convention* (Boulder, CO: Westview Press, 1993), pp. 55–72.
11. See Robin Wright, 'U.S. Leaks Word of a Secret Egyptian Chemical Warfare Plant: Cairo Issues Denial', *Los Angeles Times*, 11 March 1989, p. 11. For Israeli reaction to this 'leak', see 'Egypt and Poison Gas', *Jerusalem Post International Edition*, 13 March 1989, p. 24. In general, for the single most comprehensive survey of CW programmes, see Gordon M. Burck and Charles F. Floweree, *International Handbook on Chemical Weapons Proliferation* (New York: Greenwood Press, 1991), pp. 222–38. It should be noted that reports on the Egyptian (and other Arab states) programmes are often from Israeli sources and are therefore subject to some possible bias. On the other hand, Israeli sources are frequently the most well-informed about such matters. See Anthony H. Cordesman, *Weapons of Mass Destruction in the Middle East* (London: 1991), pp. 141–4. It should be emphasized that it is not clear what the status of current Egyptian capabilities is with respect to nerve gas or when it developed the weapon as such. See also W. Seth Carus, 'Chemical Weapons in the Middle East', *Policy Focus*, Number Nine, Washington Institute for Near East Policy, December 1988, p. 3.
12. For evidence of the Egyptian use in Yemen, see the inspection report documents of the International Red Cross, the full text of which was published in 'How Nasser Used Poison Gas', in *U.S. News and World Report*, 3 July 1967, p. 60.
13. Robin Wright, 'U.S. Leaks Word of Secret Egyptian Chemical Warfare Plant; Cairo Issues Denial', op. cit., p. 11.
14. On the possibility that Egypt has developed a nuclear weapons programme, see the negative assessment by Leonard Spector with Jacqueline R. Smith, *Nuclear Ambitions: The Spread of Nuclear Weapons* (Boulder, CO: 1990), p. 144. According to Spector, Egypt is believed to have sought Chinese aid in developing nuclear arms in the 1960s, but since signing the peace agreement with Israel in 1979 and the Nuclear Non-Proliferation Treaty in 1981, its 'nuclear intentions appear to be entirely peaceful' (p.144). On the possibility of a BW programme, see Efraim Karsh, Martin Navias and Philip Sabin, *Non-Conventional Weapons Proliferation in the Middle East* (Oxford: 1993), Introduction, p. 3. See also Cordesman, *Weapons of Mass*

Destruction, op. cit. p. 143. According to this assessment, Egypt 'seems to have carried out extensive research on biological weapons and could go rapidly into production', p. 143. It should be noted that Egypt is not generally listed in public sources as possessing an offensive BW programme. On this point see the list in *Proliferation of Weapons of Mass Destruction: Assessing the Risks* (Washington, DC: Office of Technology Assessment, United States Congress, 1993), Chapter 2, 'Assessing the Risks', Table 2–8, 'Countries Generally Reported as Having Undeclared Offensive Biological Warfare Programs', p. 65.

On the development of ballistic missiles, see Cordesman, *Weapons of Mass Destruction*, op. cit., pp. 142–4. Egypt has reportedly developed an improved version of the SCUD B with North Korean assistance, possibly stepping up its efforts to improve that missile after Israel's testing of the Jericho II. See also W. Seth Carus, *Ballistic Missiles in Modern Conflict* (New York: Praeger, 1991), p. 85. See also Robert G. Nagler, *Ballistic Missile Proliferation: Emerging Threats* (Arlington: Systems Planning Corporation, 1992), on Egypt's collaboration with Argentine to produce a solid propellant, inertial-guided missile, the Condor II, with a range estimated at 800–1000 kilometres. Egypt withdrew after Iraq refused to pay for missiles used in the Iran–Iraq War. The Egyptian version of 'Condor', known as 'Vector', could have targeted the major political capitals in the region.

15. See, for example, Cordesman, *After the Storm*, op. cit., pp. 345–7.
16. See Joseph S. Bermudez, 'Egypt's Missile Development', William C. Potter and Harlan W. Jencks, *The International Missile Bazaar: The New Suppliers' Network*, (Boulder, CO: Westview Press, 1994), pp. 23–46, esp. 31–41.
17. Cited in Cordesman, *After the Storm*, op. cit., pp. 374, n. 434. The author specifies several sources for these 'rumours': *Jane's Defence Weekly*, 17 February 1990, p. 295 and *The Financial Times*, 21 November 1989, p. 1; *Washington Post*, 20 September 1989.
18. See the comment by William Lewis on the importance of the psychological dimension in the evaluation of Middle East military capabilities in 'The Military Balance: Change or Stasis', Chapter 3, in Phoebe Marr and William Lewis (eds), *Riding the Tiger: The Middle East Challenge after the Cold War* (Boulder, CO: Westview Press, 1993), p. 83.
19. *Proliferation of Weapons of Mass Destruction*, op. cit., p. 66, Figure 2–3, 'Suspected Weapons of Mass Destruction Program'. For a description of Iraq's efforts to rebuild its military, see 'Iraq's Reborn Military', *The Washington Times*, 1 June 1993. According to this report, Iraq has rebuilt 80 per cent of its tank production capability. In addition, it has reportedly rebuilt 200 munitions factories and revived its international arms network; see the sub-committee staff report of the House Committee on Foreign Affairs referenced in Jeanne Kirkpatrick, 'Iraq Proves the Frailty of Nuclear Restraints', *The Sun*, 14 July 1993; for an indication of the horrific and ambitious weapons projects sponsored by the Hussein regime, see 'Britain Tells of Effort to Sell Supergun Parts to Iraq', *The New York Times*, 1 July 1993; for an assessment by the Central Intelligence Agency on Iraq's ability to produce intercontinental missiles, see Bill Gerz, 'North Korea, Iran, Iraq, Capable of Developing ICBM', *The Washington Times*, 24 December 1993;

Kenneth Timmerman, 'A Nuclear Iraq – Again', *The Wall Street Journal*, 12 November 1993. For a report on Iraq's alleged effort to save the bulk of its BW programme, see the testimony by Gordon Oehler of the Central Intelligence Agency.

20. For an early account of the Iranian CW capability, see 'Iranian Says His Country Is Able to Make its Own Chemical Arms', *New York Times*, 3 April 1984, p. 12; Tom Diaz, 'Syria Said to Have Offered Chemical Weapons to Iran', *Washington Times*, 9 December 1985, p. 4; 'Making Chemical Arms Iran Says; Planes Next', *Los Angeles Times*, 28 December 1987, p. 5. According to Cordesman Iran had produced significant amounts of mustard and nerve gas by the August 1988 ceasefire, but never succeeded in effectively using CW. More recently, Iran has established a significant CW production capability and may have obtained CW material from India, North Korea, West Germany [*sic*] and China. *Weapons of Mass Destruction*, op. cit., pp. 83–4. On recent developments, see Ed Blanche, 'Iran Close on Missile That Could Hit Israel', *The Washington Times*, 23 October 1993, p. A5; 'North Korea's Air Force Chief Visits Iran for Closer Ties', *The Washington Times*, 25 February 1994. According to Leonard S. Spector, Iran will probably be the second Islamic country, after Pakistan, to possess a nuclear weapon. See Leonard S. Spector, 'Islamic Bomb West's Long Term Nightmare', *The Washington Times*, 19 January 1994, p. A20; 'China Gives Iran Nuclear Boost', *The Washington Times*, 5 July 1993.
21. According to Cordesman, op. cit., 'there are strong indications' from experts that Iran is working on biological weapons, p. 84.
22. The IRAN-130 is probably a solid-fueled rocket. Iranian officials announced a successful test of a missile with a 160-kilometre range in July 1988. See Teheran Domestic Service, 31 July 1988, as translated by the Foreign Broadcast Information Service, Daily Report: Near East and South Asia, 2 August 1988, p. 52. For a report on a 200-kilometre-range missile, see Teheran IRNA, 17 April 1989, as reported in Foreign Broadcast Information Service, Daily Report: Near East and South Asia, 18 April 1989, p. 52. For a report on a missile with a 320-kilometre range, see Teheran Domestic Service, 14 April 1988, as translated by the *Daily Report: Near East and South Asia*, 15 April 1988, p. 51.
23. *Proliferation of Weapons of Mass Destruction: Assessing the Risks*, op. cit., see Table 2–9, 'Classification of Indigenous Production Capabilities of Ballistic Missiles', p. 67.
24. A point made by Joseph S. Bermudez and W. Seth Carus, 'Iran's Growing Missile Forces', op. cit., p. 126.
25. See Joseph S. Bermudez, 'Iran's Missile Development', in William C. Potter and Harlan W. Jencks (eds), *The International Missile Bazaar: The New Supplier's Network* (Boulder, CO: Westview, 1994), pp. 47–74, esp. p. 65.
26. Evidence for Iranian political ambitions can be found in the statements of the leadership. See Graham E. Fuller, *The Center of the Universe: The Geopolitics of Iran* (Boulder, CO: Westview Press, 1991), pp. 241–3, 261–74. It should also be appreciated that such hegemonial aspirations are duly noted in areas of the Persian Gulf that are on the receiving end of such threats.

27. Shahram Chubin, 'The Middle East', in Mitchell Reiss and Robert S. Litwak (eds), *Nuclear Proliferation after the Cold War* (Washington, DC: Woodrow Wilson Press, 1994), p. 50.
28. Anthony H. Cordesman, *Iran and Iraq: The Threat from the Northern Gulf* (Boulder CO: Westview Press, 1994), p. 84.
29. In 1985, the U.S. Deputy Assistant Secretary of Defence, Douglas Fieth, asserted that the Syrians had 'been interested in chemicals for many years'. See Tom Diaz, 'Syria Said to Have Offered Chemicals to Iran', *Washington Times*, 9 December 1985, p. 4; William Webster asserted in a prepared statement that Syria began CW agent and munition production shortly after Iraq did so in the 1980s, Senate Committee on Governmental Affairs, 9 February 1989, p. 5.
30. On the Egyptian sources, see Aharan Levran (ed), *The Middle East Military Balance 1986* (Jaffee Center for Strategic Studies, Tel Aviv University; Boulder, CO: Westview Press, 1987), pp. 94–5; Jack Anderson and Dale Van Atta, 'Iran May Turn Chemical Tables on Iraq', *Washington Post*, 2 October 1985; Ze'ev Schiff, Tel Aviv, *Ha'aretz,* 18 June 1986, p. 7. On Soviet sources, see Jack Anderson,'The Growing Chemical Club', *Washington Post*, 26 August 1984, Section C, p. 7.
31. On the alleged Syrian supply to Iran, see Jeff Abramowitz, 'Intelligence Briefing: Chemical Warfare', *IDF JOURNAL*, 3, no. 4 (Autumn, 1986), pp. 18–23, referenced in Burck and Floweree, op. cit., p. 219.
32. Marie Colvin and John Witherow, 'Syrian Nerve Gas Warheads Alarm Israel', *Sunday Times*, 10 January 1988; Jack Anderson and Dale Van Atta, 'Israel May Hit Syrian Nerve Gas Plant', *Washington Post*, 24 February 1988, p. D14. Citing a Central Intelligence Agency report the authors assert that the Syrians have made a special warhead to carry the gases atop Soviet-made SCUD-B and SS-21 missiles. The CIA is quoted as assessing the Syrian CW programme as 'the most advanced chemical warfare capability in the Arab World'.
33. Michael Eisenstadt, 'Syria's Strategic Weapons', *Jane's Intelligence Review*, April 1993, p. 169.
34. Ibid., p. 169.
35. Ibid., p. 169.
36. Michael Eisenstadt, 'Syria's Strategic Weapons', op. cit., p. 169.
37. Ibid. The SCUD-B and -C are mobile battlefield surface-to-surface tactical artillery missile systems. They include missiles, transporter-erector, re-supply units, propellant tanker and a command and control unit. The payload is up to 800 kilogrammes of chemical or conventional munitions. Guidance is derived from a strapdown inert guidance system; course correction is by means of jet vanes. Propellant is a single-stage liquid rocket motor. Set-up time for these missiles is slightly less than one hour, including both position identification and wind measurement. See *The World's Missile Systems, Eighth Edition* (Pomona, CA: General Dynamics Corporation, August 1988), pp. 244–5.
38. See the discussion of SCUD technology and development in Steven J. Zaloga, 'Ballistic Missiles in the Third World: SCUD and Beyond', *International Defence Review*, November 1988, p. 1426; W. Seth Carus, 'Trends and Implications of Missile Proliferation', 10 April 1990, a paper

presented at the annual conference of the International Studies Association, 13 April 1990, pp. 18–22.

39. The SS-21 Scarab is the direct replacement for the unguided ballistic rocket FROG-7. A single missile is carried by the launcher vehicle. This missile uses solid fuel. Guidance is according to inertially-corrected ballistic course using jet vanes for steering. See *World's Missile Systems*, op. cit., pp. 242–3.
40. Eisenstadt, 'Syria's Strategic Weapons', op. cit., p. 172.
41. Steve Weissman and Herbert Krosney, *The Islamic Bomb* (New York: Times Books, 1981), pp. 60, pp. 211–12.
42. Leonard Spector and Jacqueline R. Smith, *Nuclear Ambitions: The Spread of Nuclear Weapons, 1990* (Boulder, CO: Westview, 1990), Chapter 2, Libya, pp. 175–83. In this book, Binder, a respected authority on proliferation, gives due weight to the political factors for the first time in his series on nuclear proliferation. In addition, he acknowledges for the first time the political-doctrinal links between nuclear weapons and chemical weapons. See esp. pp. 179–80.
43. On the activities of corporate suppliers in Libya and Iraq involved in proliferation, see Kenneth R. Timmerman, *The Poison Gas Connection: Western Suppliers of Unconventional Weapons and Technologies to Iraq and Libya*, A Special Report by the Simon Wiesenthal Center from Middle East Defense News (MEDNEWS), Los Angeles: 1990, pp. 45–52.
44. Yoseff Bodansky and Vaughn Forrest, 'Chemical Weapons in the Third World, Libya's Chemical-Biological Warfare Capabilities', Task Force on Terrorism and Unconventional Warfare, House Republican Research Committee, US House of Representatives, Washington DC, 12 June 1990, p. 3; El-Hussini Mohrez, *Soviet Egyptian Relations* (New York: St. Martin's Press, 1987), p. 187.
45. See the discussion of 'Rabta' in Burck and Floweree, op. cit., pp. 277–98; William Webster, as Director of Central Intelligence, averred that the Rabta plant was 'as large as anything we have seen' in a speech to World Affairs Council in October 1988, but he later qualified that statement by saying that 'it may be the single largest chemical warfare production plant in the Third World'. The factory 'is expected to soon begin large scale production of mustard and nerve agents – potentially tens of tons per day'. See Webster's prepared statement quoted in Burck and Floweree, op. cit., p. 297.
46. On the plant fire at Rabta, see 'Libyan Poisonous Gas Plant Burns', *Washington Times*, 15 March 1990, pp. A1, 8; on the hoax fire thesis, see Adel Darwish, 'Libya Fire Almost Certainly a Hoax', *The Independent*, 10 April 1990, p. 12. On the possibility of a second CW site in Libya, see Patrick E. Tyler, 'Poisonous Gas Facilities in Libya Monitored by U.S.', *Washington Times*, 19 June 1990, p. A17; Bill Gertz, 'Second Chemical Arms Plant Spied in Libya', *Washington Times*, 18 June 1990, pp. A1, A6.
47. *Proliferation of Weapons of Mass Destruction*, op. cit., p. 65, Table 2-8 – 'Countries Generally Reported as Having Undeclared Offensive Biological Warfare Programs'.
48. *Jane's Soviet Intelligence Review*, July 1990, pp. 298–300; *Jane's Defence Weekly*, 25 June 1985, pp. 1226–27.
49. Dick Palowski, 'Changes in Threat Air Combat Doctrine and Force Structure', 24th Edition, General Dynamics DWIC-91, Fort Worth Division,

February 1992, pp. 1–65 and 110–17, cited in Cordesman, *After the Storm*, op. cit., p. 172, fn. 99.

50. Ibid., p. 153.
51. Lora Lumpe, Lisbeth Gronlund, and David C. Wright, 'Third World Missiles Fall Short', *The Bulletin of Atomic Scientists*, March 1992, pp. 30–6.
52. *Flight International*, May 23–9, 1990, p. 18.
53. See Cordesman, *After the Storm*, op. cit., p. 156.
54. See Leonard Spector, 'Nuclear Proliferation', in Efraim Karsh, Martin Navias and Philip Sabin (eds), *Non-Conventional Weapons in the Middle East* (Oxford: 1993), pp. 151–3. For the original revelation that Israel was developing an arsenal far beyond the scope of consensus assessments, see the revelations by Mordechai Vanunu, 'Revealed: The Secrets of Israel's Nuclear Arsenal', *The Sunday Times*, London, 5 October 1986. See also the important revelations on the possibility of a fusion and neutron capability by S. M. Hersh, *The Samson Option* (New York: 1991).
55. See the comments on the Israeli programme in Gordon M. Burck and Charles F. Floweree, *International Handbook*, op. cit., pp. 191–4. Noted here is the 'unanimous assessment of western intelligence' that the Israelis have had a CW offensive capability since before the October War of 1973 (p. 191). Less certain are the size and age of the stockpile.
56. For an intriguing examination of Israeli nuclear complexes using recent Russian and French imagery, see Harold Hough, 'Israel's Nuclear Infrastructure', *Jane's Intelligence Review* (London: November, 1994), pp. 508–10. According to the author, the placing of the nuclear weaponry in the Judean foothills is evidence of an Israeli defensive doctrine; centred as it is at, presumably, one of the last areas to fall in an invasion, it is an appropriate site at which to house devices that would be used only as a desperate measure against the final threat of annihilation.
57. Anthony H. Cordesman, *Weapons of Mass Destruction in the Middle East* (London, Brassey's:1991), p. 27.
58. For an interesting and comprehensive discussion that includes some insights about Israel's ventures with South Africa and China, see Gerald M. Steinberg, 'Israel: Case Study for International Missile Trade and Non-proliferation', in Potter and Jencks, *Missile Bazaar*, op. cit., pp. 235–54, esp. 239–47.
59. Robert G. Nagler, *Ballistic Missile Proliferation: An Emerging Threat* (Arlington: 1992), p. 42. For an excellent survey of Israeli Air Force assets, see Bill Gunston, *An Illustrated Guide to the Israeli Air Force* (London:1982), esp. pp. 100–11, 132–5, 140–3; on Israel's extensive international weapons trade, see 'China, Israel Show Dubious Honors in Arms Marketing', *The Washington Times*, 4 April 1994, p. A 11; Daniel Williams, 'U.S. Offers to Sell Israel Upgraded Fighter Jets', *The Washington Post*, p. A 31; Michael R. Gordon, 'Israel Sells Arms to China', *The New York Times*,, 13 October 1993, p. 12; 'Why Does Israel Arm China?', *The New York Times*, 15 October 1993, p. 9.
60. Cordesman, *After the Storm*, op. cit., pp. 128–9.
61. See Spector, *Nuclear Ambitions*, op. cit., pp. 205, 233.
62. Cordesman, *After the Storm*, op. cit., p. 128.

63. This political survey is based on Cordesman, *After the Storm*, op. cit., pp. 116–21.
64. For the point that military regimes tend to spend more on their own corporate-military interests, see Eric A. Nordingler, *Soldiers in Politics: Military Coups and Governments* (Englewood Cliffs, NJ: Prentice Hall, 1977), p. 171; Miles D. Wolpin, *Militarism and Social Revolution in the Third World* (Totowa, NJ: Allanheld, Osmun and Co., 1981), pp. 140, 151.
65. For a strategic-oriented argument that Algeria does not have a nuclear programme, see Shahram Chubin, 'The Middle East', *Nuclear Proliferation after the Cold War* (Washington, DC: Woodrow Wilson Press, 1994), p. 54. He argues that Algeria has no compelling threat to seek nuclear weapons. I would agree that Algeria is not surrounded by threatening states, but my analysis suggests another possible source of motivation: the quest for status and prestige that has driven nuclear proliferation developments since at least the time of Charles De Gaulle.
66. On the poignancy of defeat by the technologically superior West or Western surrogates and its implication, see Fouad Ajami, *The Arab Predicament: Arab Political Thought and Practice since 1967* rev. edn (New York: Cambridge University Press, 1992), pp. 30–86. The sense of technical backwardness and humiliation was reflected in a comment by Saddam Hussein – with a kicker: 'The Arabs could do nothing but ride camels...but how could such a people who only knew how to ride camels produce an atomic bomb?' quoted in Efraim Karsh and Inari Rautsi, *Saddam Hussein: A Political Biography* (London: 1992), p. 127.
67. Huntington, op. cit., pp. 374–6. See also J. F. C. Fuller on the 'dominant weapon' concept in *Armament and History* (New York: 1945), pp. 7–8.
68. Cordesman, *After the Storm*, op. cit., pp. 51–2.
69. Huntington, op. cit., pp. 370–2.
70. Andrew Borowiec, 'Weapons Sales Defended', *The Washington Times*, p. A8; Daniel Williams, 'U.S. Offers to Sell Israel Upgraded Fighter Jets', *The Washington Post*, p. A31; Row Scarborough, 'Pentagon Criticized for Loose Reign on Technology for Israeli Missile', *The Washington Times*, 24 August 1993, p. A4.
71. The Reagan Administration consistently refused to back congressional efforts to impose sanctions against Iraq for the use of CW against Iran; presumably this was because the potentially victorious Iran was feared as a potential source of political instability in the region.
72. On Israel's 'opaque' posture with respect to nuclear weapons possession, see Shlomo Aronson with Oded Bush, *The Politics and Strategy of Nuclear Weapons in the Middle East: Opacity, Theory, and Reality, 1960–1991, An Israeli Perspective* (Albany, NY: 1992); Chapter 9, 'The Doctrine of Opaque Nuclear Monopoly', pp. 167–84; for a relatively early statement by a major political proponent of the programme, see Moshe Dayan's comments in *Yediot Aharonot*, Tel Aviv, 14 March 1976, in FBIS/MENA, 18 March 1976, p. N7; Robert E. Harkavy, 'Future of Israel's Nuclear Strategy', *The Washington Quarterly* (Summer 1991): pp. 161–78.
73. Dr Andrew Rathmell, 'Saudi Arabia's Military Build-Up – An Extravagant Error?', *Jane's Intelligence Review*, November 1994, op. cit., pp. 500–5. According to this analysis, Saudi Arabia will need to spend about $14.5

billion for the rest of the century to maintain and operate its current level of armed forces (p. 501). The author asserts that several aspects of the Saudi defence posture are particularly rankling to Iran: (1) Saudi Arabia's protective orientation – directly under the US nuclear umbrella, (2) the large number of highly sophisticated weapons in the Saudi arsenal, particularly with respect to the development of its air force, and (3) the large number of foreign technicians in Saudi Arabia, an infrastructure that could become the basis for foreign intervention.

74. A partial list of these technologies would include the following: space satellite systems, airborne reconnaissance planes, night vision equipment, navigational aids such as global positioning systems, stealth attack bombers, diverse electronic countermeasures, and precision-guided missiles. See Yahya M. Sadowski, *Scuds or Butter?: The Political Economy of the Arms Race in the Middle East* (Washington, DC: 1994), pp. 68–9.

75. Between 1990 and 1992, Iran received approximately 20 MiG-29 fighters, a dozen Su-24 fighter-bombers and about 50 other combat aircraft. Other reports indicate Iran was buying three diesel submarines from Russia, 250 T-72 tanks, and SCUD missiles, Sadowski, op. cit., pp. 64–5. According to *The Military Balance 1992–1993* (London, The International Institute for Strategic Studies: 1992), the Iranians had less than 50 per cent of their US-origin fighter-bomber aircraft (i.e. 60 F-14D/E and 60 F-5D/E) types serviceable.

76. A partial list of the most sought-after technologies would include planes, night-vision equipment, navigation aids such as global positioning systems, stealth attack aircraft, diverse electronics countermeasures, and precision guided missiles and munitions. See Yahya M. Sadowski, *Scuds or Butter: The Political Economy of the Arms Race in the Middle East* (Washington, DC: 1994), pp. 68–9.

Conclusion: Change, Continuity and Prospects for Peace

M. E. Ahrari

A retrospective look at a major theme of this book – change and continuity – also forces one to look at the Middle East in terms of what it was during the Cold War years, what it is becoming in the aftermath of the Cold War, and what shape its strategic affairs are likely to take in the next century.

The initiation of peace negotiations between Israel, the PLO and other Arab states has indeed altered the very nature of politics in that area, a development that I previously labelled as 'mega-change'. One can only contrast this with the prolonged Arab refusal to have a dialogue with Israel with a view to solving the Palestinian Question during the Cold War years. However, this mega-change, like all major changes, has encountered more than its fair share of problems.

The negotiations between Israel and the PLO, the most crucial aspect of the overall peace process, appear to be facing what may prove to be their most serious challenge in the beginning of 1995. The Islamicist extremist groups have caused enough problems through their violent acts that the chances of further Israeli withdrawal from the West Bank appear to be rather dim. As I discussed in my chapter on the peace process, both sides want the kind of concessionary measures that neither side is capable of offering. The Israeli leadership expected Arafat to control Hamas and the Islamic Jihad, or at least that he would be able to co-opt them into going along with the negotiated solution. The Islamicist groups, for their part, continue to view the negotiated solution as heretical to Islam and inimical to Palestinian nationalism. Their continued intransigence towards a political solution might edge the PLO–Israeli conflict into a long-term impasse, or, worse still, towards its unravelling.

From the Palestinian side, the peace process is not being viewed as the beginning of the emergence of an independent Palestine which is a very clear objective of the PLO. Israel has not only refused to dismantle the Jewish settlements in the Occupied Territories, but is continuing to build more of them. On this issue, neither the Israeli public not its leadership is willing to offer concessions. Without the removal of these settlements, the chances for a negotiated solution to the conflict are virtually non-existent.

As one examines the dynamics and intricacies of the settlement issue, one wonders where or how exactly any breakthrough should emerge. Should the Palestinians as a community renounce violent acts *before* a majority of the Israeli public agrees to dismantle the settlements, as a real gesture toward the resolution of this conflict? Any such renunciation of violence by a majority of the Palestinians is not likely to come in the increasingly hostile environment towards the peace process that prevailed in the beginning of 1995. Or should some sort of public demonstration of an Israeli willingness to remove these settlements come *first* before Yasser Arafat can go to Hamas and the Islamic Jihad and say that the Israelis are really moving towards the creation of an independent Palestine? In any case, the settlement issue has to be resolved in a way that is acceptable to both sides. Even then, ample resentment is likely to be left on both sides for their respective extremists to undermine the process through violent acts.

In 1995, Prime Minister Yitzhak Rabin was considering a policy of separating the two peoples by creating barbed wire fences around the Palestinian population centres. This policy is also doomed to failure, because it will only increase the resolve of the extremists in both camps to look for opportunities to express their hatred towards the other side through acts of terror. Moreover, by initiating the process of separating the two peoples, the Rabin government is edging, albeit unwillingly, towards the creation of an independent Palestine, a concept that is not yet a part of official Israeli policy. The very nature of this process (i.e. the *de facto* creation of a separate Palestine through the separation of the two peoples) is based upon mutual distrust, hatred and pessimism, instead of confidence-building, incremental – albeit halting – trust and optimism between the Palestinians and Jews. The evolution of this policy does not bode well for the prospects for peace in Israel.

I have not thus far mentioned the Jerusalem issue, which is at least equally, if not more, explosive. If the aforementioned policy of separating the Jews and the Palestinians were to materialize, no Israeli government would be able to negotiate any sharing of sovereignty over Jerusalem. By the same token, viewing it from the Palestinian side, no final solution of the Israeli–Palestinian conflict is likely to last long if the status of Jerusalem is not resolved. The religious emotions on this issue are very intense on both sides.

The Jordanian–Israeli peace process appears to be progressing well. However, no one can guarantee a continuation of smooth progress even on this front, if the Israeli–PLO peace process were to unravel. The Syrian–Israeli peace process has been making slow progress. On this front, my sense is that Israel and Syria are likely to come to some sort of agreement sooner or later. The political realities of the Middle East in the mid-1990s do not favour Hafez Assad. He might be considering his own longevity – both personally and politically. He might also be thinking about the potential advantages of negotiating with Rabin as opposed to dealing with a possible Likud successor, if Rabin's party is ousted in the next Israeli elections. The Lebanese–Israeli peace process, as discussed in my chapter on this subject, will not be too difficult to handle now that Israel and Syria have come to some sort of agreement on the future sovereignty of the Golan Heights. In summary, the peace process, though it produced remarkable changes in the 1990s, that might be long-lasting, is also characterized by manifestations of old phobias, intransigence, obscurantism and extremism.

The Kurdish issue is not one of great strategic significance beyond the fact that there will be no independent Kurdistan in the foreseeable future. The Kurds have played a minor role in the Byzantine relationship between Iran and Iraq, Turkey and Iraq, and Iran and Turkey. In all likelihood, they will continue to play that role in the future. The present autonomous status enjoyed by the Kurds in Iraq only stems from the fact that it is one aspect of the continued punishment that the United States, the UK and France have been using against Saddam's regime. Even this autonomy is likely to disappear once Saddam Hussein is ousted.

Iran's role in the Persian Gulf and North Africa is one of the most significant issues of this study. Even though the strategic importance of Iran has diminished with the disappearance of the Soviet Union, there is likely to be no peace or stability in the Persian Gulf if Iran is excluded from future security arrangements. Washington's policy of 'dual containment' – i.e. containing Iran and Iraq – reflects the outmoded solution of the Cold War years. Iran is still too important a protagonist in that area for it to be contained or isolated. Even Saudi Arabia would not be an enthusiastic supporter of such a policy. By advocating it, the Clinton Administration appears to be creating the impression that American influence can be promoted and safeguarded in the area only by isolating Iran. Iran has tremendous potential to play a major role, and to remain engaged and involved in the multifaceted strategic affairs of the Persian Gulf. At the same time, Iran must abandon its Janus-faced policy, and return to the fold of conventional nation-states.

Any permanent changes in Iranian foreign policy – especially a stable manifestation of conventional foreign policy behaviour – are only likely to ensue once the pragmatists in that country gain the upper hand. However, since the domestic tug-of-war in Iran is also inextricably linked to the success of the present pragmatic Iranian rulers in improving the standard of living of their subjects, no one can state with certainty that the pragmatist forces in that country will prevail in the near future. In fact, as economic conditions continue to deteriorate in Iran, even the chances of long-term survival of the Islamic government appear to be somewhat shaky. If there were to be another cataclysmic political change in Iran, the Persian Gulf region would once again be likely to undergo a period of turbulence and instability such as the world witnessed during the Cold War. In this sense, the strategic affairs of the Persian Gulf region appear to reflect the continuity of the Cold War years.

Islam's role as a source of change and continuity is perhaps the least predictable variable of the strategic affairs of the Middle East. The 'Islamic alternative', as imprecise as it appears to be, serves as an ultimate source of promise for the believers. For the past fourteen hundred years, the notion of Islamic government has remained alive, practised in different forms by various dynasties and individual rulers. Its ultimate strength emanates from the fact that the Prophet Muhammad practised it. And as long as believers strive to emulate the Prophet's example, the Islamic alternative will remain highly relevant in the Middle East.

How much deviation is likely to be allowed from the model of government the Prophet practised is a major source of controversy. Even the notion of *Ijtihad* is not of much help in enabling Muslim politicians to develop models of Islamic government that would be in harmony with the issues of governance in the twenty-first century.[1] This, an important dimension of Islam – one which is not at all new – is how to adapt Middle Eastern governments and make them appear more Islamic. At the same time, this issue conflicts with the beliefs of those who want to see the states of that area march on the road to democracy. These countries must find a balance between democracy and Islam.

I, for one, do not see severe disagreements between Islam and democracy. However, I want to reiterate that when I talk about the prospects of democracy in the Middle East, I am not thinking of the liberal Western democracy that is in operation in the United States and in numerous other Western countries. If my understanding of the Middle East is correct, democracy in that part of the world must accommodate Islam. *It is not likely to be the other way around.* Aspects of democracy that are in harmony with Islam are likely to be incorporated. Those which are not will be discarded. The end result is likely to be an Islamic democracy, in which freedom of expression would not be absolute and in which the separation of sexes will be practised, to cite only two examples. At the same time, the continued separation of sexes should not be equated with the exploitation or mistreatment of women. Such practices in the Middle East, as shameful as they are, predate Islam. In fact, Islam has brought significant changes in this regard; however, much progress is urgently warranted on this issue in the Muslim Middle East.

No discussion of democracy in the Middle East can ignore the role of secularism. Given the overall dim view of secularism that prevails in the region, one cannot hope that this phenomenon will be incorporated in many countries in coming years. In fact, Egypt – the largest and leading secular country – is slowly edging away from secularism. On this issue, one cannot realistically expect a rapprochement between the secularists and the Islamicists, because there is no basis for a compromise. The secularists are as categorical about separating religion from politics as the Islamicists are against it. I am not sure that any Islamicist group can compromise on the issue of emulating the Prophet by not establishing an Islamic government. About the only topic of debate may be how orthodox an Islamic government ought to be. The two examples that come to mind are what is being practised in Jordan and Morocco, two states that are maintaining a balance between the demands of the Islamicist groups and others. However, even in these countries, the public debate is not about whether the government should incorporate practices that are aimed at separating Islam from issues of governance.

As the government of Egypt retaliates against the violent acts of the Islamicist extremists, one can only expect a continuation of this cycle and an escalating spiral of violence in that country. In addition, a discussion of cycles of violence between the government and the Islamicists in that country must also be examined from the perspective of worsening economic conditions, high birth rates, urban decay, mass unemployment among the young and educated sectors of population, growing corruption among government officials, a socialistic economy, and a notoriously bloated, inefficient and corrupt bureaucracy. Even the cosmetic application of elections in Egypt is aimed at maintaining the present inept and corrupt rulers in power. So, how are the Egyptians going to bring about political change? What measures – short of assassination attempts – can they adopt to bring to power new and honest rulers, given that those who are in power refuse to step down by allowing free and fair elections? As the 'competitive violence' between the Islamicists and the government of Egypt continues to escalate, extremist elements on both sides – especially from the Islamicist side, since it has less power than do the government officials – are destined to get an upper hand, thereby further condemning that country to cataclysmic change. The example of Algeria is too obvious in this regard.

Post-Cold War security in the GCC states will be significantly affected by future developments in Iranian foreign policy, and following a change of regime in Iraq. The types of incidents that occurred as a direct outcome of Saddam's invasion of Kuwait – the manner in which his troops withdrew from that emirate, the looting, the reported violation of women, the burning of the oilfields, his brutal suppression of the Kurds and the Marsh Arabs – underscore the fact that the only insurance against a repetition of these inhuman acts is his removal from power. Anything short of that is not acceptable to the civilized community of nations. However, the removal of Saddam has to be left to those who are bearing the brunt of his tyrannical rule – the Iraqis themselves. The intra-GCC differences and boundary disputes are minor enough to be resolved by them, as long as the economic and security-related *raison d'être* of this organization keeps them together.

The stability of the Persian Gulf is likely to improve if the arms race is curtailed in this region. On the Arab side of the Gulf, Saudi Arabia, Kuwait and the UAE are big spenders on arms purchases. On the other side of the Gulf, Iran has been spending huge sums on weapons. In the aftermath of the Gulf War of 1991, it was generally hoped that the big five arms-sellers of the globe – the United States, Russia, UK, France and the People's Republic of China – would come up with mutually agreed mechanisms with which to stem the flow of weapons into this area. However, even by the mid-1990s, such agreements had not materialized. Since the end of the Cold War, the defence sectors of these countries appear to rely increasingly on the foreign sales of weapons for long-term survival and for the continuance of their capital-intensive research and development programmes. And, given the high capability of the Persian Gulf countries to purchase weapons, this area has remained a highly lucrative market for the United States, the UK and France. The Russian and Chinese advantage in the weapons trade emanates largely from the fact that their sales agreements are the least politicized and will not be nullified in the foreseeable future for political reasons as might those for weapons from the West. Consequently, a country like Iran has remained a major customer, since Western weaponry is not available to it.

The arms race involving Syria, Israel and Egypt might not be intensified in coming years largely because the buying power of the two Arab states is under tremendous pressure due to their growing economic problems. Consequently, the military supremacy of Israel is guaranteed, at least through this decade. In fact, even if Egypt and Syria were to suddenly get enormous amounts of hard currency, their military capabilities are unlikely be matched with those of Israel within a span of a few years. As Alvin and Heidi Toffler have argued persuasively in their study, *War and Anti-War*, in the 'third wave' era (i.e. the information era), the ultimate military strength of countries stems from their ability to integrate technical knowledge and military technology, and their ability to merge defence and commercial technologies.[2] In this sense, Israel is decades ahead of its two Arab neighbours. However, the peace process-related changes promise to de-escalate the arms race in the Levant and Egypt. Jordan has already made tremendous strides in this direction by signing a peace agreement with Israel in October 1994. Even though Egypt and Israel continue to disagree over signing the Nuclear Proliferation Treaty, the fact that they have been at peace with each other for over fifteen years shows that this disagreement poses no threat to peace in that region.

In the Persian Gulf area, however, an ongoing dialogue between Iran and Saudi Arabia as the leading representative of the GCC states is warranted. What may be an important impediment in the way of such a dialogue is the fact that the United States is bent upon excluding Iran from future security arrangements. If the arms race in the Persian Gulf is to de-escalate, a multilateral security arrangement must be worked out among all those involved, with the exception of Iraq, for now. The inclusion of Iraq has to wait for the post-Saddam era. Saudi Arabia, Kuwait and Iran would not want anything less than that.

The countries of the Middle East, while attempting to curtail the arms race, must also focus on improving their respective capabilities in the realm of economics. Major economic disparities are not prevalent in states on the Arabian peninsula, with the exception of Yemen. Elsewhere in the Middle East, serious economic miseries prevail in Egypt, Sudan, Algeria, Tunisia, Jordan and Syria. Within the Occupied Territories, the Gaza Strip is the epitome of appalling economic conditions. If one needs to point to one source of instability and political turbulence throughout the Middle East that can cause endless problems if it continues to be neglected, the obvious choice is the growing economic misery in the aforementioned countries. It is almost a cliché to state that acute economic inequities serve as a breeding ground for extremism of all sorts. In this sense, a number of Middle Eastern countries have not changed significantly as far as economic prosperity is concerned.

In the post-Cold War years, the Middle East did not experience a deluge of changes in the same way as the Eastern European countries or the states that came into existence as a result of the break-up of the Soviet Union. However, a number of changes occurred in the area, the most noteworthy of which was the progress made by a number of countries in the resolution of the Arab–Israeli conflict. These multi-frontal attempts, when brought to a successful conclusion, are likely to permanently alter the nature of the interstate politics of the Middle East. The states of the region might then also be able to focus on finding workable arrangements to deal with another very serious and equally intricate problem that is afflicting most of them – acute economic underdevelopment. The intractability and obduracy of this problem indeed requires Arab–Israeli collective attention. Any progress on this front is also likely to deal a serious blow to all sorts of extremist movements which have fed on the acute economic miseries in many countries in that area for the past fifteen years or so. The defeat of extremism will open up new vistas for peaceful resolution of all conflicts. A region that has produced the world's three great religions deserves nothing less than that.

NOTES

1. *Ijtihad* is applied to those questions that are not covered by the Quran, *sunnah* (i.e. the example of the Prophet), *taqlid* (i.e. precedent), or *qiyas* (direct analogy). *Ijtihad* 'is always necessary because of the need to act in situations which are new or unique, or because information is lacking or competent authorities not present'. Cyril Glasse, *The Concise Encyclopedia of Islam* (NY: Harper & Row, 1989), pp. 182–3.
2. Alvin and Heidi Toffler, *War and Anti-War: Survival At the Dawn of the 21st Century* (Boston: Little, Brown, 1993).

Index